SHAKESPEARE IN CHINA

A Comparative Study
of Two Traditions and Cultures

Xiao Yang Zhang

Newark: University of Delaware Press
London: Associated University Presses

Associated University Presses
440 Forsgate Drive
Cranbury, NJ 08512

Associated University Presses
16 Barter Street
London WC1A 2AH, England

Associated University Presses
P.O. Box 338, Port Credit
Mississauga, Ontario
Canada L5G 4L8

The paper used in this publication meets the requirements of the American National Standard for Permanence of Paper for Printed Library Materials Z39.48-1984.

Library of Congress Cataloging-in-Publication Data

Zhang, Hsiao Yang, 1949–
Shakespeare in China : a comparative study of two traditions and cultures / Xiao Yang Zhang.
p. cm.
Includes bibliographical references and index.
ISBN 0-87413-536-2 (alk. paper)
1. Shakespeare, William, 1564–1616—Stage history—China.
2. Literature, Comparative—English and Chinese. 3. Literature, Comparative—Chinese and English. 4. Chinese drama—History and criticism. 5. English drama—Appreciation—China. 6. Theater—China—History. 7. East and West. I. Title.
PR3019.C6Z48 1996
822.3'3—dc20   95-30444
                                                  CIP

To my father, Professor Zhang Si Yang, Vice Chairman of the Shakespeare Association of China, who helped me to love Shakespeare's works when I was a boy.

To my mother, Hu Feng Yun, who although a chemist took great pains with my upbringing and supported my desire to be a literary critic.

To my wife, Zhang Qing, whose loving support has made this project possible.

To my son, Mu Yang, who is also a Shakespeare enthusiast although just eleven years old.

Contents

Editorial Note

ALL references to Shakespeare are from the Riverside edition of *The Complete Works of Shakespeare* (Boston: Houghton Mifflin Co., 1974). All quotations from traditional Chinese drama are taken from *The Ten Greatest Classical Chinese Tragedies*, ed. Wang Ji Si (*Zhong Guo Shi Da Gu Dian Bei Ju Ji*) (Shanghai, 1983; abbreviated in English as *Classical Chinese Tragedies*) and *The Ten Greatest Classical Chinese Comedies* (*Zhong Guo Shi Da Gu Dian Xi Ju Ji*) (Shanghai, 1983; abbreviated in English as *Classical Chinese Comedies*). All books, journals, magazines, and newspapers published in China are in Chinese, so all quotations from Chinese drama and all Chinese references are my translations, unless otherwise indicated. Chinese names are spelled according to the Scheme for the Chinese Phonetic Alphabet worked out by the Chinese government in 1958. All Shakespearean quotations are from *The Riverside Shakespeare*, ed. G. Blakemore Evans (Boston: Houghton Mifflin Co., 1974).

Acknowledgments

First I thank James L. Smith for his encouragement and advice throughout the writing of this book. I also remember with affection and gratitude the care and advice of the late Professor A. J. Smith. I am also grateful to Professors F. T. Prince and John Peacock for kindly reading and commenting on the manuscript. To my editor at the University of Delaware Press, I owe special thanks for her meticulous scrutiny and insightful comments.

I wish also to thank Professor Zhang Si Yang for his interest and suggestions. Professors Mason Wang, Qiu Ke An, Meng Xian Qiang, and Dr. Larry Tang have helpful reactions and advice on the central argument of the book midway into the project. I am indebted to Cao Shu Jun and Sun Fu Liang, whose book (in Chinese) *Shakespeare on the Chinese Stage* (Harbin: Harbin Press, 1989) provided useful information on Shakespearean production in China.

Introduction

As a "cultural hero" Shakespeare has not only been a major figure in Anglo-American culture, but he has also had a great impact on many cultures the world over. The exploration of the interaction between Shakespeare and these societies has consequently become an important part of Shakespeare studies.

Ever since his introduction into China at the beginning of the twentieth century, Shakespeare has exerted a tremendous influence upon Chinese theater and culture. The Shakespeare industry in China has flourished rapidly since the New Cultural Movement in 1919, and his works have been widely read, interpreted, and performed by the people. The enthusiasm of the Chinese for the playwright has remained high, particularly after the Cultural Revolution. Westerners are unaware of how ardently Shakespeare is admired and worshiped by the Chinese people. In literary and artistic circles, he is considered the god of art. For the reading public, his writing is regarded more highly than that of any other Western author.

The reasons why Shakespeare occupies such a high position in the cultural landscape of China are evident. On the one hand Shakespeare has greatly affected traditional Chinese drama and infused new blood into an old dramatic tradition. Helping to form a new dramatic concept, he has also had an impact on the formation and development of modern Chinese theater, which is centered on the practice of spoken drama. On the other hand Shakespeare has entered into numerous domains of Chinese culture and exerted a widespread and profound influence upon them as well. In a sense, as an "institution maker," Shakespeare has made a great contribution to the formation of the "New Culture" of China (a combination of traditional Chinese culture with some elements of Western culture) and has permeated Chinese life as no other great Western cultural figure has done.

During his transplantation into Chinese culture, Shakespeare's drama has inevitably undergone some transformation. As Hanna Scolnicov writes,

> the problem of the transference of plays from culture to culture is seen not just as a question of transplanting the text, but of conveying its

meaning and adapting it to its new cultural environment so as to create new meanings.[1]

It is obvious that in being adapted to the cultural environment of China, Shakespeare's plays have ended up looking quite different to the Chinese. Understandably his works have been interpreted and reshaped from the perspective of Chinese cultural tradition, resulting in the creation of a "Chinese Shakespeare." The study of the interaction between Shakespeare and Chinese culture needs to become an important part of Shakespearean studies. It provides a valuable perspective from which to consider the nature and implication of the universal appeal of the dramatist, after allowing for the striking cultural discrepancies between Western and Eastern cultures. The distinctive interpretation of Shakespeare by the Chinese will make the study of Shakespeare more varied and diverse. Yet it is a pity that Shakespearean studies and production in China are so little known in the West, with only a few published articles giving simple accounts of activities concerning Shakespearean criticism and production in the country.[2] The nature and significance of the interaction between Shakespeare and Chinese theater and culture have not been examined in depth in either Chinese or Western academic circles. This book is thus an attempt to fill this gap.

The interaction between Shakespeare and traditional Chinese drama reflects the nature of the exchange between Western and Asian theater in the twentieth century and forms a substantial part of the tendency towards the interculturalism of the postmodern theater. This tendency, as critics have pointed out, demonstrates that realism-oriented Western theater shows an interest in the "distancing sense" and stylized techniques of Asian theater, while the nonrealistic Far Eastern theater tries to imitate the naturalistic dramatic techniques of Western theater.[3] The interaction between Shakespeare and Chinese culture in a sense represents in microcosm the relationship between Western and Chinese cultures. A prevalent belief in China, shaped by the changing economic and political contexts, holds that the two great cultural traditions conflict with each other. Some radical intellectuals maintain that the Chinese people should completely abandon their tradition and replace it with Western culture. Conversely, some conservative politicians try to resist the invasion of Western culture, fearing that they may lose a long-standing cultural tradition as well as their power. Admittedly the introduction of Western culture into the country has indeed caused a certain degree of crisis in conventional culture in the short term, as we will see from the initial influence of Shakespeare on traditional Chinese drama. But as I demonstrate, in the long term Chinese culture will benefit from the impact and reinvigorate itself by absorbing the strong points of Western culture. One can therefore safely say that the two great cultures in fact complement each other.

This study was undertaken from the viewpoint of cultural materialism. This approach did not come about merely because the topic is based on cultural studies, but rather because the principal ideas of the book are closely related to relevant cultural contexts. For example, I trace the different characteristics of Shakespeare and traditional Chinese drama back to their cultural origins, which helps to explain the formation of such differences. In addition, I contrast the interaction between Shakespeare and traditional Chinese drama against the social and cultural backgrounds of the country since it is far more than an interaction between two types of drama. More important, the reception, interpretation, and reconstruction of Shakespeare by the Chinese cannot be accurately and deeply examined without relating them to the cultural context of China. Jonathan Dollimore and Alan Sinfield believe that

> Shakespeare's text is reconstructed, reappraised, reassigned all the time through diverse institutions in specific contexts. What the plays signify, how they signify, depends on the cultural field in which they are situated.[4]

The Chinese perception of Shakespeare is by no means a simple, monochromatic, and frozen vision conjured up by the universal appeal of the dramatist or any authentic interpretation. On the contrary, it is a complex, colorful, and changeable vision created by the changing social, cultural, and historical contexts of China.

The first part of this book describes many differences and similarities between Shakespeare and traditional Chinese drama and finds their source in relevant cultural circumstances. Earlier studies of Shakespeare and traditional Chinese drama have tended to list only a few superficial differences and similarities between individual Shakespeare plays and traditional Chinese plays, rarely exploring the cause in their cultural traditions.[5] In this section I emphasize traditional Chinese drama and its cultural context to clarify the discussion of Shakespeare's experience in China later in the study. Chapter 1 compares tragedy and comedy against their cultural backgrounds, concentrating on the tragic concepts and comic patterns that relate frequently to the argument in Parts II and III. Chapter 2 uses general artistic characteristics such as the mixture of tragedy and comedy, deployment of time and space, characterization, poetic quality, and the use of imagery to explore Shakespeare and traditional Chinese drama. The relevant cultural circumstances are also analyzed.

Part II examines the nature and significance of the interaction between Shakespeare and traditional Chinese drama. Chapter 3 begins with a brief survey of the introduction of Shakespeare into modern China, including translation and performance, and looks particularly at the impact of the dramatist on Chinese drama in academic, theatrical, and literary circles. Chapter 4 investigates the possibility and advantages of performing Shakespeare's plays in the form of traditional Chinese drama and discusses the achievements of some Shakespearean productions presented in the major types of traditional Chinese drama such as Beijing, Kunju, Shaoxing, and Huangmei operas. The chapter also looks at other metamorphoses of Shakespeare's plays on the Chinese stage and pays special attention to the significance of these sinicized productions to both Shakespearean theater and traditional Chinese drama in contemporary China.

Part III explores the interaction between Shakespeare and Chinese culture. Chapter 5 discovers the widespread and profound influence of the dramatist on Chinese culture, including the customs and daily life of the Chinese, and shows how his plays flourish and function in varied and diverse cultural forms. This chapter also discusses the use of the dramatist in the country as a means of constructing cultural meaning. Chapter 6 analyzes the factors that operate culturally, socially, and historically in the assimilation of Shakespeare into Chinese culture and explores the multiple perspectives of the Chinese on the dramatist, showing how greatly they affect the Chinese interpretation of Shakespeare and considering the different functions of these perspectives in the formation of the general Chinese vision of Shakespeare.

SHAKESPEARE
IN CHINA

Part I

1

Tragedy and Comedy: The Culturally Produced Differences and Similarities

ONE feature of the new interest in comparative literature in the last two decades has been the examination of the distinctions of literary works belonging to the same genre but coming from different literary traditions. Such research in a sense serves as an easy way to understand the features of foreign cultures because literary characteristics usually are culturally produced and the parallel study of different literary traditions helps to explain the interaction between them. Shakespeare and traditional Chinese drama, as the representatives of two great dramatic traditions, are particularly fascinating to the audiences. Although they share some common features, there are many striking differences between them. A study of the nature of these differences is an essential first step toward understanding the interaction between the two types of drama in modern China. The differences and affinities between Shakespeare and traditional Chinese drama are especially obvious in their tragedies and comedies. Shakespeare's tragic concept clearly differs from that of traditional Chinese drama, though both command pity and sympathy; his comic concept is roughly akin to that of traditional Chinese drama, although their different comic patterns interestingly display the influence of their cultural circumstances.

The archetype of tragedy is usually related to the suffering and death of a protagonist, but since the particular themes of Shakespeare's tragedies vary so greatly, it is hard to group them by theme, as some Shakespeare critics have pointed out.[1] For the convenience of this study, I classify Shakespeare's tragedies into three categories according to subject matter: love tragedies, political tragedies, and a combination of these two categories, as is found in *Antony and Cleopatra*. The classification of traditional Chinese tragedy follows this pattern as well. Of the ten best-known traditional Chinese tragedies, which have been generally accepted as the ten greatest classical Chinese tragedies by Chinese theatrical circles in the 1980s,[2] there are more love tragedies and fewer political tragedies than in Shakespeare. A fair number of love-political tragedies appears in the traditional Chinese dramatic heritage, and in fact three of them are included in the "top ten."

Shakespearean political tragedies are linked by the theme of a struggle for power in a royal family or among the leading figures in the political arena, while most traditional Chinese political tragedies recount the conflict between virtuous ministers and treacherous ministers, as in *The Flag of Loyalty (Jing Zhong Qi)*, *The Story of the Honest Subject (Qing Zhong Pu)*, and *The Orphan of the House of Zhao (Zhao Shi Gu Er)*. The last one, *The Orphan of the House of Zhao*, was introduced to Europe in the eighteenth century and adapted by French, English, and other European playwrights. In 1759, an English adaptation by Arthur Murphy of this famous classical Chinese tragedy was presented at the Theatre Royal in Drury Lane, with the principal character played by David Garrick.[3] Like Voltaire, Murphy adapted the play by changing some characters and plots to suit the national taste. Moreover, one of his main aims, as he stated in the added prologue, was to introduce Confucian morals and exotic settings to the audience.[4] Some traditional Chinese political tragedies have justice or law as their central theme, as for instance the well-known Yuan play *The Injustice to Dou E*, in which Dou E, the heroine, was executed on an unjust charge. This theme seems to be rather similar to one encountered in Shakespeare's "problem plays."

It is easier to generalize about the theme of traditional Chinese love tragedies than about Shakespearean love tragedies. All of them are concerned with the conflict between lovers and feudal ethics. In most cases, like Romeo and Juliet, the tragic fate of the lovers clearly derives from pressures in their environment such as parents, immoral suitors, and a rigid community that represents the doctrine of Confucianism.[5] In ancient China, freedom of marriage was inconceivable and the younger generation could only accept its parents' decision. Three love tragedies appear among the ten greatest classical Chinese tragedies: *The Sad Story of Lady Wang (Jiao Hong Ji)*, which has been called the "Chinese *Romeo and Juliet*," *The Story of a Pipa (Pipa Ji)*, and *The Tower of Lei Feng (Lei Feng Ta)*.

The themes of traditional Chinese love-political tragedies are more complex than those in Shakespeare's tragedies. These plays deal with not only the incompatibility of the desire for love and the desire for power, as in *Antony and Cleopatra*, but also with the way the pleasures of love are destroyed by the great turbulence of Chinese history. Thus in the plays the lovers encounter desperate situations caused by domestic troubles and foreign invasions, as in *Autumn in the Han Palace (Han Gong Qu)* and *The Fan of Peach Blossom (Tao Hua Shan)*. *The Hall of Longevity (Chang Sheng Dian)* parallels *Antony and Cleopatra* in this category of traditional Chinese tragedy with its sad story about Emperor Tang Ming and his favorite concubine, Lady Yang. In the play, the more they indulge in their love pleasure, the more the emperor neglects his official duties, which eventually results in an armed rebellion. To escape from the calamity, the emperor has to issue, with great reluctance, an order to execute Lady Yang to calm down the soldiers, whose resentment against her is running high. With evident cultural bias, the thematic treatment of this play differs from that of *Antony and Cleopatra*. The author's marvelous illustration of this popular historical event in the Tang dynasty[6] more or less embodies a conventional Chinese political idea that beautiful women are the root of social upheaval. However, Hong Sheng, the playwright, has transcended this traditional dramatic motif and made his play rather complex and ambiguous.

A striking contrast between Shakespearean and traditional Chinese tragedy lies in the treatment of the protagonists. In Shakespearean tragedies the chief characters are mainly great heroes of high degree such as kings, princes, or the leaders of states. They need not obey anyone nor follow any conventional moral doctrine. Since they are their own masters and can exercise great freedom of choice, they are unlikely to become victims of other people's wills. By contrast, traditional Chinese tragedy is concerned with people in relatively lower social positions. They are often characters in political tragedies, such as Zhou Shun Chang in *The Story of the Honest Subject* and Yue Fei in *The Flag of Loyalty,* or ordinary people in love tragedies, such as Zhao Wu Niang in *The Story of a Pipa* and Lady Wang in *The Sad Story of Lady Wang*. These are people who cannot decide their own actions, who are not the rulers but the ruled. They have to submit to the authority of a monarch or comply with the moral doctrine of Confucianism. Some powerful rulers, usually emperors, appear in the plots of traditional Chinese tragedies, but they are not leading or significant characters because they do not appear onstage and serve only as backstage manipulators and arbitrators, like the kings in Molière's comedies. Their decrees are at times announced by courtiers, particularly in the final scenes. A few traditional Chinese love-political tragedies are exceptions in this aspect. In *Autumn in the Han Palace*, the main plot is concerned with the love between Emperor Han Yuan and his concubine Wang Zhao Jun against the political setting of a threat of foreign invasion. In *The Hall of Longevity*, as I described before, Emperor Tang Ming and his favorite concubine, Lady Yang, might be seen as the two leading characters in the play. But I would argue that the real protagonists in these two plays are the two women, Wang Zhao Jun and Lady Yang, not the two emperors. They are the characters who suffer most from the calamities in these two tragedies, which ultimately destroy them.

Another interesting phenomenon in the treatment of the protagonists is that Shakespeare's tragedies revolve around men and traditional Chinese tragedies encompass women. Of the ten greatest classical Chinese tragedies, seven plays have women as principal characters, such as Dou E in *The Injustice to Dou E*, Wang Jiao Niang in *The Sad Story of Lady Wang*, Zhao Wu Niang in *The Story of a Pipa*, Bai Niang Zi in *The Tower of Lei Feng*, Li Xian Jun in *The Fan of Peach Blossom*, as well as Lady Yang and Wang Zhao Jun. The tragic effects of Shakespeare's tragedies come from the death of the male protagonists, but the tragic mood in the Chinese plays is created by the suffering and destruction of the women, which appeals strongly to the audience's sympathy and pity.

The difference in the social status of the protagonists in the plays of the two traditions is rooted in very different theatrical, literary, and cultural traditions. The origin of European literature can be traced back to Greek myth and epic, which depict the deeds of gods and noble heroes. Tragedy as a dramatic genre also emerged soon after this heroic time, and their playwrights took stories from Greek myth and Homeric epic for their subject matter. Geoffrey Brereton defines the traditional Western concept of tragedy as "Great people are engaged in great events, both appropriate to the noble genre of tragedy."[7] Elizabethan dramatists inherited the theatrical convention of tragedy largely from their Greek and Roman predecessors, so it follows that Shakespeare has great heroes as his tragic protagonists.

By contrast, classical Chinese literature at first developed with lyric poetry rather than any narrative literary form.[8] These lyric poems, such as those in the famous poetry collection *The Book of Songs (Shi Jing)*, represent mainly the realistic thoughts and feelings of ordinary people with few supernatural elements. Thus at the very beginning of Chinese culture, a literary tradition was established that did not emphasize great heroes. Chinese scholars commonly believe that Confucianism tends to exclude the supernatural, so myth has had very little influence on classical Chinese literature.

To a certain extent most well-known traditional Chinese tragedies resemble classical Chinese poems transformed into plays and having two major themes: the complaints of *shi* (educated officials in or out office) about frustrations in their political careers and the sorrows of *qie* (concubines, or women from the middle or lower classes) over their misfortunes in love. Consequently it is easier to understand why traditional Chinese tragedies rarely have all-powerful rulers as protagonists and why ordinary subjects (commissioned *shi*) and women (*qie*) become leading characters.

A minor factor that affects the social status of protagonists in traditional Chinese tragedy is that the golden age of traditional Chinese drama occurred in the Yuan dynasty (1271–1368, see Appendix), when townspeople formed a growing social class in big cities. The playwrights of the Yuan dynasty had to suit their theatrical style to the taste of ordinary urban audiences. To achieve this goal they often drew materials from the oral narratives and folktales of the Song dynasty that described the lives of ordinary people. This is partly the reason for the lower social strata of the protagonists in traditional Chinese tragedies. More indirect reasons are to be found in the depth of Chinese culture. I shall return to this subject later.

In his *Poetics* Aristotle emphasizes that the protagonist of a tragedy must not be perfect but should rest somewhere between the extremes of good and evil. This means that we can always see some moral weakness or defect in the character of a tragic protagonist. In this aspect of tragedy Shakespeare seems to follow Aristotle strictly. It is fair to suppose that the notion of a "tragic flaw" is in accordance with Shakespeare's idea of human nature, which can be seen, for example, in the passage where Hamlet criticizes the bad customs found in Denmark (1.4.14–38). Shakespearean tragedies rarely have a perfect principal character. Even Hamlet, the embodiment of Shakespeare's humanistic ideal, does not behave as firmly and resolutely as a noble hero should in the face of his unshirkable duty of revenge. Filled with disgust at the world and life and indulging in endless meditations on the philosophical meaning of existence and death, Hamlet's soul is wracked by his own hesitation (although this is, ironically, the very reason why we like him). There are also apparent defects in the chief characters of other Shakespearean tragedies, as, for instance, the willfulness of King Lear, the self-deception and jealousy of Othello, the ambition of Macbeth, and the arrogance of Coriolanus.

As for traditional Chinese tragedies, the formula of a tragic flaw cannot be applied to their protagonists because they are almost perfect either morally or aesthetically. No obvious weak points in their natures exist to bring about their destructions. All the male principal characters are virtuous and loyal officials. They are always concerned for their monarch, their country, and their people, but seldom worry about themselves. For instance, Zhou Shun Chang, the hero of *The*

Story of the Honest Subject, was an honest and upright senior official. He continued to worry about the desperate situation at court even after he was ousted from his post by a corrupt minister. He was very poor, although he had been in office for ten years, since he had never accepted a bribe or even a gift from a friend. His English counterparts can be found in Shakespearean tragedies and historical plays such as Kent in *King Lear* and the Duke of Gloucester in *Henry the Sixth.* The female leading characters in traditional Chinese tragedies are as sweet-natured and lovely as the leading women in Shakespearean comedies. Unfortunately, for their virtues life brings them not happiness but suffering and death.

Serving as an ambiguous dramatic personage, the imperial concubine Lady Yang in *The Hall of Longevity* may invite some doubt about the perfection of all Chinese protagonists. In the play Lady Yang is presented as both the root of Anshi Rebellion and as an unswervingly loyal lover. In fact, it is unfair to put the blame on her, considering that she is a victim of the corrupt feudal political system and the scapegoat of Emperor Tang Ming. To vindicate the absolute authority of monarchy, conventional Chinese political ideas tend to shift the faults of the rulers onto their subjects. Emperor Tang Ming makes every effort to please Lady Yang, including appointing her relatives to high positions, which evokes strong resentment in the court. But the more he gives her, the greater the danger he puts her in, which eventually leads to the destruction of his love. As A. C. Bradley says, the situation demonstrates that "Everywhere in this tragic world, man's thought, translated into act, is transformed into the opposite of itself."[9] As Shakespeare did in *Antony and Cleopatra,* Hong Sheng, the playwright, also presents public responsibility as the opposite of love. Having no obvious imperfections, Lady Yang to the Chinese people is an embodiment of the saying "Beautiful women are born unlucky";[10] consequently her misfortune and death strongly evoke the sympathy and pity of the Chinese.

The principal characters of traditional Chinese tragedies come to us with clear and unambiguous moral keynotes. As positive characters they must earn the audience's respect and sympathy or as negative characters their hatred and contempt. People usually find it simple to determine the moral status of a character in a traditional Chinese tragedy. By contrast the characters in Shakespearean tragedy are not so easily typed. So many paradoxes appear in the traits of Shakespearean tragic characters that one does not know how to evaluate them properly. For example, Edmund is presented both as a sinister villain and as a dynamic young man. Although generally we dislike him, we still find a little sympathy for him in our hearts. Lear, Othello, Macbeth, and most other major characters in Shakespearean tragedies also evoke complex and ambiguous responses in audiences. Since Shakespeare obviously understands human nature so well, his characters are more true to life than those of traditional Chinese drama. To some extent, as mentioned earlier, Lady Yang and Emperor Tang Ming in *The Hall of Longevity* do appear similar to Shakespearean characters in that they have complex natures.

Stemming from his notion of conflict, Hegel opened up a new field exploring the essence of tragedy. Some later theories of tragedy, including that of Engels, have either been directly derived from or have leaned heavily upon the Hegelian account. As Hegel's English disciple, Bradley applied this notion of conflict to the analysis of Shakespearean tragedy. These theories of Hegel and his followers have been attacked by some modern dramatic critics. Dissatisfied with the Hegelian historical approach to tragedy, they believe that it overemphasizes the attempt to find the "real presence" of the character and the author's mind.[11]

The Hegelian notion of conflict led to a critical formulizing of literature in most socialist countries, especially in China during the 1960s and 1970s. In China this movement was characterized by commentary on literary works in the light of popular sociology and the principles of class struggle. In spite of these negative influences, Hegel's notion of conflict remains a valuable perspective from which to view tragedy, showing us that all tragedies indeed contain conflicts in different forms.

The numerous and apparent conflicts in Shakespearean tragedies are represented dialectically, without static or superficial description. In his tragedies the general ethical viewpoint is obvious, but Shakespeare is not satisfied with an approach that divides the antagonists into "good" and "evil" according to the play's moral doctrine. Carefully examining the motives of both sides, he identifies them with the relevant sociopolitical circumstances and shows the historical justification of all characters.

Hamlet is neither a play with bloody revenge as its theme nor a play centered on the moral struggle between a usurper and a hero who consciously defends a monarchy. What impresses us most about the conflict here is the strong skepticism caused by the striking contrast between humanistic ideals and cruel reality, which extends to a meditation on the general human condition and the meaning of life. In *Julius Caesar* it is also difficult for us to judge Caesar's and Brutus's morality.

In contrast to the varied conflicts in Shakespearean tragedies, those in traditional Chinese tragedies seem explicit and stereotyped. Chinese dramatists are interested in presenting the outward form of a tragic conflict. Believing that the ultimate power in the tragic world is a moral order, they divide the two forces into good and evil. The moral order presented by these dramatists is not universal, as it is in Shakespeare's mature tragedies, but rather is a special one formed by Chinese cultural conventions and based on Confucian ethical doctrines.

Traditional Chinese tragedies have two major types of conflict. The first is a conflict between two social forces in which one strives for the realization of *ren* and the other disrupts it. *Ren* is an ultimate social ideal of Confucianism based on ancient Chinese patriarchal society. The good in *ren* is to maintain harmonious family relationships between father and son, husband and wife, elder brother and younger brother, and so forth. Over time the authority of father and husband and the obedience of son and wife are increasingly stressed. Confucianism extends this family harmony to the entire empire. Since the relationship between colleagues or friends compares to that between brothers, while the relationship between emperor and subject is analogous to that between benevolent father and filial son, the whole social order is conceived of in terms of family relationships. Thus different moral rules (*li*) must be observed such as *zhong* (loyalty) for the subject, *xiao* (filial piety) for the son, *jie* (chastity) for the wife, *yi* (loyalty to friends) for anyone. *Li* serves only as a means to achieving *ren*. In the later dynasties, however, *li* was carried to extreme and became very strict and rigid, which violated the original spirit of *ren*. Thus came about the second type of conflict in traditional Chinese tragedies, that between *ren* and later *li*.

The first type of conflict is presented mainly in traditional Chinese political tragedies. For instance, in *The Orphan of the House of Zhao*, the treacherous general Tu An Jia is a leading evil force against *ren*, and he brings about massacres and disorder to the country. The opposing force is composed of loyal subjects such as Zhao Dun and Gong Sun Chu Jiu, who follow *li* and fight for *ren*. The second type of conflict appears mostly in love tragedies. In these plays the young lovers strive for the freedom to choose their mates while the parents persist in the rigid principle that the marriage of young people must be arranged by the older generation.

There is yet another difference in the handling of tragic conflict between Shakespearean tragedies and traditional Chinese tragedies. Shakespeare usually presents a conflict between an individual will and a social order. His hero acts from personal desire or passion rather than from moral purpose. In traditional Chinese tragedy, however, a conflict between two moral tendencies always arises. The principal character always acts with clear moral intentions. In *The Injustice to Dou E,* when confronted with the threat of Zhang Lur, a villain who forces Dou E to marry him, the heroine's first response is not to reprimand him for his wickedness, but to express her moral faith:

> A good horse does not change its saddle,
> A chaste woman will never remarry,
> I would die rather than marry you,
> I shall go to the court with you.
> (Act 4, "Qiao Pair," *Classical Chinese Tragedies,* 24)[12]

Through the conflicts and the deaths of the chief characters, the authors of traditional Chines tragedies reaffirm the supremacy of the existing feudal political system and the justification of the Confucian moral order. However, in Shakespearean tragedies, particularly in his greatest ones, the playwright seems to have little interest in affirming a particular political system or moral doctrine, but tends instead to uphold a universal justice, the dignity of humankind, and the value of life. As Dorothea Krook remarks,

> By being reconciled to the suffering as necessary, we reaffirm the supremacy of the universal moral order, and by this act of recognition and submission to the universal moral order, which the reaffirmation of its supremacy implies, we express and affirm the dignity of man and the value of human life.[13]

The reason why Hamlet revenges his father's death on Claudius is not that he conscientiously defends a hereditary monarchical system, but that his father, as a model of a perfect human being, has been murdered by a base person, so that he must bring disjointed justice back to its proper course.

In traditional Chinese tragedy the dividing line between the two antagonistic groups is clear and firm. In most cases a group cannot cross this line and convert to the other side. In accordance with both Chinese moral ideas and aesthetic standards, a good man always does good works and a bad man does evil deeds. If a playwright changes a positive hero into a villain or a villain into a virtuous person, he will then violate the principle that "good will be rewarded with good and evil with evil" and his play will lose its moralizing function. A character like Macbeth was not available to an audience in ancient China.

In tragic conflict, Shakespeare's heroes always take the initiative in their action because they have great freedom of choice. By contrast, the leading characters in traditional Chinese tragedies are passive in their confrontation with the opposing force due to their subordinate status. As a Chinese scholar said recently, "The characters of traditional Chinese tragedies, in most cases, are forced to act. They never intend to do something to change or improve the existing social structure."[14]

In *Hamlet*, after the Prince of Denmark is aware of the truth of his father's death and in spite of reservations, he still takes a series of actions (pretending to be insane, arranging a play to verify the story of the ghost, killing Polonius) that arouse the suspicion of Claudius, who then plots against Hamlet's life. In tragic conflict Shakespeare's heroes take offensive positions while the principal characters in traditional Chinese tragedies form defensive stances. The heroes and heroines of Chinese plays rarely overstep their own social place in order to act. As subjects and wives they strictly stay within their social positions, as set by feudal society. They refuse to react until the evil forces attack them fiercely.

In political tragedies such as in *The Flag of Loyalty, The Story of the Honest Subject,* and *The Orphan of the House of Zhao,* we first see the full antics of the corrupt ministers (deceiving the emperors and holding great powers, framing faithful officials). Then the loyal subjects begin to react by exposing the plots of the evil ministers, risking their lives to persuade the emperors to punish the ministers, and so on. In love tragedies such as *The Sad Story of Lady Wang,* the chief characters dare not disobey their parents' will or outwardly reject the suitors chosen for them. As a result they suffer from stress and eventually die of despair. They do not act as bravely as Romeo and Juliet. However, Lady Bai of *The Tower of Lei Feng* can be singled out as a different type of heroine. Like those of Shakespearean comedies, she is more active and fearless than those in traditional Chinese tragedies because she has an unusual advantage: she is a supernatural snake.

Critics have said that the general development of tragic drama has been from the outward form of human beings to the inner world of human nature. In Shakespearean tragedy inner conflict is the main method used to illustrate interiority and contributes largely to the play's drama. The playwright concentrates more on inner than outward conflict because the former delineates the predicament of humanity and the essence of life more subtly than the latter. When seeing Shakespearean tragedies we are always electrified by the inward struggle in the hero's soul. Hamlet, King Lear, Othello, Macbeth, and other great heroes are all torn, shaken, and driven by the conflict between their personal passions and impersonal principles.

By contrast, the inner conflict in traditional Chinese tragedy is not as deep or wide as that in Shakespearean tragedy, due to the theatrical conventions of ancient China. Classical Chinese playwrights usually did not write long soliloquies in their works, so there was no vehicle for a hero to pour out his innermost thoughts and feelings. Inner conflict in traditional Chinese tragedy is usually limited to the hero's reaction to a predicament and is not extended to the wide range of philosophic problems such as the human condition, the mystery of the universe, and the meaning of life and death that Shakespeare's heroes confront. For example, in act 3 of *The Injustice to Dou E,* after she has been condemned to die, Dou E is anguished by her wrongful treatment and the threat of death. The inner conflict produced by this situation is simply a hatred for the unjust law and a lament that even heaven and earth do not uphold justice:[15]

The sun and the moon hang high in the sky,
The gods and the ghosts control the life and death of man.
Heaven and Earth should distinguish between good and evil,
But they confuse the virtuous person with the villain:
Why are good people always poor and short-lived
And vile creatures rich and long-lived?
O, Heaven and Earth also fear the strong and oppress the weak,
They only push the boats floating with the current.
O Earth, you should not be called Earth
If you fail to discriminate between good and evil.
O Heaven, you are called Heaven in vain
When you mistake the sage and the fool!
Ah, you only leave me alone with tears in my eyes.
     (Act 3, "Gun Xiu Qiu," *Classical Chinese Tragedies,* 19)
It is all because officials don't care for justice,
People in turn dare not to speak out.
                     ("Yi Sha," ibid., 22)

In some plays the playwright deliberately avoids delineating possible inner conflict to highlight the courage and moral steadfastness of the chief characters. In *The Story of the Honest Subject,* at the very moment when Zhou Shun Chang, the leading character in the play, is to be arrested by the corrupt minister, he still is calm and fearless although his entire family is consumed with great sadness. His strong moral fiber suggests the character of Titus Andronicus, who also shows an unhesitating suppression of personal desire and the softer emotions.

In *The Orphan of the House of Zhao,* which, like *Hamlet,* has revenge as its central theme, when the orphan has grown up and is aware that the whole household of the Zhao family had been killed by the corrupt minister Tu An Jia and that his foster father is none other than his personal enemy Tu An Jia, he, unlike the Prince of Denmark, decides to avenge himself immediately and without delay:

> I'm burning with anger after
> The whole truth has come out,
> I must capture that vicious old man
> And force him to pay with his life
> For the murder of the honest officials
> And the massacre of the whole family!
> (Act 4, "Pu Tan Le," *Classical Chinese Tragedies,* 90)

Common sense tells us that there must be some hesitation in the orphan's soul because Tu An Jia is both his enemy and the benefactor who brought him up. But the playwright let his hero redress the injustice firmly and quickly, eliminating a chance to show the inner struggle in the hero's heart, which would have been more satisfying to both Elizabethan and modern Chinese audiences.

The dramatists of traditional Chinese tragedy, however, are good at depicting a great range of feelings in exquisite verse, giving an audience entry into a hero's innermost thoughts, and moving it deeply. Some of these feelings may arise from genuine inner conflict, particularly those that are produced by the struggle between two spiritual forces, such as a heroine's dilemma over whether to follow her parents' will or to chose her own lover. However, many of the hero's emotions cannot be attributed to a true inner conflict as when, for example, they come from the sorrow of a woman on missing her departed lover. Generally speaking, the feelings described in traditional Chinese tragedy are gentle and sentimental ones, not the strong and vigorous emotions found in Shakespearean tragedy.

People often take it for granted that a tragedy must have a tragic ending. Traditional Chinese tragedy, however, is unusual in having happy endings. Shakespearean and other Western tragedies usually end with the destruction of the hero and his enemy, but in Chinese tragedies, after the suffering and death of a principal character, a happy event always serves as the final ending of the play. These happy endings can be grouped into three types.

First, in political tragedies, some enlightened emperors or upright officials punish the corrupt ministers or villains and announce the chief characters' rehabilitations, as in *The Story of the Honest Subject, The Flag of Loyalty,* and *The Injustice to Dou E.* Second, in love tragedies or love-political tragedies, the lovers reunite in a fairyland or dreamland at the end of the plays, as in *The Sad Story of Lady Wang*, *The Hall of Longevity*, and *Autumn in the Han Palace*. Finally, in some political tragedies and love tragedies a later generation descended from the tragic characters takes revenge on the enemy or strives for the liberation and rehabilitation of the characters, as in *The Orphan of the House of Zhao* and *The Tower of Lei Feng*.

The happy ending in traditional Chinese tragedy performs at least two functions. The first is to punish the evil force and, accordingly, to reaffirm the supremacy of the moral order. In these tragedies, as discussed earlier, the positive moral force is not strong enough to resist the evil force; it cannot wipe out evil while being destroyed by it, as occurs in Shakespearean tragedy. This task has to be left to a more powerful defender of moral order. The second function of the happy ending is to give the principal characters an opportunity to realize the aspirations that have not come true during their lifetimes. The first type of happy ending is a logical consequence produced by the fundamental principle of these plays that evil must always be punished and the second appears to be a product of wishful thinking. Yet it too can be clearly connected to Chinese cultural tradition, as I will explain later in this chapter.

To some extent the aims of the happy ending in traditional Chinese tragedy share a common ground with "poetic justice" in seventeenth-century Europe, which emphasizes that prosperity and adversity are distributed in proportion to the merits of heroes in literary works. But the Chinese happy ending by no means changes the essence of these tragedies. In the plays, after all, the suffering and death of the characters are accomplished facts and the basic elements of tragedy are present everywhere, yielding an essentially tragic vision. However, the happy ending has another obvious function in providing tragic relief, which lightens the heavy atmosphere at the end of the plays and comforts the audience.

It is a dubious enterprise to explore the source of tragedy, for a tragic calamity is brought about by many elements. Nevertheless one may roughly classify all the possible sources of tragedy into two main categories: internal and external causes. Internal causes include all the personal elements of a protagonist: his or her weakness, guilt, passion, self-will, or blindness in the face of the future. External causes come from the world outside the play. They can be exceptional villainy or criminality such as that shown by Iago, Claudius, and Edmund in Shakespearean tragedies. They can also involve social circumstances such as inhumane laws, rigid moral doctrines, or even outdated conventions. There is no doubt that all tragedies are brought about by both internal and external causes, and none by a single cause. Generally speaking, the sources of Shakespearean tragedy are produced by internal causes—that is, by the hero's mistake or guilt, a flaw in his nature, or by the stubbornness and blindness of his will to transcend his limitations, as Nietzsche remarked:

> Man's aspiration to transcend his limit entails sacrilege and suffering, being at bottom an attempt to reimpose the original unity of life. The cost of that heroic effort is the annihilation of the individual hero: he suffers the primordial contradiction in his own person.[16]

In traditional Chinese tragedy, on the contrary, tragic fate is most often created by external causes. As I discussed earlier, the principal characters in traditional Chinese tragedies are usually unflawed persons having no guilt, passion, or even extravagant hopes. It is the evil nature and injustice of the law or rigid moral doctrine that destroy them. Therefore, one might think that Shakespearean tragic heroes in a sense deserve their catastrophes, but that the protagonists in traditional Chinese tragedies do not. Thus it can be said that Shakespearean tragedy is a tragedy of the individual and traditional Chinese tragedy is one of society.

This brief comparison of Shakespearean and traditional Chinese tragedy makes clear that there are striking differences between the two forms in terms of tragic concept, although both imply disaster, suffering, and death. For the convenience of this comparison, I will simply summarize the typical Shakespearean tragedy as the story of a highborn man with an apparent weakness in his character. He is driven by his will, desire, or passion to suffer eventually from an exceptional calamity that leads to his destruction.

Correspondingly, a typical traditional Chinese tragedy is the story of an innocent and perfect woman or man in a subordinate position who fails to defend the moral order or his or her basic personal happiness, suffers from a disaster, and is destroyed by the external force of society. If both types of tragedy come from the same dramatic genre, why do they have such different characteristics? If we consider the problem from the angle of cultural tradition, some answers may be clear.

Philosophy is the foundation of many cultures because every group uses it to interpret the phenomena of nature, history, and human society. In drama philosophical ideas influence tragic elements of the play, and in most tragedies people can observe the process of history, the human predicament, and the interpretation of this struggle. In Greek tragedies, the tragic fact that heroes battle bravely with a mysterious fate shows that the ancient Greeks were unable to explain the calamities that they encountered and attributed them to the gods' will. In Shakespearean tragedies, as Bradley writes, "we find practically no trace of fatalism in its more primitive, crude and obvious form"[17] because by the Renaissance people recognized that human disasters derive mainly from human actions and the conflict that results when individual desire confronts the moral order. Chinese culture, on the other hand, is celebrated for its early rationalism. The ancient Chinese philosophers paid great attention to the secular world and ignored the divine world. Thus, in traditional Chinese tragedy the connection between the hero's tragic end and its source is clear, unclouded by mysterious supernatural elements.

Chinese philosophy provides a convincing interpretation of the happy ending in Chinese tragedies. Unlike the Greek philosophers, who center their studies on the origin of the universe and objects, classical Chinese philosophers concentrate on the relation between objects, conceiving *yin* and *yang* as the paramount antithesis of the universe and the relation between five elements (metal, wood, water, fire, and earth) as the main pattern of the relationship between other objects.[18] According to the yin and yang principle, there is a corresponding relationship between nature and human beings, like the macro-and microcosmic relationship in the Middle Ages and the age of Shakespeare. Therefore, like nature, human society moves in the same cyclic way: a decline must be followed by new prosperity, disaster by good fortune, and so on. Thus the ancient Chinese took life's changing phenomena for granted.

Naturally, this mode of thinking has had great influence on the works of traditional Chinese tragic dramatists. It is assumed that dramatists would not stop at the moment when a protagonist has suffered or been destroyed by evil forces; they must show the whole cycle and bring good fortune to the protagonist to atone for his misfortune, even if only by wishful thinking. Consequently, almost all Chinese tragedies have happy endings, a pattern that obviously derives from the belief in cyclical recurrence. Although Chinese tragedy does expose life's contradictions, they are concealed by a happy ending in which confidence, hope, and optimism triumph over the existing political system and moral order.

By contrast, Shakespearean tragedy covers a wide range of problems of the period and of the general human condition, without reference to any idealized or deified political system—although Tillyard thought that he had found them in Shakespearean historical plays. Shakespearean tragedy arouses doubts, scruples, hopelessness, sometimes even pessimism and nihilism, feelings that are basically in tune with the contradiction in the philosophy of this age:

> Shakespeare's drama reflects conflict between traditional views, as in Aquinas, for whom value may be present and bound up in the object, and newer views of such figures as Bruno, with his aesthetic relativism, and Hobbes, with his notion of value as relative to a market-situation.[19]

Shakespearean tragedy represents a general trend of the Renaissance in which people began to criticize conventional ideas and establish new ideological and value systems. To some extent, Shakespearean and Chinese tragedies demonstrate one of the main differences between modern Western and traditional Chinese cultures. Since the European Renaissance Western culture has become a dynamic "culture of regeneration" with the ability to constantly produce new ideas. On the other hand, Chinese tragedy clearly shows that although unique and rich, Chinese culture had become a static and closed system—or a "culture of preservation"—since Buddhism was mingled with Confucianism and Taoism during the Song and Ming dynasties (about A.D. 1000–1400; see the Appendix).[20] Chinese philosophical and political ideas also account for the general tendency of tragedy to portray subjects and women but not rulers. In ancient China, an emperor had absolute power and divine right, which was based on Confucian ethics and strengthened by the philosophy of Taoism. It is impossible for Chinese dramatists to present the suffering and destruction of emperors, for this would go against both public opinion and the authority of the monarchy. During some periods of Chinese history, as in the Ming dynasty, special laws prohibited players from acting as emperors or speaking any lines that blasphemed them. Offenders would have been punished severely and even put to death.[21]

In comparison, Shakespearean tragedy comes to us with a different social and ideological background. Historically England, as well as most other European countries, was not a country with a fully developed, centrally controlled political system strictly ruled by a monarch. The relationship between a ruler and his or her subjects was relatively loose. Unlike Chinese subjects, English citizens were not taught to obey their kings unconditionally. Moreover, as the dominant religion in England and Europe, Christianity did not emphasize the authority of secular power. Thus it can be said that in Western history, the supremacy and divine right of kingship were not reaffirmed and reinforced by philosophical, religious, and political ideas.[22] Consequently, the suffering and death of kings could be used as subject matter. Even corrupt and cruel rulers could be presented, as Shakespeare did in his tragedies and histories.

Conventional political ideas and social institutions can help us account for the representation of officials and women in traditional Chinese tragedy. As I discussed above, in ancient China the social positions of a subject, a son, and a wife are subordinate and unstable. The good relationship between ruler and subject and between husband and wife depends on the behavior of subject and wife, but not on ruler and husband. A subject and a wife must make every effort to maintain a harmonious relationship with his ruler and her husband through strict observance of Confucian ethics (*li*), which demands the absolute submission and loyalty of a subject and the absolute submission and chastity of a wife. The process of seeking and maintaining good relationships with ruler and husband is often full of hardship and suffering and liable to result in misfortune. Therefore, it is inevitable that subjects and wives would fill tragic roles on the historical stage.

Shi (Confucian politicians and officials) are a very special social class in Chinese history, serving as representatives of Confucianism. In many ways no one can understand Chinese culture well without some knowledge of *shi*. It is difficult to find its English or European counterpart in Western history because it was created by a unique examination system in ancient China that selected civil officials according to ability but not to family status. A *shi* is not simply an official but is usually a trinity of Confucian scholar, official, and poet or writer. His experience can be divided into three rough periods: first, as a student or scholar studying classical learning, especially that of Confucius, and practicing writing poems and articles; second, as an official (after passing the imperial examination) serving the emperor in government at levels as high as a minister or as low as a junior official; third, as a poet or writer engaging in literary creative works, particularly when relegated to a lower position or ousted from his post or framed by a corrupt minister.

To the Chinese *shi* stand as both defenders and the victims of the feudal political system in the minds of Chinese people because their careers are full of frustrations. As a rule emperors tend to trust the corrupt officials who always flatter them and avoid the upright officials who give frank and honest advice. The position of a faithful official, therefore, is quite unstable. It is very likely for him to be treated wrongly by his superior or the emperor at any time, and sometimes even to be executed by a corrupt courtier carrying out an order issued by the emperor, as we see in political tragedies such as *The Flag of Loyalty* and *The Story of the Honest Subject*. Being both poets and writers at the same time, *shi* express their indignation and complaints directly in poems and indirectly in drama and novels. But their resentment, no matter how high, never causes them to question the supremacy of the emperor. They never rebel against the emperor, as do some characters in Shakespearean tragedies and histories, even if they know he is wrong, because conventional Confucian and Taoist principles require unconditional loyalty. Instead they divert their indignation onto the corrupt courtiers, believing that it is they who deceive the emperor and bring about chaos in the court and society; therefore the root of their misfortune is the corrupt courtiers but not the emperor. It is not hard to see how these beliefs lead to stereotyped conflict in traditional Chinese political tragedies and happy endings in other tragedies.

Thus at least two evident facts partly account for the appearance of officials as protagonists in Chinese tragedies: *shi* are liable to meet with misfortune and they are writers. However, I do not mean to imply that any writer necessarily describes his own experience or social class in his works, but only that it is a natural inclination to depict what is familiar. Shakespeare, of course, is one of a few great writers whose creative activities are not limited by personal experience.

Women are often presented as protagonists because in past centuries their position was the lowest in society. They had no personal freedom and existed totally as appendages of men. According to Confucian ethics a woman must follow the principle of "the three obediences and the four virtues." The "three obediences" are that a woman must obey her father before marriage, obey her husband after marriage, and obey her son after the death of her husband. The last obedience means she must live with her son and not remarry after her husband dies. The "four virtues" pertain only to a married woman. When she comes into her husband's family after marriage, she must take good care of her parents-in-law, serve her husband with all her heart, have a good relationship with her sister-in-law, and get on well with neighbors. She is the person who works hardest in the family and is also the one most likely to be blamed, as in the situation of Zhao Wu Niang in *The Story of a Pipa*. Moreover, she is likely to be cast off by her husband or by her parents-in-law through her husband if they do not like her. Some poorer women have to become prostitutes, thereby meeting with more misfortune. This is how prostitutes also come to appear in tragedies such as Li Xian Jun in *The Fan of Peach Blossom* and Du Shi Niang in *Du Shi Niang*. Traditional Chinese tragedy typically reflects the miserable reality of women in ancient China. Although women in the Elizabethan age were also submissive and powerless, as some critics have pointed out,[23] comparatively speaking their situation was better than that of women in ancient China. At least Elizabethan women had fewer spiritual fetters imposed on them than their Chinese counterparts. Chinese tragedy, like the rest of traditional literature, displays a tendency to support feminist ideas by describing the oppression of women in a cruel patriarchal society and by showing great sympathy for them. This support arises because not only did Chinese women suffer from physical and mental oppression, as I discussed above, but they were also victims of many inhumane customs such as footbinding. Another reason, however, stems from the multiple status of classical Chinese dramatists and writers, which made them express their own grievances through the similar plight of women. There is no doubt that Shakespeare's plays, especially the comedies, also represent some feminist ideas, though critics have argued vigorously about the dramatist's feminist perspective,[24] but in comparison, the feminist tendency in Chinese tragedies seems to show a closer connection to its cultural circumstances.

Every culture has its own religious and moral doctrines that are enormously influential in molding its tragic concept. Through an examination of a culture's religion and ethics we can further analyze some aspects of the differences in tragic concept between Shakespearean and traditional Chinese tragedy. For instance, why is there a "tragic flaw" in Shakespeare's protagonists and a state of perfection of the principal characters of Chinese tragedies? Shakespeare is said to have inherited the cultural traditions of Greece, Rome, and Christianity, mingling them with the newly rising humanism of his age. In accordance with the religious faith of the ancient Greeks and Romans, the gods are perfect, powerful, and dominate human fate. Correspondingly, humanity is imperfect and weak and is constantly punished by the gods for its crimes and mistakes, as in Greek and Roman tragedies. The Christian concept of Original Sin makes it clear that people are born sinful and can only achieve happiness in the next life by atonement for their sins. Humanism interprets good and evil in terms of human nature and advocates that human beings are not perfect but have potential tendencies toward both good and evil. This makes it easier for us to understand why some flaws or frailties appear in the protagonists of Shakespearean tragedy, even though they are great heroes who command our respect. The main purpose of the concept of human fallibility in the Greek and Christian religions seems to be to intimidate or teach uncivilized people, to make them recognize their limitations and become humble and modest.

By contrast, Chinese culture, even in its early stage, appears to have more rationality and a less theological bias. It uses reason rather than religion to help people realize why they should follow moral principles and teaches that both individuals and society will benefit from courtesy and good behavior. Confucianism holds that people are born basically good. There is no notion that God is perfect and man is sinful in Confucian ethics because Confucius did not measure human behavior in the light of divine nature when he established his moral doctrine. Unlike the philosophy of ancient Europe, the core of Confucianism is learning how to become a perfect and virtuous person. To achieve this goal, one should first cultivate moral character and then administer one's affairs in such a way that all members of the family live together in perfect harmony. Finally one serves the monarch, manages state affairs, and brings about great order in the land. To be virtuous, as I discussed above, a woman must observe the three obediences and the four virtues. The most important virtue is her fidelity to her husband. Having yin and yang as an archetype of antithesis in the universe, the ancient Chinese saw good and evil as an antithesis in human society and took their existence for granted. Thus a positive leading character in tragedy and other works must be a person of the highest virtue, striving after the social ideal of Confucianism or against evil forces. Accordingly, the perfection of their moral nature arouses deep respect and their suffering and destruction sympathy in an audience, allowing its members to consciously or unconsciously model themselves after the virtuous characters. In this way traditional Chinese tragedies serve to instruct the people, which after all was the prime goal of their dramatists.

The cultural elements discussed so far are only secondary and external influences upon the concepts of tragedy as developed by Shakespeare and the ancient Chinese dramatists. The major influence upon both concepts is aesthetic ideas, which serve as fundamental criteria by which to judge the artistic merits of literary works. Aesthetic standards obviously vary with different cultures, and different criterions of tragedy are to be found in Shakespearean and Chinese tragedies. When we watch both types of tragedy being performed we sense that the plays are beautiful and impressive. Yet the emotional effects they bring about are entirely different. The effect of Shakespearean tragedy, caused by the suffering and death of the noble protagonists, is to arouse fear, shock, depression, sublimity and mystery, and pity in the audience. On the other hand, the effect of traditional Chinese tragedy, produced by the suffering and destruction of virtuous, decent, and weak characters, evokes respect, love, sorrow, and great sympathy and pity. Influenced by Greek, Roman, and Spanish tragedies, which pay great attention to horror and fear, Shakespeare heightens the climate of death and horror in his tragedies and includes sensational scenes to shock his audience. Compared with traditional Chinese tragedy, however, the attempt to arouse sympathy and pity in Shakespearean tragedy seems weak. This is not merely because all Shakespearean protagonists are strong, independent, self-confident, and self-contained persons who demand no protection from others and require no sympathy and pity until they suffer greatly and are destroyed at the end. Rather it is mainly because the catastrophe partly derives from their own defects and errors. In a sense they deserve their tragic fates, which weakens their sympathetic appeal. Only a few of the innocent protagonists such as Hamlet and Romeo and Juliet may earn the compassion of a Chinese audience.

In comparison, Chinese dramatists rarely play up horror and death and never write terrifying and thrilling scenes. They concentrate instead on the effect of sympathy and pity. According to the aesthetic standard of the ancient Chinese, only a virtuous person, not a defective one, can command respect. The same is true for a weak person but not a strong one. Therefore, in their tragedies Chinese dramatists create characters with inner virtue and physical beauty to win the admiration and respect of an audience. Any suffering and death happening to these characters would weigh heavily on Chinese playgoers.

Of the many sad events in human life, which is the one that should be regarded as possessing aesthetic value and a basic tragic sense? Traditional Western and Chinese cultures approach this question in different ways. Because of the origin of their culture—Greek myth and epics—Westerners tend to choose the suffering and downfall of a great person or the destruction of something great and extraordinary as the fundamental tragic sense in literature. This is not a tragic sense caused by ordinary social life. It is instead a sense of sadness throbbing with sublimity, strength, and vigor; as a Shakespearean scholar says, "As a rule, to be properly called tragedy, the disaster has to have an element of heroic pathos or some sensational and astounding quality."[25]

This basic tragic sense, through medieval heroic epics, Christian romance as in the stories of King Arthur, and the works of early Elizabethan dramatists, was handed down to Shakespeare. To these influences he added the great agony caused by the split of human nature and the consciousness of the general predicament of the human condition. Thus his use of tragedy is unique and ranks as the greatest in the world on the assumption that

Any great tragedy touches on the fundamental questions of the ultimate cause of human suffering, the origin and nature of evil in man, and the existence of a destructive or benevolent fate. It is an expression of a universal desire to come to terms with these disturbing uncertainties.[26]

Bearing some resemblance to the type of tragic sense characterizing modern Western drama and novels, such as in Ibsen's plays or in Thomas Hardy's novels, tragedy as conceived by the ancient Chinese resulted from sorrowful events occurring in the lives of ordinary people such as the parting of friends, homesickness, unhappy love affairs, the suffering and death of a beautiful woman forsaken by her husband, chaos of war, and so on.[27] These misfortunes were chosen by two standards: value and beauty. In summary, the fundamental tragic sense of early Chinese culture can be said to be a feeling caused by the loss and destruction of somebody or something valuable and beautiful. This sadness, mingled with sentiment and gentleness, served as the major emotional tone throughout Chinese poetry and gradually permeated into dramas and novels, even affecting music.[28] To be sure, more vigorous elements appear in the Chinese literature of some periods, as in the poetry of the Jian An period, the Tang dynasty, and the South Song dynasty,[29] but these qualities are mainly heroism and patriotism, and not tragic feelings. Therefore, the uniqueness of Chinese literature is largely based on this gentle, sentimental feeling of sadness. Almost all the masterpieces of Chinese poetry, novels, and drama, especially tragedy, are imbued with this emotion. Examples are the often-quoted and widely loved ancient poem "A Spring Moonlit Night on the River" ("Chun Jiang Hua Yue Yie") by Zhang Ruo Xu and the great novel *The Dream of the Red Mansion* (*Hong Lou Meng*) by Cao Xue Qin. This aesthetic convention may help to explain from another angle why the Chinese playwrights tend to use women as tragic protagonists. The suffering and destruction of a beautiful woman would produce the very emotions that the Chinese people appreciate most.

Behind this "beauty of gentle sadness" was the general Chinese aesthetic principle of the "beauty of balance and restraint," a concept based on the Confucian philosophy of "the doctrine of the mean" that dominated many types of art in ancient China. Knowing this, one can understand more easily why the tragic sense in traditional Chinese tragedy was never as strong as that of Shakespearean tragedy. By the principle of the "beauty of balance and restraint," all the feeling and emotion presented in a work of art must be kept in moderation and never carried to an extreme, otherwise the beauty of the work would be damaged. Confucian aesthetic theory advocated that man's feeling was "generated by disposition and controlled by moral sense,"[30] so a talented Chinese artist always keeps a good balance of emotion and reason in his works.

The "beauty of balance and restraint" principle may well be the main reason for the happy endings found in traditional Chinese tragedies. To avoid too strong an impact upon an audience, on the assumption that this would damage the play's dramatic merit and violate the principle of the "beauty of balance and restraint," playwrights created happy endings to moderate tragic feelings. This principle also explains why in traditional Chinese tragedy there are few representations of abnormal psychological states, which are often found in Shakespearean tragedies. In Chinese tragedies, emotion is so carefully controlled that the characters do not display obvious mental disorders.

This brief comparison of Shakespearean and traditional Chinese tragedy has pointed out the striking difference between the two types of plays in particular tragic elements and in the basic tragic concept, as well as their connections with Western and Eastern cultures. In general one can find more profound philosophical thoughts in Shakespearean tragedy than in its Chinese counterpart and a clearer moral purpose in the latter than in the former. Having said this, I must add that the strong moral sense in traditional Chinese tragedy does not damage its dramatic merit, due to the fact that in most cases one cannot divorce moral from aesthetic concerns in literary works and that the best Chinese tragedies have come down to us with relatively little moralization. In terms of aesthetics, Shakespearean tragedy mingles sadness with sublimity and vigor—as Schopenhauer says, "Our pleasure in tragedy belongs not to the faculty of beauty, but to that of sublimity"[31]—while traditional Chinese tragedy presents sadness mixed with beauty and gentleness. Therefore, the principal tragic spirit of the two types of tragedies may be summarized as the destruction of greatness and the destruction of beauty.

The tragic concept of classical Chinese dramatists obviously differs from that of Aristotle, who thought that the downfall of a virtuous character would not raise terror or sympathy. However, the logic of the Chinese does not completely contradict that of Aristotle since they use the happy ending as a remedy for the undeserved misfortune of the protagonist. Although the tragic concepts of Shakespeare and traditional Chinese playwrights are different, some parallels between the two forms of tragedy do exist. For instance, *Hamlet* is, to some extent, similar to a Chinese political tragedy and *Romeo and Juliet* resembles a Chinese love tragedy. A more interesting parallel is to be found between traditional Chinese tragedy and the English sentimental melodrama of defeat in the eighteenth century. This type of melodrama presents innocent and pure protagonists (often women) whose downfall is caused by undeserved misfortune and external forces. The drama is based on an optimistic faith in human nature and has an explicit moral goal. The emotional effect of the melodrama also has an affinity with that of traditional Chinese tragedy:

> a tragic hero's fall releases complex feelings: pity touched by fear and awe, admiration tempered by moral reservations or even qualified by irony and laughter . . . melodramas of defeat are simpler and more imme- diately appealing. For the spectacle of totally unmerited misfortune our tears flow freely and our admiration knows no bounds. After all, such feelings cost us nothing and attest the sensibility and moral beauty of our souls.[32]

Despite the striking contrast between Shakespearean and tradi- tional Chinese tragedy, the two types resemble each other faintly in that both suggest a tendency for characters to renounce the world. In Shakespearean tragedy the tendency is presented directly and ex- plicitly, as in *Hamlet, Macbeth, Timon,* and other plays, and it seems to be caused by the inherent tragedy found in the human condition. In traditional Chinese tragedies, mainly in the later tragedies of the Qing dynasty (see Appendix), this renouncement is represented indi- rectly and implicitly (as in *The Hall of Longevity, The Fan of Peach Blossom,* and the tragedies adapted from the great novel *The Dream of the Red Mansion*), yet still with the distinctive aura of gentle sadness caused by disillusionment with the mortal world, a concept that derives from the spirit of Taoism. Beautiful imagery often poeti- cizes this idea of resignation, as for example "life is a dream."

We have seen striking contrasts between Shakespearean tragedy and traditional Chinese tragedy, but we shall see similarities in the two cultures' treatment of comedy. The two traditions, however, reach the same goal by different routes. That is, although the basic comic concepts are similar, the particular comic patterns, which are deeply affected by their cultural surroundings, are quite different.

Most Shakespeare critics classify Shakespearean comedies into three categories: romantic, problem, and tragicomedy (romance). Of the three romantic comedy predominates because it exhibits the ma- jor characteristics of all types of Shakespearean comedy.

Traditional Chinese comedies are usually classified according to two general types: they either attack vice, folly, or foolish behavior, or they describe the achievement of happiness or praise virtuous action. The first type includes satirical comedy and in the second is "laudatory comedy" (for lack of a better term; some Chinese scholars also call it humorous or lyrical comedy).[33]

Since it is difficult to draw a clear distinction between satirical and laudatory comedy, one can detect a fair number of Chinese comedies having both types. Most Chinese comedies, however, are laudatory comedies. Satirical comedies occupy only a small proportion of the canon and most of them were written with less dramatic skill. *The Ten Greatest Classical Chinese Comedies* lists seven laudatory comedies: *The Romance of the Western Chamber, Li Kui Carries Thorns, Looking over the Wall, The Secluded Boudoir, The Story of a Jade Hairpin, The Green Peony,* and *The Errors of a Kite.* Two of them, *The Green Peony* and *The Errors of a Kite,* are in fact combinations of both laudatory and satirical comedy. There are three satirical comedies in this collection: *A Slave to Money, Rescued by a Coquette,* and *The Wolf in Mount Zhong Shan.*

The general characteristics of Chinese laudatory comedies are very similar to those of Shakespearean romantic comedies. They share many comic elements such as theme, characterization, atmosphere, pattern, and ending. It is interesting that most laudatory comedies were also called romances by ancient Chinese dramatists. There are some parallels between those Chinese comedies having a mixed style of satire and extolment and certain Shakespearean romantic comedies such as *Love's Labor's Lost, The Merchant of Venice,* and *Twelfth Night.* We can even see some problem comedies in traditional Chinese comedy, but unfortunately they are not considered comedies by modern Chinese scholars because the general climate in these plays is too serious to amuse audiences in spite of a happy ending. For these reasons, this present comparison between Shakespearean and traditional Chinese comedy will center on Shakespearean romantic comedies and traditional Chinese laudatory comedies.

Most Shakespeare critics agree that the major themes of Shakespearean comedy are love and friendship. Similarly almost all the Chinese laudatory comedies are concerned with love and marriage and some of them with friendship. The two types of comedy are also linked by minor themes such as family relationships, money, corruption, and other social problems that are usually found in Shakespeare's problem comedies and Chinese satirical comedies.

The theme of love, combined with other themes, runs through Shakespeare's early and mature romantic comedies and his problem plays and romances. Against varied settings, Shakespeare's young lovers strive for ideal love, overcoming every impediment that faces them because, as A. R. Humphreys says in the introduction to the

Arden Shakespeare edition of *Much Ado About Nothing*, "the course of true love never did run smooth, and in the romantic comedy, though seldom in real jeopardy, it has amusing or touching impediments to surmount."[34] The love stories in Shakespearean comedies serve not only to create a delightful atmosphere and happy endings, but also describe vividly the psychological subtlety of the characters in love and explore a wide range of problems relating to love and marriage.

Unlike Shakespearean love comedies, which are so varied that it is hard to generalize about them, traditional Chinese love comedies have a clear pattern that shows their connection to conventional Chinese ideas of love, marriage, and happiness. Most of the plays have a similar format: a young gifted Confucian scholar (usually with low social status) meets by chance a beautiful young woman (usually from a wealthy family or a great house). They fall in love at first sight, but unfortunately they are kept from each other by social barriers such as their difference in social status, parental opposition, and sometimes the prior claims of a rival. The lovers, therefore, become secretly engaged to each other. When their love affair is exposed to the parents, a compromise allows the young man to marry the woman on condition that he must pass the imperial examination to become a high-ranking official. (It should be remembered that in ancient China, only men were eligible to sit for the imperial examination. Although some women of wealthy families were educated, their training was mainly for enhancing their accomplishments.) Then the young man goes to the capital to take the imperial examination. The comedy ends with the return of the young man with a title of Zhuang Yuan (the first-place rank on the examination list) and a new official position, as well as the happy wedding of the hero and heroine. The famous Yuan play *The Romance of the Western Chamber* most typifies this pattern. This basic format obviously resembles Greek New Comedy and the comedies of Plautus and Terence. It also suggests, in some respects, the plot of Shakespearean comedies such as *A Midsummer Night's Dream* and *The Merry Wives of Windsor*, in which the lovers marry the partners of their choice against their parents' will.

The plots of some traditional Chinese love comedies are slightly different from the above pattern. In *The Secluded Boudoir*, the love between Jiang Shi Long and Wang Rui Lan does not take place in the garden of a house or a monastery but during their flight from the chaos of a war. In the turbulence caused by foreign invasion, Jiang Shi Long is separated from his sister and Wang Rui Lan, whose father is a defense minister in the court, is separated from her mother.

In the wilderness Jiang Shi Long encounters Wang Rui Lan. She asks him to help her escape with him in spite of her reluctance to approach a strange man because it would be very dangerous for a beautiful woman to travel alone. To avoid suspicion she has to agree that they will pretend to be a couple. This clever device, as expected, brings about a series of dramatic situations. The rest of the story resembles the general formula of traditional Chinese love comedies. After many setbacks, Jiang Shi Long passes the imperial examination, winning the title of Zhuang Yuan, and obtains a high-ranking appointment. The play ends with the reunion of the families and the formal wedding of the hero and the heroine. This love theme, mingled with the separation and reunion of a family, seems to be a universal comic device and as such can be found in some Shakespearean comedies, as, for instance, *The Comedy of Errors, Twelfth Night,* and most of the romances. Two other popular Chinese love comedies, *The Green Peony* and *The Errors of a Kite,* also feature unique plots. In *The Green Peony,* the action of the lovers is played out before a social setting related to the literary activities of the Confucian scholars. It is not easy to find its parallel in Shakespearean comedies, for the main action in this play is closely concerned with Chinese cultural tradition.

The claim for free choice in marriage has been emphasized more in traditional Chinese love comedies than in Shakespearean comedies because, as I discussed earlier in this chapter, women in ancient China were firmly fettered by a feudal ethical code and controlled by their parents. Thus the message to shake off the bonds of old marriage customs resounds through these plays. In *The Romance of the Western Chamber,* although Ying Ying's mother dislikes Zhang Sheng because of his low social status, Ying Ying still secretly marries him. In *Looking over the Wall,* Li Qian Jin elopes with her lover, Pei Shao Jun, and secretly lives with him for seven years in Pei's house. When Pei's father learns the truth and upbraids her, she bravely argues in justification of her action. At the end of these plays the heroes and heroines express their common aspiration: "We wish all the lovers in this world could marry their beloved ones" (as, for example, in *The Romance of the Western Chamber, Classical Chinese Comedies,* 5.4, "Qing Jiang Yin," 157).

The situation of an ideal partner involves not only the general assumption of love, but also particular social circumstances and cultural biases. Shakespeare's comedies do not emphasize the objective condition of the lovers such as wealth and family background, but stress instead subjective qualities such as looks, manner, virtue, and so forth. This general tendency is in harmony with the concept of love popular during the Renaissance. Like Shakespeare, Chinese playwrights usually describe heroines in terms of their beauty and sweet natures. Heroes, on the other hand, are valued for their literary talents rather than allover virtue and accomplishment, as Shakespeare does in his comedies. In the beginning of *Looking over the Wall* Minister Pei talks about the talent of his son Pei Shao Jun, the hero in the play:

> My son Shao Jun is a rare genius. He could speak at the age of three and read when he was five. He wrote very well when he was only seven years old. At the age of ten, he was able to compose a poem impromptu. (Act 1, *Classical Chinese Comedies*, 35)

In *The Romance of Western Chamber*, Zhang Sheng writes poetry to Ying Ying to express his deep affection, eventually winning her love. In *The Green Peony*, the two heroes, Xie Ying and Gu Chan, marry their sweethearts and defeat their rivals, two ignorant dandies, through their outstanding literary gifts. Why literary skills should be so important in Chinese culture relates to the country's emphasis on classical—mainly Confucian—learning (including literature, history, and philosophy). Only by possessing outstanding literary talent could a young man pass the imperial examination and obtain a high official position in ancient China, thus making this skill the most important factor in evaluating a young man.

Scholars agree that Shakespeare's comedies show a great variety of love patterns such as falling in love at first sight (*As You Like It*); love triangles (*The Two Gentlemen of Verona*); winning love by struggle and wit (*The Merchant of Venice* and *All's Well That Ends Well*); and finding love by chance (*Twelfth Night*)—all of which are in tune with Shakespeare's romantic concept and the general literary and dramatic tendencies of the Renaissance. Traditional Chinese comedies have fewer patterns than Shakespearean comedies, yet they have their own distinctive motifs. In most of these plays, falling in love at first sight is the main topic, as in *The Romance of the Western Chamber*, *Looking over the Wall*, and *The Story of a Jade Hairpin*. In some comedies two other themes are evident: affection between the lovers that is bred by their mutual experience in adversity (*The Secluded Boudoir*) and affection that comes first through creative literary activity (*The Green Peony* and *The Errors of a Kite*). These two motifs command scholarly interest not only because of their dramatic use in the plot, but also because of their close connection to Chinese historical and cultural backgrounds. As stated earlier, in *The Secluded Boudoir*, Jiang Shi Long and Wang Rui Lan fall in love while fleeing from the turmoil of war. This setting relates to Chinese history in that the chaos of war and famine are two major disasters that have occurred frequently. In *The Green Peony*, the affection of the two heroines, Sheng Wanr and Che Jing Fang, for the two heroes, Xie Ying and Gu Can, comes from their appreciation of their literary talent, even before they meet them. The ancient Chinese believed that a person with outstanding talent and high virtue must also be handsome and have an attractive manner, a philosophy based on the ideal aesthetic assumption that beauty is always associated with intelligence and virtue and ugliness with foolishness and stupidity. Thus this love pattern can be singled out as the most frequently recurring motif in traditional Chinese love comedies. It bears the imprint of an evident Chinese cultural bias, and its parallel is difficult to find in Shakespearean comedies.

Another difference between Shakespearean and Chinese comedies involves the initiative of men and women in love affairs. In Shakespearean comedies both heroes and heroines seek love actively. Many of the heroines even begin a love affair, as do Viola in *Twelfth Night*, Rosalind in *As You Like It*, and Helena in *All's Well That Ends Well*. By contrast, the active role in love is nearly always played by men in traditional Chinese comedies. The reason, as I mentioned earlier, is that women in ancient China were kept at home and had no opportunity to participate in social intercourse, whereas men possessed absolute freedom in all social activities.

The love themes in Shakespearean and traditional Chinese comedies are also influenced by marital relationships. In Shakespearean comedies men and women appear to be almost equal in love affairs and marriage; only in a few plays are the motifs characterized by male supremacy, as in *The Taming of the Shrew* and *The Comedy of Errors*. Yet in Chinese love comedies, although love and marriage are highly idealized, one can easily find the imprint of male domination. In most of these plays, when the lovers meet secretly, particularly before they decide to make love, the heroine always expresses concern that her lover may forsake her after his passion is satisfied. Then the hero must swear to be loyal to her forever. In *The Romance of the Western Chamber*, after many setbacks Ying Ying eventually promises to meet Zhang Sheng secretly in the garden. Before they consummate their love, she says:

> I shall give you tonight
> My precious virgin body.
> I'll commit my whole life to your care.

Don't abandon me on some later day
And leave me to sigh time away in loneliness.

(4.1, *Classical Chinese Comedies*, 126)

When Zhang Sheng passes the imperial examination, wins the title
of Zhuang Yuan, and waits for the emperor's appointment in the
capital, Ying Ying asks his servant boy to send him something special
to remind him of his oath. These examples reflect the lower social
place of Chinese women in the past and the fact that they were
viewed only as appendages to men.

Friendship is another important theme in both types of comedies.
In his comedies Shakespeare extols true friendship and criticizes dis-
loyalty. Antonio in *The Merchant of Venice* is a typical honest friend
because he not only generously helps his friend with money but also
risks his life to help Bassanio seek love and happiness. Interestingly,
his action resembles an old Chinese saying that defines the highest
level of friendship: "To help your friends, you must be brave enough
to stab your chest with a knife." On the other hand, in *The Two
Gentlemen of Verona*, to satisfy selfish desires Proteus commits a
double treachery: he is disloyal to both his friend Valentine and his
love, Julia. Friendship (*yi*) is also represented in traditional Chinese
comedies. In *The Romance of the Western Chamber*, Du Jun Shi,
who is a good friend of Zhang Sheng, the hero, passes the imperial
military examination and becomes a general. When Zhang Sheng and
his beloved, Ying Ying, are threatened by a rebellious general who
intends to take Ying Ying by force, Du Jun Shi immediately leads
his troops to rescue his friends. At the same time he helps to bring
about their marriage to further protect Ying Ying from being married
off by her family. A similar subtheme of friendship is found in *The
Secluded Boudoir*. Here Jiang Shi Long risks his life to save a young
warrior, Tuo Man Xing Fu, causing them to become sworn brothers.
Later Tuo Man Xing Fu also saves Jiang Shi Long and his love, Wang
Rui Lan, from execution. At the end, both Jiang Shi Long and Tuo
Man Xing Fu pass the imperial examinations and marry their lovers.

Much of the fascination of Shakespearean comedies and traditional
Chinese comedies stems from characterization. Although Shakespeare's complex plot devices attract the attention of an audience,
what impresses it most is the colorfulness and subtlety of his
comic characters:

Less satiric than Jonson or Molière, less continuously witty than Con-
greve, less cerebral than Shaw, less funny than many lesser writers,
Shakespeare presents us with a variety of lively and attractive characters,

with whom audiences become friends, and he invests them with the riches of his poetry.[35]

In traditional Chinese comedies, the heroes and heroines who are held up to our admiration are not just models of morality. They are vividly portrayed young men and women with flexible moral codes and personal desires. Minor characters are also lifelike people with a variety of traits, even if some of them are only lightly sketched.

When I contrasted Shakespearean and traditional Chinese tragedies above, I found that one of the main differences between them in the treatment of protagonists is that their leading characters have different social statuses. Interestingly, however, the social standings of the characters in both types of comedy are quite similar. In most of his comedies Shakespeare represents the love affairs and friendships of young aristocrats, the business and domestic affairs of the middle class, and the daily lives of working people. Similarly, traditional Chinese comedies do not usually illustrate political court struggles—one of the central themes of traditional Chinese tragedies—so one rarely sees high-ranking officials such as ministers as leading characters in the comedies. Most of them have only supporting roles, chiefly as rigid parents opposing their children's desire to choose a mate and insisting on family status in marriage. In general, Chinese comedies have two groups of characters: young men and women from the middle and upper classes (landlords and officials) and ordinary people such as servants, porters, charlatans, pedants, shopowners, monks, nuns, matchmakers, soldiers, outlaws, prostitutes, and so on. Most of the comedies center on the love affairs and friendship of the young men and women, interwoven with the daily life of ordinary people.

The comparison of Shakespeare's tragic protagonists with those of Chinese tragedies discovered an interesting fact: Shakespeare's tragedies feature a world of men while traditional Chinese tragedies concentrate on women. More interestingly, the reverse occurs in the comedies. As many critics have pointed out, in his comedies Shakespeare favors female characters, or as some feminist critics have maintained, Shakespeare privileged the masculine Self in tragedy and the female Other in comedy.[36] This assumption can be used, in reverse order, to define gender and genre in traditional Chinese drama, for the tragedies are built around the female Other, as I discussed earlier, and the comedies around the masculine Self. A masculine dominance can be clearly seen in traditional Chinese comedy. First, in most of these plays it is the men who take the initiative in love affairs: they make every effort to approach female beloved ones and actively woo them. When the women weaken from the opposition of parents and other obstacles, it is the men who persuade and encourage them to make their own choices. Finally, at the ends of these plays it is also the men who pass the imperial examination by their erudition and talent, thereby meeting the parental requirement on social status and eventually winning their sweethearts. Second, Chinese comedies, particularly love comedies, in fact depict how young Confucian scholars obtain bliss because, as an old Chinese saying goes, the happiest moments of a man's life are the first night in the bridal chamber and the day when he sees his name on the imperial examination list. So basically one can safely say that traditional Chinese comedy is a world of men. Having said this, however, I must add that there are a few exceptions. For instance, in *Looking over the Wall,* the heroine appears more brave and decisive than the hero in their love affair. The privilege of the masculine Self in the comedies, however, by no means signifies that feminist ideas are denied. Women in the plays actually cooperate with men and serve as the embodiment of beauty and goodness. In this sense gender in traditional Chinese drama can be explained in the light of aesthetics. The first section of this chapter described the aesthetic archetype of traditional Chinese tragedy as the destruction of beauty, or beauty lost. And it is probably not far-fetched to say that the aesthetic archetype of traditional Chinese comedy is beauty regained. By "beauty regained" I mean that the dramatists of these plays present the process of seeking beauty. While deplorable, it is nonetheless understandable that classical Chinese dramatists emphasized the seekers (men) and not the objects of their search (women).

There is an evident pattern in the constitution of comic characters in Chinese comedies. Traditionally gifted scholars and beautiful women are the main characters. But besides the hero and the heroine, we also see in most comedies a conservative and strict parent serving as the embodiment of an old ethical code (such as Ying Ying's mother in *The Romance of the Western Chamber* and Defense Minister Wang in *The Secluded Boudoir*); a warm and resourceful servant (such as Hong Niang in *The Romance of the Western Chamber* and the servant of Han Shi Xun in *The Errors of a Kite*); a foolish rival, usually a playboy from a great house (such as Zheng Yuan in *The Romance of the Western Chamber* and Wang Gong Zi in *The Story of a Jade Hairpin*); and other lowlife people whose function is mainly to add comic atmosphere to the plays (for example, the quack Weng Tai Yi in *The Secluded Boudoir*). Although this basic pattern is very similar to that of Roman comedies and French neoclassical comedies, it is not found in Shakespeare because it is very difficult to discover a character type formula in his comedies. Even so there is a certain resemblance between the character patterns of the two comedies.

Besides young lovers, Shakespeare's comedies also feature their parents, some of them rigid and some quite open-minded, foolish rivals (such as Sir Andrew in *Twelfth Night* and Portia's suitors in *The Merchant of Venice*), and servants helping the lovers. We even find the English counterpart of Hong Niang, the waiting-girl to Ying Ying in *The Romance of the Western Chamber,* in *The Two Gentlemen of Verona.* Moreover the scene in which Lucetta delivers Proteus's love letter to Julia suggests the very dramatic moment in which Hong Niang passes the love poems of Zhang Sheng to Ying Ying, who pretends to be angry and blames Hong Niang. In Shakespearean comedies a great many characters belong to the lowest class and do much to create an amusing atmosphere for the audience. One might also say that Shakespeare's comic characters are more complex than those of Chinese comedies since his characters have more distinctive traits. For instance, clowns rarely appear, as they often do in Shakespeare's comedies, although one of the major role types in Chinese comedy is called *chou* (clown or fool). The *chou* in traditional Chinese drama is either a negative or a lowlife character whose main function is to add to the comic atmosphere. Yet Shakespeare's clown is not only a joke-maker but often a critic. Other special Shakespearean characters appear nowhere in Chinese comedies, as for example the degenerate knight (Falstaff), the melancholic (Jaques in *As You Like It*), and the fairies (in *A Midsummer Night's Dream*). This difference in character type is caused partly by social and cultural structures and partly by literary and dramatic convention.

Unlike characters in Chinese tragedies, who tend to be unflawed and uncomplicated, characters in the comedies are more human and colorful. This change results from certain evident factors. First, in the tragedies, men—as the embodiment of Confucian social ideals—are largely idealized. Yet in the comedies male activities revolve around one's private life and effort to seek personal happiness rather than social and political responsibility. Thus men may behave in ordinary ways, showing weak qualities or occasionally doing ridiculous things. Second, since the main purpose of Chinese comedy is to delight, not to teach, the playwrights felt free to create a carefree climate instead of a serious moral atmosphere and to portray a variety of characters without being limited by moral standards.

As an anthropological critic and a systems-builder, Northrop Frye gave an important impetus to postwar Shakespearean criticism. Frye believes that all comedies, including Shakespeare's romances, are self-contained conventions and structures rather than mirrors of life.[37] Frye takes the opposite approach to A. C. Bradley, who concentrated on character and lifelike reality. The dramatic merit of a great comic playwright is not based on how well he or she uses appropriate archetypal structures and conventions, for even the most mediocre writer can easily adopt them. Accordingly, Shakespeare's universal appeal does not derive from his use of conventions.

However, there is often a grain of truth in an extreme opinion. As an important approach to the study of Shakespearean comedies, Frye's criticism complements that of the Coleridge-Bradley tradition since it is difficult to divorce the reality of life from convention in all works of literature and art. In this chapter I pay attention to Frye's theory because my comparison of Chinese and Shakespearean drama has a cultural base, and archetypal structures usually stem from cultural traditions. Certain comic structures in traditional Chinese comedies clearly show their close connection to long-standing Chinese culture. But I should point out that the conventions and structures in Chinese comedy can hardly be traced back to primitive Chinese myth because, as I have mentioned earlier, Confucian scholars tend to ignore the supernatural; hence primitive Chinese legends and myths were not systematically collected, collated, and preserved. What remain today are only some fragments that cannot stand comparison with Greek and Roman myths. Nevertheless the archetypal structures in Chinese comedies have been shaped by Chinese feudal culture since the Spring and Autumn period (770 B.C.; see Appendix).

In *A Natural Perspective*, Frye divides the general structure of Shakespeare's comedies into three phases:

> This structure, then, usually begins with an anticomic society. . . . It often takes the form of a harsh or irrational law. . . . Most of these irrational laws are preoccupied with trying to regulate the sexual drive, and so work counter to the wishes of the hero and the heroine. . . .
>
> The second period of confusion and sexual licence is a phase that I may call the phase of temporarily lost identity. . . . most frequently a loss of sexual identity. . . .
>
> The third and final phase is the phase of the discovery of identity. This may take many forms, but I may generalize them as social (A identified with B) and individual (A identified as himself).[38]

The general structure of Chinese comedy is similar to that outlined by Frye. Most of the comedies also have an anticomic society and an irrational law (feudal ethic code) that is preoccupied with trying to regulate sexual drive and serves as an obstacle to the desire of the hero and the heroine. For example, although the protagonists love each other deeply, they are still prohibited from marrying by an old law that states that any marriage without parental consent is illegal. In *Looking over the Wall*, even though Pei Shao Jun and Li Qian Jin have been secretly married for seven years and have two children, Pei's father still brutally dissolves the union when he learns the truth.

The structure of Chinese comedies rarely has a phase like Frye's "temporarily lost identity." Only a faint shadow of it can be found, for classical Chinese writers seldom used the device of disguise. An example is a popular classical Chinese tragedy, *Liang Shan Po and Zhu Ying Tai*, in which Zhu Ying Tai disguises herself as a boy to study in a private school and falls in love with her classmate Liang Shan Po. Traditional Chinese comedy has indeed used the device of identity confusion, but usually it is presented in a different way. In some of the plays the heroes and heroines do not know their real identities until the end. For instance, in *Looking over the Wall*, the secret marriage of Pei Shao Jun and Li Qian Jin is regarded by others, and even by themselves, as illegal, although they were already engaged to be married by their parents some years previously. Sometimes the confusion of identity is caused by mistakes and misunderstanding. For example, *The Green Peony* and *The Errors of a Kite* have so many confusions of identity that the characters cannot tell who their lovers are. This phase can be termed a change of social status, for in most of the comedies the parents always ask the young man to pass the imperial examination and get an official appointment before they will consent to the marriage. This is obviously a key point leading to the final happy ending.

A parallel to the third phase, the discovery of identity, can easily be found in the structure of traditional Chinese comedies. At the ends of these plays the lovers are finally united and characters discover their real identities. Outwardly the happy endings of these comedies look like those of Shakespeare's comedies. A joyous wedding and a jubilant banquet celebrate the formal marriage of the lovers, as well as the reunion of a family. Behind this typical festive scene emerges a new society—a peaceful, happy, and harmonious society. In most cases the young lovers and their friends are also reconciled with the anticomic force, which can include their parents and the immoral rival, just as in the last phase of Shakespearean comic structure. Some exceptions to the pattern exist in both types of comedy, however. Shakespeare has characters like Shylock, Jaques, Don John, and Malvolio, and in *The Romance of the Western Chamber*, the loutish rival Zheng Yuan is not only defeated by the hero Zhang Sheng and his friends, but also commits suicide. In *The*

Story of a Jade Hairpin, the rival Wang Ren is heavily punished for his vice.

At the same time there are also some differences between the two comic structures. First, at the beginning of most Chinese comedies, another factor besides irrational law serves as an important anticomic force: social turbulence or the chaos of war. In *The Romance of the Western Chamber*, a rebellious band of soldiers robs people of their money and rapes women. In *The Peony Pavilion*, *The Story of a Jade Hairpin*, *The Secluded Boudoir*, and many other plays, the characters and their society are faced with the threat of foreign invasion. Compared to the second phase of the structure of Shakespearean comedies, as I have pointed out, Chinese comedies tend to present a change of social status instead of lost identity. Obviously there are also some differences in comic ending between the two types of comedy. First, after passing the imperial examination, all the heroes have their social status upgraded to match the family status of the heroines or just to satisfy the level of the particular Chinese audience. Second, the new harmonious society appearing at the end of the plays also marks the termination of the turbulence or chaos of war. Third, an imperial edict often rewards the hero and heroine or other concerned characters, which heightens the joyous atmosphere of the wedding and banquet.

The structure of traditional Chinese comedy can be traced to the ancient rituals and cultural conventions of China. In primitive Chinese society, people often celebrated their harvest and hunting gains with festive singing and dancing. Later, in Chinese slave society performances of singing and dancing for special occasions such as weddings or victory celebrations also affected the structure of comedy. The rituals and social conventions of Chinese feudal society, however, have left an obvious mark on the structure of these plays. During the long years of this period, people—especially those who belonged to the court, local government, or a wealthy house—would always hold a ceremony or give a banquet to celebrate a happy event such as a wedding, passing the imperial examination and getting an official position, rendering outstanding service in a war, and in particular receiving an award or honor from the emperor. These rituals have gradually shaped the basic conventions and ultimate goals that the plays were expected to achieve. In contrast with the structure of Shakespeare's comedies, which Frye maintains has evolved from religious rituals and myths, one can say that the structure of Chinese comedy derives largely from secular social and political practice.

The cycle of nature and movement from death to rebirth is considered by Frye as one of the major conventions of Shakespeare's comedies and is typically expressed in the romances.[39] This pattern can also be roughly applied to Chinese comedy, though it is not presented as overtly as in Shakespearean comedy. Using ancient Chinese literature as prototypes, classical Chinese writers often related spring to birth and hope and autumn and winter to death and hopelessness. In most Chinese comedies it is difficult to find an obvious movement from birth to death and back again to rebirth, yet this pattern appears in most tragedies. Almost all traditional Chinese tragedies have happy endings, and in most cases the heroes or heroines become celestial beings or spirits, a spiritual development that bears some resemblance to Christianity. An example of this pattern in the comedies can be found in *The Peony Pavilion*. In this play Du Li Niang, the heroine, dies of longing for her lover, Liu Meng Mei, whom she meets in a dream. She is resurrected when the real-life Liu Meng Mei digs up her grave and opens her coffin, an ending that may seem odd to Elizabethan audiences since it has no parallel in Shakespearean romances. This play belongs to the genre of tragicomedy and, by an interesting coincidence, also to the romances of traditional Chinese drama. The key point behind the death and rebirth of Du Li Niang is that the feudal ethical code makes people die and natural emotion and desire let them live again. This device was used by the dramatist Tang Xian Zu to criticize the rigid Confucian scholars of the Ming and Qing dynasties who pushed Confucian ethics to an extreme and to justify the role of human nature. Thus the use of this death-rebirth pattern in *The Peony Pavilion* shows a clear Chinese cultural influence, compared to the same pattern in Shakespeare's comedies, which embodies a more universal meaning.[40]

The presentation of the cycle of nature in traditional Chinese comedies is worth notice because there is a unique pattern of seasonal change in the plays. Unlike the cycle of nature in Shakespeare's comedy, which serves as an invisible superstructure, the change of season in Chinese comedy is designed mainly to support the comic action of the plays. For instance, in *The Romance of the Western Chamber*, *The Secluded Boudoir*, *The Story of a Jade Hairpin*, and other famous comedies, when the lovers are in an awkward predicament the action is always played out against a seasonal setting of autumn or winter; likewise an enchanting spring scene heightens the atmosphere when all the anticomic barriers are overcome and the lovers are finally united. This pattern stems from Chinese literary tradition, especially classical poetry, where the ancient poets tended to express their particular emotions through the appropriate seasonal scenes. The major difference between Shakespearean and traditional Chinese comedy in the use of the cycle of nature, then, is that in the former this pattern represents philosophical meanings and in the latter it serves as an expression of emotion.

There is, as some critics have pointed out, a unique structure in some Shakespearean comedies that shows us a forest scene or "green world." Coincidentally, there is also a small green world—not a dense forest but an exquisite garden—in most traditional Chinese comedies, as in *The Romance of the Western Chamber, Looking over the Wall, The Peony Pavilion, The Story of a Jade Hairpin,* and others. The garden is the principal setting where the comic action takes place. It is in this garden where the protagonists meet each other and first fall in love, unburden themselves of their grievances, finally become united, and where the whole family enjoys a festive celebration after the hero passes the imperial examination and becomes a high-ranking official. The garden setting, a typical convention of traditional Chinese comedy, is closely connected to Chinese cultural tradition. In ancient China, most wealthy families had a formal garden characterized by traditional Chinese horticultural practices and architecture. It was an ideal place for members of the family, particularly the women, to relax, play, and enjoy the sight of artificial rockeries, pools, paths, pavilions, and so on. Since the young women were kept inside the house all year round, this garden became the only outdoor place where they could act freely and enjoy themselves. In the history of Chinese literature and art, the garden scene has served as one of the major symbolic conventions in many masterpieces.

Both the forest world of Shakespeare's comedy and the garden world in traditional Chinese comedy come across to the audience not as simple settings but as profound symbols. In Shakespearean comedies the forest seems to be an embodiment of natural society, in contrast to the grim outside world. Such a contrast between the green world or natural society and the aristocratic or sophisticated world should be taken as one of the most distinctive conventions of Shakespeare's comedy. The tendency to cherish a pastoral or natural world descended from the courtly love tradition that has run through the history of European literature. It is also a reflection of social reality since Europe had begun to enter a kind of early industrial civilization during the Renaissance, possibly causing people to become worried that nature would be spoiled by a corrupt society. The green world of Shakespeare's comedy seems to suggest a utopia—an embodiment of an ideal world made necessary by increasing industrialization.

On the other hand, the garden of traditional Chinese comedies can be understood from a different point of view, for it stems from a different cultural background. Even so, the function and symbolic meaning of the garden bear a resemblance to those of the green worlds of Shakespeare's comedies. In China the garden usually serves as a symbol of a secluded earthly paradise, in contrast with the harsh outside world. It is a free and happy place where everyone has a right to make his or her own choices. The garden is a harmonious haven in which people enjoy open and equal relationships. In contrast to the forest world in Shakespeare's comedies, the garden in traditional Chinese comedies is not designed to present a striking contrast between the natural society and the sophisticated material world. At that time (from approximately 1271 to 1911), the Chinese did not see human society as separate from nature since ancient China had retained its natural economy and feudal political system and was still a long way from becoming an industrialized society. Thus the garden represented an ideal and proper place where the principle of life was in keeping with the basic and rational demand of human nature and at the same time was not violating the conventional ethical code. Such a representation was based on a general ideological tendency to change rigid feudal ethics and create more room for personal will during the Yuan, Ming, and Qing dynasties.

Unlike Jonson, Shakespeare excels in an English tradition of comedy that runs from Chaucer to Bernard Shaw. His comedies are less didactic than Jonson's or most other English comic writers and he mingles moral instruction with pleasure so perfectly that his comedies seem to be written for today's entertainment industry. In a sense one could say that the main purpose of Shakespeare's comedy is to represent life, particularly its happy side, through poetic imagination.

I have already mentioned that classical Chinese playwrights have fewer lessons to teach in their comedies than in their tragedies, although the moralizing of comedy was still emphasized by a few Chinese writers such as the famous classical dramatic critic and writer Li Yu, the author of *The Errors of a Kite*. But in practice classical Chinese comic writers often mixed moral instruction with lighter themes, sometimes even exhibiting an antifeudal attitude, just as Tang Xian Zu did in his play *The Peony Pavilion*. This is the very reason why so many brilliant comedies were attacked by orthodox Chinese critics, who believed that the first and most important purpose of drama was to propagate the Confucian ethical code. In the sixteenth century a heated argument between critics ensued over which play was better, *The Secluded Boudoir* or *The Story of a Pipa*. The debate in fact reflected the conflict between critics who emphasized moralizing and those who favored the representation of emotions.[41] Generally, however, like Shakespeare's comedy, the main purpose of traditional Chinese comedy is to represent the emotions, aspirations, and ideals of the ancient Chinese. Comedy should reflect life and not be designed to resemble a morals textbook.

In the history of comic criticism, satire has been regarded as an indispensable part of the comic concept. European comedy features a satiric tradition beginning with Aristophanes and continuing through Jonson and Molière to Bernard Shaw. The satiric element in traditional Chinese comedy can also be traced back to the early Can Jun plays in the Tang dynasty (see Appendix). The original purpose of these plays, which had only two actors, was to satirize the corruption of officials. Compared to most other European comic writers, Shakespeare is unusual in this connection because we rarely see satiric elements in his comedies. Like European comedy, the Chinese comic tradition has two parallel types: satiric and romantic comedy (laudatory comedy). In the early stages of traditional Chinese comedy the satiric tradition played a leading role, for we see more satiric comedies in the Tang, Song, and Yuan dynasties, as for example the Yuan plays *A Slave to Money* and *Rescued by a Coquette*. From the Ming dynasty on, the form of traditional Chinese drama was changed from short *zaju* into long "romance" plays; subsequently laudatory comedy became more dominant, along with the increase of more narrative elements in the plays. Today Chinese drama critics admit that the typical traditional Chinese comedy is laudatory comedy, not satiric comedy. In this way the overall attitude of classical Chinese comic writers toward satiric elements in comedy agrees with that of Shakespeare.

Take *The Green Peony* and *The Errors of a Kite* as examples. The satiric elements in the two plays are so gentle that they should not be called real satiric comedies, like those of Molière. Although we laugh at the absurdity of the evil rivals in these plays, we forgive them at the end. Both Shakespearean and traditional Chinese comedy apparently have the same purpose in laughter: we are invited to laugh when the principal characters are in absurd situations or do ridiculous things. This is friendly laughter. We are also asked to laugh when minor characters whom we do not like show their weaknesses and follies. This may be unfriendly laughter, but in most cases it tends to be a remedy, not a whip.

Generally speaking, the comic concepts of Shakespearean and traditional Chinese comedy are similar in most aspects. Both are designed mainly to delight or to create lifelike characters and to represent life with poetic imagination, but not especially to teach.

Both admire virtues and wisdom, presenting a bright and optimistic view of life, but do not satirize. Both are intended to represent the realization of personal happiness and the harmonious order of society. And both, with their unique devices of the utopian forest and the heavenly garden, set up for humanity brilliant and lofty social ideals.

2

General Artistic Characteristics and the Related Cultural Contexts

In the first chapter I discussed, through brief comparisons, the differences and similarities between Shakespearean and traditional Chinese drama in tragedy and comedy and explored the related social and cultural backgrounds that helped to shape the features of the two dramas. A general comparison between the artistic characteristics of the two dramas will now provide us with a wider field of vision to see even more clearly the distinctions between Shakespeare's plays and traditional Chinese drama, which in turn paves the way for a full understanding of the discussion of the interaction between Shakespeare and traditional Chinese drama in later chapters.

The feature of mixing comic and tragic scenes, while serving as one of the main characteristics of Shakespeare's works and often debated by Shakespearean critics, is also a distinctive characteristic of traditional Chinese drama, evoking controversies among modern Chinese dramatic critics when they tried to classify traditional Chinese drama by the Western criteria of tragedy and comedy. Hence this shared characteristic deserves more consideration. We shall find, through the obvious similarity between the two dramas in this aspect, many subtle differences concerning its function and related theatrical and philosophical traditions.

The mixture of tragedy and comedy, which I term a "mingled mode," is a typical and important factor in nearly all of Shakespeare's plays. While the dominant atmosphere in Shakespearean tragedy is sadness, it is sometimes suspended by comic scenes. Likewise, the comedies also have tragic scenes. This commingling is especially evident in traditional Chinese drama.

As I pointed out in the first chapter, the comic element is so strong in traditional Chinese tragedies that most of the plays have happy endings even though the allover mood is sad. Besides the happy endings in tragedies, however, comic scenes and characters often appear in the course of the plot.

A tragedy that incorporates both moods is *The Story of a Pipa,* the famous drama of the Yuan dynasty. Just after scene 11, in which the heroine, Zhao Wu Niang, and her parents-in-law have suffered greatly from a famine after her husband, Cai Bo Jie, left for the capital to take the imperial examination, the audience's attention shifts rapidly to a comic scene in which Prime Minister Niu asks a matchmaker to talk to Cai Bo Jie and get him to marry Niu's daughter after he passes the imperial exam and wins the title of Zhuang Yuan. The matchmaker is a very funny character who carries an axe and a balance that she uses as her business sign. When Prime Minister Niu asks her why she takes these two objects with her, she explains that according to an old saying, "You need an axe to cut firewood and a matchmaker to find a wife," so she takes an axe as one of her business signs. The balance, she says, is used to weigh the good and bad points of men and women to make the prospective marriages firm. Both the humorous language and action of the matchmaker explicitly contrast with the tragic mood of the preceding scene.

Like Shakespeare, traditional Chinese dramatists sometimes use a mingled mode in a single scene, as in the churchyard scene in *Hamlet.* A typical example is scene 17 of *The Story of a Pipa,* in which some local officials provide relief grain to the people in the disaster area who are suffering from the terrible famine, including the heroine. The basic mood of this scene is somber because it depicts the corruption of the officials and the miserable situation of the poor people. It also describes Zhao Wu Niang's bad treatment by the officer in charge of the relief grain and subsequent attempt at suicide. Nevertheless, the scene has a comic element in that the speech and actions of the corrupt officials are foolish and ridiculous. Except for the heroine, the poor people also are amusing even though they are in miserable circumstances. This scene is reminiscent of a ludicrous scene in Shakespeare's *King Henry the Fourth* (part 1, 3.2) in which Falstaff recruits soldiers for the war. Both are presented in comic mode but contain a tragic undertone.

Chinese comedies also have tragic scenes. As I discussed in the first chapter, some tragic themes of the tragedies reappear in the comedies. Many traditional comedies such as *The Romance of the Western Chamber, The Secluded Boudoir, The Story of a Jade Hairpin,* and *The Errors of a Kite* take place in a time of great social turbulence and war chaos, a common background in Chinese tragedies. The scattering and separation of a family serves as an important device in both Shakespearean comedies and traditional Chinese comedies. Yet it shows a more explicitly tragic tone in the latter than in the former, since it is also one of the main themes of traditional Chinese comedies. In *A Slave to Money*, a famous traditional Chinese comedy that could be the Chinese counterpart of Molière's *The Miser*, a poor couple, suffering from hunger and cold, have no alternative but to sell their son to the rich miser Jia Ren. This sad scene is enough to draw tears from the audience. (*The Secluded Boudoir* and *The Story of a Jade Hairpin* also have tragic scenes of family separation caused by wartime.)

The mingled mode in both Shakespeare's plays and traditional Chinese drama is of great importance to their dramatic merits. Yet this technique existed for many years before it was properly understood by critics. In Shakespeare's plays it was lamented and faulted by many critics, most particularly the neoclassicists, who thought that mixing grief and joy might be distracting and create an inconsistency of mood. The device as used in traditional Chinese drama has also been misunderstood and criticized by both Western and Chinese scholars. Some Western critics doubt whether the optimistic philosophy of the Chinese can produce real tragedy; others are even unconvinced that Chinese drama contains tragedy at all since the plays have so many comic elements.[1] Many modern Chinese critics have lamented the fine distinction between tragedy and comedy in traditional Chinese drama, which had taxed the ingenuity of the critics attempting to classify the plays. Some young scholars in contemporary China complain that Chinese civilization has failed to produce genuine tragedy and comedy. I will deal with this issue in detail in chapter 3.

It would seem that the mixture of tragedy and comedy in Shakespeare's plays and in traditional Chinese drama could cause an inconsistency of dramatic mood. Yet a careful examination shows that it has not damaged the general dramatic effect of the two types of drama, particularly Shakespeare's plays. Furthermore, this device demonstrates a special artistic function and purpose. In Shakespearean tragedies the comic scenes seem to serve as interludes or burlesques, but they actually closely contribute to the central theme of the play. In *Hamlet* the churchyard scene is not a simple comic interlude. Rather it deals with the eternal truths of death and life, although they are presented in an ironical way. The function of the porter scene in *Macbeth* also transcends that of a comic interlude.

Critics have often considered one of the major purposes of the mingled mode to be comic relief. This term might apply more to traditional Chinese drama than to Shakespeare, considering the happy endings of Chinese tragedy. However, these scenes sometimes do indeed function as comic relief in Shakespearean tragedies, but in a more complicated way. The mixture of sorrow and joy in Shakespeare's plays is more subtle and complex, which is consistent with the complicated structure of human psychology. When Dr. Johnson vindicated Shakespeare logically and psychologically, he also pointed out that the blending of the two modes in his plays represented the complex change and movement of passion in life.[2] But perhaps its most important purpose in Shakespeare is to serve as a way to demonstrate that life is never just one single happy or sad event but is filled with a variety of happenings that produce different emotions. In fact, combining tragedy with comedy shows the dialectical movement of the two sides of life.

Compared to its use in Shakespeare's plays, the mingled mode in traditional Chinese drama exhibits a similar yet slightly different function. Its main effect is to produce special emotions. Traditional Chinese plays usually are designed to create two types of emotion: humor and compassion. In the tragedies the comic scenes, while appearing to be comic interludes or burlesque, try to produce amusing and funny effects. In the comedies, sad scenes are used to move the audience and to evoke sympathetic feelings. The comic elements in traditional Chinese tragedies obviously serve more as comic relief, considering the happy endings of these plays. But sometimes this effect is so strong that it weakens the principal tragic atmosphere of the plays and makes them appear more like tragicomedies, although as a whole they are categorized as tragedies. As with Shakespeare, one of the main effects of mixing tragedy and comedy in traditional Chinese drama is to represent all sides of life. Living in a society means that some people are happy and successful while others experience loss and misfortune. Therefore, as a stage presentation of life, a play must imitate both happy and sorrowful phases of life, combining the two modes to accomplish the task.

The distinctive mix of comedy and tragedy in both Shakespeare's plays and traditional Chinese drama can be traced back to their dramatic traditions and cultural backgrounds. Shakespeare's method contradicts the academic tradition of his age, yet its connection with the popular theatrical tradition is readily apparent because it was an often-used theatrical convention in Elizabethan age, as Sidney described in his "An Apology for Poetry."[3]

Shakespeare's unique characterization is another reason why he combined tragedy and comedy. Since he intended to present a wide range of characters, his plays always have both serious and funny characters. Most important, however, is the fact that his dramatic concept differed from those of his professional predecessors and successors. Shakespeare saw his drama as a mirror of nature, not merely as a means of moralizing or giving pleasure. For him the world was a big stage and a stage a miniature world, just as Antonio says in *The Merchant of Venice:*

> I hold the world but as the world, Gratiano,
> A stage, where every man must play a part,
> And mine a sad one.
>
> (1.1.77–79)

Blending comedy with tragedy, then, was the most suitable way for Shakespeare to realize his creative ideas and to depict the colorful and complex world of nature.

The mingled mode in traditional Chinese drama is more easily explained than in Shakespeare's plays because its connection with classical theatrical tradition, dramatic concept, and cultural background is quite apparent. Unlike Western drama, traditional Chinese drama makes no distinction between comedy and tragedy. Although general tragic and comic modes exist in traditional drama and in other literary works, one cannot find these genres in the traditional Chinese dramatic heritage. The classification of the two genres was actually formulated by modern Chinese critics in the light of Western dramatic traditions. Therefore it is easy to understand why traditional Chinese playwrights mixed comic with tragic elements so often in their works: they had no rules to observe and incurred no criticism for their blended style.

The use of characterization in traditional Chinese drama is another factor that affects the mixing of moods in the plays. The characters in traditional Chinese drama, as I remarked in the first chapter, tend to be stereotypes. Four or five types of character usually can be found in a play. One of them is a comic character (*chou*) whose function is to create an amusing atmosphere by impromptu comic gestures, remarks, and tricks. This explains why even in the most serious plays a few comic characters and scenes are usually present.

The mingled mode in traditional Chinese drama can be traced back directly to the basic creative principle of classical dramatists. The principle holds that one should not separate tragic events from happy ones or grief from joy. The best plays are those in which different emotions are blended subtly. In *The Fan of Peach Blossom*, for example, through the speech of a character in the Prologue, the author expresses his idea about the expected emotional effect of the play:

> This production will please you as well as grieve you. Sometimes you will be made to laugh, and sometimes you'll shed sad tears.
>
> (Prologue, in *Classical Chinese Tragedies*, 779)

When he discussed dramatic concepts in his book *On Drama,* the famous classical Chinese playwright and critic Li Yu[4] pointed out that in order to avoid pedantic and stale moralization in stage presentations, a writer must "mingle seriousness with levity, sorrow with joy."[5]

More important reasons for classical Chinese playwrights to use the mingled mode in their works can be found in the underlying structure of the country's traditional culture. For example, Chinese philosophy advocates a dialectical relationship between things. Hence, good fortune may bring about disaster, and disaster may be followed by good fortune. Joy taken to an extreme will produce sadness, while sadness often contains potential joy. Such a way of thinking would surely influence Chinese playwrights, causing them to keep tragic and comic elements together. Traditional aesthetic ideas, as I mentioned in the first chapter, also contribute to the use of the mingled mode in Chinese drama. "The beauty of balance and restraint," the fundamental aesthetic idea in ancient China, asks Chinese writers to restrain their representation of emotions. This may help to explain the use of the mixed mode, particularly the comic relief found in traditional Chinese drama.

It would appear that the mingled mode in Shakespeare's plays has a more philosophical purpose than that of Chinese drama, which uses it for emotional effects. By this I mean that profound meanings can always be found when Shakespeare uses the mingled mode in his plays. In traditional Chinese drama, however, one sometimes feels that certain mixed scenes are out of keeping with either the themes or moods presented. They are designed for certain character types, particularly for the comic role (*chou*). For example, in *The Hall of Longevity,* there is a comic scene after the death of Lady Yang in which Emperor Tang Ming decides to dig up the body and bury her formally. After receiving an imperial decree, a local official recruits four hundred women for the grave-digging work. After finding that one of the women is a disguised man, the official decides to check the rest by touching their bodies. This scene is somewhat obscene, compared with the solemn mood generated by the central theme of the play. On the other hand, however, this example shows clearly how Chinese dramatic conventions are responsible for comic scenes and characters in every play. It also tells us that, just like Shakespeare's works, traditional Chinese drama suits both refined and popular taste. Like Shakespeare, classical Chinese dramatists did not avoid sexual matters in their works.

Plot-making has been regarded as an important technique in building a play, for almost all playwrights must tell stories in dramatic form, although a few modern Western dramatists have indeed created stage productions without plots, as Samuel Beckett and other playwrights of the Theater of the Absurd have demonstrated. Shakespeare frequently prefers a double plot, which naturally contains more incidents and events than a single plot and is hence suitable for representing his vast artistic world. Typical examples of double plots can be found in many of his popular plays, especially *King Lear, Twelfth Night,* or the two parts of *Henry IV.* Shakespeare's use of double plots was highly skilled and showed great variety. A common type is the "parallel double plot" in which the subplot almost exactly parallels the main plot. The two plots are closely interrelated throughout and the two sets of characters parallel and reflect each other, as in *King Lear.* Another type of Shakespearean double plot may be called the "contrast double plot" in which the main plot and subplot form a clever comparison. Because each plot has opposite features set against each other, such a contrast often produces a special aesthetic effect. A typical example of this plot type can be found in the two parts of *Henry IV,* in which courtly life and low life are contrasted. As a rule most of the plots in Shakespeare's plays are tightly knit, particularly in his tragedies. Occasionally Shakespeare uses an episodic plot characterized by a series of loosely related incidents, as in the three parts of *Henry VI* or *Love's Labor's Lost.*

In turning to Chinese drama, one finds that the plays in the early and middle periods (mainly during the Yuan dynasty; see Appendix) tend to use a single plot while the plays in the later periods (the Ming and Qing dynasties) usually have double plots. In most of Yuan plays (the plays of the Yuan dynasty represent the golden age of traditional Chinese drama), the simple stories need only a single plot, as in major tragedies such as *The Injustice to Dou E, Autumn in the Han Palace,* and *The Orphan of the House of Zhao* and in important comedies as *Looking over the Wall, The Romance of the Western Chamber,* and *A Slave to Money.* Yuan playwrights can use a single plot in their works because their plays are much shorter than Ming and Qing plays and have relatively few events to include. A typical Yuan play is approximately only one-fourth the length of a Shakespearean play.

As in Shakespeare's plays, the later Chinese plays use double plots. As I stated earlier, the plays written in this period have been called "romances" by both classical and modern Chinese critics because they are much longer than Yuan plays and their stories are more complex. Thus the double plot is useful since it provides room for more spatial representation and groups of characters. Double plots are employed in the most famous of the Ming and Qing tragedies such as *The Flag of Loyalty, The Story of Lady Wang, The Story of the Honest Subject,* and *The Fan of Peach Blossom,* and in comedies such as *The Story of a Jade Hairpin* and *The Errors of a Kite.* However, double-plot patterns in these dramas are different from those in Shakespeare's plays. For example, parallel double plots are rare in traditional Chinese plays, as are contrast double plots. The plot in *The Story of a Pipa* may be called a contrast double plot, however, because the sad main plot, which recounts the suffering of the heroine during the famine, and the more cheerful subplot, in which the hero passes the imperial examination, obtains a high position, and marries the daughter of the Prime Minister, form a striking contrast in mood. The principal pattern of a double plot in traditional Chinese plays is designed so that the main plot describes the actions of the leading characters and the subplot provides the related social and historical background. Take *The Errors of a Kite,* for example. The main plot recounts the love story of the principal characters while the subplot illustrates the turmoil of a war caused by a tribal invasion. The two plots are sometimes related, particularly at the beginning and at the end.

Shakespeare displays his superb technique in plot-making when he uses a multiple or a quadruple plot in some plays. It is surprising that in *A Midsummer-Night's Dream* Shakespeare is able to relate four plots so harmoniously and show us such a fantastic world. Traditional Chinese drama rarely uses the multiple plot, although the later plays contain many different stories. The plot of *The Fan of Peach Blossom* is seemingly like a multiple plot but in a strict sense is actually a double plot. On the other hand, the plot is not as tightly knit as that of *A Midsummer Night's Dream.* There are more plays having episodic plots in traditional Chinese plays than in Shakespeare's plays. Influenced by the narrative literary tradition in the Song and Ming dynasties, especially the historical novels, the later classical Chinese dramatists tend to use this type of plot in many works, generally following a natural chronological order that recounts historical events, just as Shakespeare does in the three parts of *Henry VI.*

Traditionally the Chinese like a complete story, hence almost all their plays have finished plots. A play with an incomplete story, like Shakespeare's *Love's Labor's Lost,* would be unacceptable to any Chinese audience before the modern period. In comparing the plot design of traditional Chinese plays with that of Shakespeare's plays, some Chinese critics believe that Shakespeare sometimes used the "closed plot," which classical Chinese playwrights never used. The so-called closed plot is a play that starts from the middle of the story or even at a point very near the end of an event. If a play begins from the very beginning of an event, it would logically be called an open plot. Almost all traditional Chinese plays have open plots, as do most of Shakespeare's plays, but occasionally Shakespeare used a closed plot in plays such as *Hamlet* and *The Tempest*.[6] Compare, for example, *Hamlet* and the famous Yuan tragedy *The Orphan of the House of Zhao*. Both plays recount a story of revenge. As a play using an open plot, *The Orphan of the House of Zhao* starts from the very beginning of the event, showing how the corrupt general Tu An Jia plots to frame the virtuous minister Zhao Dun and massacre the whole Zhao household. The climax of the play is not based on the revenge itself but on the brave action of the honest officials and friends of the House of Zhao, who protect the orphan of the Zhao House from the massacre. Actually, the revenge of the orphan on his enemy serves only as the resolution of the play. As a play with a closed plot, however, *Hamlet* begins with the revenge itself, leaving all the previous events to be recounted in narrative. This contrast shows that the plot of *Hamlet* is tight and concentrated, whereas the plot of *The Orphan of the House of Zhao* as a whole tends to be episodic and somewhat loose.

There is a striking similarity between Shakespearean and traditional Chinese drama in dramatic techniques. That is, both have a very free deployment of time and space. There is no fixed time limit in Shakespeare's plays because his plays cover a time period much longer than twenty-four hours. Sometimes the events in his plays last for many years, particularly in his romances. For example, in *The Winter's Tale*, the duration of the plot is sixteen years. In his plays the action often shifts from city to city, and even from country to country.

Like Shakespeare, Chinese playwrights always felt free to determine the time length of their plots. In traditional Chinese drama, very few plays take place within twenty-four hours. Most plots proceed for several days, weeks, or months, and sometimes even for many years. For example, in many short Yuan plays the events last as long as those in Shakespeare's romances. *The Injustice to Dou E* has an interval of thirteen years between the prologue and act 1 and another interval of three years between acts 3 and 4. In *The Orphan of the House of Zhao*, the orphan is only a newborn baby in the first three acts, but by the fourth act he is twenty years old and ready to be informed of the truth so that he can avenge himself on his enemy.

The deployment of place in traditional Chinese drama is also absolutely free. In plays such as *The Green Peony, The Injustice to Dou E,* and *The Romance of the Western Chamber,* the stories for the most part take place in the same location. But in most of the plays, as for example *The Hall of Longevity, Autumn in the Han Palace,* and *The Secluded Boudoir,* the events occur in two, three, or several different places.

Chapter 1 listed briefly some distinctions between tragic and comic characters in Shakespeare's plays and those in traditional Chinese drama. However, since the differences between the two cultures are quite apparent when characterization is compared, further discussion on the subject will be useful.

To readers and audiences all over the world, Shakespeare's name will always be associated with characters such as Hamlet, King Lear, Othello, Romeo and Juliet, Timon, Falstaff, Shylock, and many others. In this respect Shakespeare has made a lasting contribution to the character gallery of world literature. In contrast, however, traditional Chinese drama has offered the world fewer immortal characters, although the traditional Chinese novel has provided more. This is not merely because the methods of characterization in the two types of drama are different; it is basically because Shakespeare approaches humanity in a different way than do classical Chinese playwrights. As most of the critics in both past centuries and modern times have agreed, Shakespeare was interested in representing the general human condition while simultaneously portraying characters of a particular community, nation, or era.

Unlike Shakespeare, Chinese dramatists did not concentrate on human nature as a whole. Rather, they paid special attention to the moral and social sides of their characters. Like ancient Greek and neoclassical French writers, they tended to idealize and beautify the characters in their works. As mentioned in the first chapter, Shakespeare's characters are rarely perfect persons. Like people in real life, they have weak points as well as virtues. In traditional Chinese drama, however, the two sides of humans are presented separately. The positive characters are always perfect and the negative characters are totally vicious. Neither resemble people in real life. While Shakespeare's characters are not immoral, representing moral principles was not his main purpose. In traditional Chinese drama, however, the moral virtues of the characters are emphasized and heightened. Most of the characters tend to be moral types such as loyal subjects, patriotic generals, dutiful sons, chaste wives, and faithful friends.

In Shakespeare's plays we often find admiration for the nobility of humanity. The best example can be taken from *Hamlet:*

What a piece of work is a man, how noble in reason, how infinite in faculties, in form and moving, how express and admirable in action, how

like an angel in apprehension, how like a god! the beauty of the world;
the paragon of animals. . . .

(2.2.303–7)

But in traditional Chinese drama one rarely sees a passage in praise
of abstract and common humanity. What we often find is admiration
for some moral principle that contributed to the peace and harmony
of ancient Chinese society. These lines are usually written in beautiful verse and appear in prologues and epilogues. For example, in the
famous Yuan play *The Story of a Pipa*, the prologue and epilogue
are used to praise the piety and faithfulness of the hero and the
heroine, qualities that are regarded as fundamental to good family
relationships and harmonious order in the state.

Classical Chinese playwrights followed the general rule of dramatic creation, trying to mix beauty with goodness. Yet moral principles vary with time and nation, and sometimes Chinese plays may
not be very easily understood by a person with a different cultural
background. Some moral doctrines in the plays might seem strange
to a Western audience, such as *yu zhong*—stubborn loyalty to a
fatuous and self-indulgent ruler, as in *The Flag of Loyalty*—or *shou
jie*—the chasteness of a woman after the death of her husband, as in
The Injustice to Dou E. These concepts can form a barrier for a
Western audience and prevent it from identifying with the characters.
Sometimes even modern Chinese find it difficult to understand outworn feudal ethical codes in these plays because of the great changes
in moral principles that have taken place in twentieth-century China.

The colorfulness and complexity of his characters provide one of
the major artistic distinctions of Shakespeare's plays. By contrast,
the characters of traditional Chinese drama are relatively monochromatic and simple, having protagonists that represent certain social
classes in ancient Chinese society. These characters have something
in common with the *dramatis personae* in the plays of French neo-
classicist playwrights in the seventeenth and eighteenth centuries.
That is to say, unlike Shakespearean characters, the nature of a leading character in a Chinese play usually consists of a single trait or
passion. Chinese characterization is based not on naturalism but on
the presentation of the moral principles of Confucianism, the core
of Chinese culture.

Generally speaking, the chief characters of traditional Chinese
tragedies can be divided into four types representing four virtues.
The characters of the first type are loyal officials who personify
zhong (loyalty to the monarch), the most important virtue of the
Confucian moral code when applied to the relationship between ruler

and subject. Yue Fei, the patriotic general in *The Flag of Loyalty*, is such a type. He fights a great many of bloody battles for the sake of rescuing the two emperors, Song Hui Zong and Song Qin Zong, who are captured by an invading minority nation. At the very moment when he is to be murdered by the traitorous prime minister Qin Hui, Yue Fei weeps—not for his own life but for the two emperors.

The characters of the second type are sons and daughters who embody *xiao* (filial piety), a fundamental moral convention concerning the relationship between parents and their children. Zhao Wu Niang, the heroine in *The Story of a Pipa*, is a typical character of this category. After her husband goes to the capital to take the imperial examination, Zhao Wu Niang becomes responsible for her parents-in-law:

> Since the departure of my husband,
> A famine has hit this region.
> Selling my clothes and ornaments
> To support my parents-in-law,
> I have nothing left.
>
> . . . .
>
> I have made a plain meal
> To allay their hunger.
> I myself have to eat husk and bran
> To maintain my feeble life.
> (Scene 20, "Po Xing," *Classical Chinese Tragedies*,
> 164–65)

After the death of her parents-in-law, she sells her hair to pay for the funeral arrangements. Without tools or help from others, she makes a grave for her parents-in-law with her bare, bloody hands. This moving story faithfully reflects the primacy that the Chinese placed on filial piety.

The third type of typical character is a woman serving as an embodiment of *jie* (chastity). In ancient China, a wife was supposed to be not only loyal to her husband but also faithful to his spirit after he died, remaining a widow for the rest of her life (*shou jie*). Lady Wang in *The Sad Story of Lady Wang* is a typical embodiment of chastity. In the play, like Romeo and Juliet, Lady Wang and her cousin Shen Chun love each other deeply. When they become secretly engaged and Shen Chun worries about the possible disagreement of Lady Wang's parents, Lady Wang promises,

> Provided we are unshakable and firm,
> Our wish will surely come true.

> If we fail to marry at last,
> I shall repay your love with my life.
> (Scene 10, "Cu Pao Ying," *Classical Chinese Tragedies*,
> 376)

Since Shen Chun is a poor relative, Lady Wang's father forces her to marry a dandy from a great house. To fulfill her promise, Lady Wang resists this unreasonable marriage by killing herself. Her lover also commits suicide.

The last type, *yi*, meaning literally "loyalty towards one's friends," was a more comprehensive virtue in ancient China that is found and practiced in all social situations by people of all walks of life, from officials to outlaws. This virtue is extolled in the famous Yuan play *The Orphan of the House of Zhao*. The herb doctor Cheng Ying is a typical character with such a virtue. As a guest financially supported by the House of Zhao, Cheng Ying is grateful to the Zhao family. When the household is massacred by the corrupt minister, he risks his life to rescue the only survivor of the Zhao family, even sacrificing his own son to save the orphan.

As I discussed above, most principal characters of traditional Chinese drama are moral types rather than the individuals of passionate humanity that are a feature of Shakespeare's plays. The chief characters of traditional Chinese drama, who belong to the same type, are difficult to categorize because of their similarity. However, it is much easier to classify Shakespearean characters of the same type because each character still possesses his or her own particular personality. For example, the "treacherous man"—Claudius, Macbeth, Edmund, and Iago, for example—is a major type of Shakespearean character. The desire for power is their most common leading trait, but many other qualities distinguish their individual natures.

There are few highly individualized characters in traditional Chinese drama. For instance, we can see characters similar to Falstaff in a few Chinese plays, playboys living a dissipated life such as Zhou She in *Rescued by a Coquette* and Qi You Xian in *The Errors of a Kite*, but they are one-dimensional and are held up to our ridicule. Yet Falstaff is different. Even while we laugh at him, he also evokes wonder, admiration, delight, and exaltation, which was partly the reason why Hegel, in his *Aesthetik*, selected Falstaff as an example of Shakespeare's power.[7] Shylock is another example. A similar character can be found in the traditional Chinese comedy *A Slave to Money*. The chief character, Jia Ren, is a miser whose stinginess is presented in full exaggeration by the playwright. In comparison with Shylock, Jia Ren is (like Harpagon in Molière's comedy *The Miser*) only a simple miser, although his miserliness is vividly portrayed. On the other hand Shylock is much more than a miser because as father, victim, or Jew he arouses ambiguous emotions in us.

Character types in traditional Chinese plays have also been influenced by the country's literary tradition. For example, honest subjects are leading characters in classical Chinese historical novels such as *The History of Three Kingdoms* (*San Guo Zhi*) and *The Biography of the North Song Dynasty* (*Bei Song Shi Zhuan*). Confucian scholars also appear frequently in many genres of classical literature. Outlaws, as one of the main character types—for example, Li Kui in *Li Kui Carries Thorns*—are vividly described by classical Chinese novelists, as Luo Guan Zhong did in his well-known book *Water Margin* (*Shui Hu Zhuan*). Modern Chinese scholars thus believe that the characterization and themes of traditional Chinese drama were greatly influenced by classical Chinese novels (especially the works of the Song and Yuan dynasties).[8] As some Western critics have pointed out, Shakespeare's characters were sometimes directly associated with the old types from English and European literary traditions such as the old morality villain, the adventurous knight, and the sighing lover.[9] But Shakespeare always tried to develop these old types in his works and at the same time not to limit himself to them. By contrast, classical Chinese playwrights were keen on depicting the types they had inherited from the literary tradition and had no intention of extending the range of types.

The emphasis on morality in the characterization of traditional Chinese drama leads to a lack of psychological character types. Traditional Chinese plays rarely have melancholy characters like Jaques in *As You Like It* or a misanthrope like Apemantus in *Timon of Athens*. Generally speaking classical Chinese dramatists had no interest in describing the very odd or peculiar types of humanity to which Shakespeare paid great attention. To classical Chinese playwrights, not all human qualities are worth depicting, only those that have aesthetic and moral value. Yet because Shakespeare saw beauty in humanity itself and in the wide variety of human personality, we can find many vivid descriptions of various character types. For instance, in *The Merchant of Venice* we read:

> Now, by two-headed Janus,
> Nature hath fram'd strange fellows in her time:
> Some that will evermore peep through their eyes,
> And laugh like parrots at a bagpiper;
> And other of such vinegar aspect

That they'll not show their teeth in way of smile
Though Nestor swear the jest be laughable.

(1.1.49–56)

Another interesting type of man is described in the same play:

There are a sort of men whose visages
Do cream and mantle like a standing pond,
And do a willful stillness entertain,
With purpose to be dress'd in an opinion
Of wisdom, gravity, profound conceit,
As who should say "I am Sir Oracle,
And when I ope my lips let no dog bark!"
O my Antonio, I do know of these
That therefore only are reputed wise
For saying nothing; when, I am very sure
If they should speak, would almost damn those ears
Which hearing them would call their brothers fools.

(1.1.88–99)

In *Hamlet*, the hero vividly describes the traits of a minor character, Osric:

'A did comply, sir, with his dug before 'a suck'd it. Thus has he, and many more of the same breed that I know the drossy age dotes on, only got the tune of the time and out of an habit of encounter, a kind of yesty collection, which carries them through and through the most profound and winnow'd opinions, and do but blow them to their trial, the bubbles are out.

(5.2.187–94)

Yet in traditional Chinese drama one rarely sees this sort of description. What we see most are passages that tell the stories or express the emotions of the characters.

As many Shakespeare critics have pointed out, particularly early ones like John Dryden, Shakespeare was good at presenting the human passions such as love, hatred, anger, jealousy, honor, ambition, revenge, and so on. There can be no doubt that this is one of the main features of Shakespeare's characters, especially those in his tragedies and histories. Most of Shakespeare's famous characters are associated with certain kinds of passions, as Macbeth is with ambition, Othello with jealousy, and Antony and Cleopatra with love. The significance of Shakespeare's presentation of the passions concerns at least two aspects of his art. First, the opportunity to illustrate a variety of strong feelings would leave more room for

Shakespeare to give full play to his poetic talent, since feeling and emotion are the main food of poetry. Second, the representation of passions can be used to explore deeply the motives of the characters' action in human nature and so help us to interpret the plays.

In comparison, the main purpose of characterization in traditional Chinese drama is not the representation of strong feelings, although some are depicted in a few of the plays: jealousy in *The Hall of Longevity* and *The Sad Story of Lady Wang* (in both plays the jealous characters are heroines, not heroes like Othello); revenge in *The Orphan of the House of Zhao;* ambition in *The Story of the Honest Subject;* and love in many of the plays. As a rule, however, love in traditional Chinese drama is not represented as strongly as it is in Shakespeare's plays. In most cases it appears as a refined and restrained feeling instead of a deep, strong, and uncontrollable drive. Other passions are only slightly sketched.

The passions were ignored by classical Chinese dramatists on at least two counts. First, the ancient Chinese tended to explain the motives of human action in the light of ethics. They believed that human behavior stems from moral principles and not from instinctive desires. It was considered very dangerous if society did not restrain personal passion because wildly running emotion would damage the group's moral order. By the time of the later Confucian ethical code (mainly during the Song and Ming dynasties), human passion and desire were seen as inevitable causes of social evil and crime. Thus a playwright would be criticized if he included much passion in his works. Wang Shi Pu, for instance, was severely attacked for describing sexual love in his masterpiece, *The Romance of the Western Chamber.* Shakespeare's presentation of the passions can be associated directly with the Elizabethan age, which many historians see as a period marked by the liberation of individuality. Personal will and desire were praised in literary works written during this period of the Renaissance. Yet we see a different situation in ancient China, where people always gave priority to collectivism and where individualism was rarely encouraged.

The second reason for ignoring passion is that in the light of their literary tradition, classical Chinese writers were inclined to depict refined and restrained feelings to comply with the general aesthetic principle of "the beauty of balance and restraint," as discussed in chapter 1.

I have already mentioned that Shakespeare's characters are complex and that the characters in traditional Chinese plays are comparatively simple. The main reason for this is that Shakespeare tried to explore the depth and range of humanity's inner world, while classical Chi-

nese playwrights were generally content to describe only the outer
actions and certain emotions of human beings. Shakespeare's special
methods of revealing one's inner world (such as self-consciousness,
double nature, multiconsciousness, abnormal mentality) were not
properly understood for many years. The results of modern psychological research have proved the justification of these methods, as
J. I. M. Stewart says:

> And is it not significant, too, that Freud vindicated Shakespeare, whose
> works he had abundantly studied, as a psychologist of genius? . . . the
> late Professor C. H. Herford, remarked that modern psychology, by its
> disclosure of such phenomena as those of dual and multiple personality,
> might unexpectedly illuminate the vexed problem of an apparent incon-
> sistency in Shakespeare.[10]

In traditional Chinese drama, however, one can rarely see similar
methods for revealing a character's inner world. There is no description of self-consciousness or self-knowledge in which characters examine and understand themselves independently. There is no cynical
self-awareness like that in *Hamlet,* because skepticism has always
been excluded by traditional Chinese ideas, and Chinese people in
the past were unable to transcend their closed ideological system.
Although Taoism promoted withdrawal from the world, it never
served as a critical force underlying orthodox Chinese ideology.

The examples of double nature that appear in Shakespeare's plays,
such as Edmund in *King Lear,* often are depicted through self-
revelation. Occasionally self-revelation can be seen in traditional
Chinese plays. For example, some villains tell us of their plots to
frame innocent persons. But normally such self-revelations are not
as complex as those in Shakespeare's plays and are only simple state-
ments of villainy. Here is the soliloquy of Mao Yan Shou, the corrupt
minister in *Autumn in the Han Palace:*

> Large pieces of gold I hoard and idolize;
> Seas of blood or royal commands cannot me jeopardize.
> I want to be rich when still alive,
> And mind not people's curses after my demise.
>
> . . . .
> Truly it is said:
> He with only a little hatred is no man;
> He with but a little venom is no real human being.[11]
>
> (Act 1, *Classical Chinese Tragedies,* 42)

This typical self-revelation of a villain does not show the double
moral self-consciousness of the character that appears quite often in

the self-revelations of Shakespeare's characters, such as in the soliloquies of Macbeth or Claudius in *Hamlet*. A double consciousness or a double nature was not psychologically suited to the literary tastes of the ancient Chinese, who believed that a good man is different from an evil man. Yet Shakespeare tells us that all people are nearly alike and that everyone has the tendency to become either virtuous or vicious, depending on the particular circumstances.

Abnormal mental conditions such as insanity, somnambulism, and so on, are rarely found in traditional Chinese plays. This is not difficult to understand, considering that proper behavior and restrained emotion in ancient Chinese society are so well defined that there is little room for morbid action and mental aberration. Although sometimes Chinese characters, particularly in the tragedies, may be frustrated and upset by overwhelming disaster, they still keep their sanity and never lose their reason. Although a great many dreams are enacted in traditional Chinese plays, all of them are reflections of normal psychological activities and in most cases represent the strong desires and feelings of the characters, such as Zhang Sheng's affection for Ying Ying in *The Romance of the Western Chamber*, Zhou Shun Chang's hatred for the corrupt minister in *The Story of the Honest Subject*, and Jia Ren's desire for richness in *A Slave to Money*.

This brief comparison between Shakespeare and traditional Chinese drama suggests that the type of characterization found in traditional Chinese drama may not satisfy Western audiences since they are used to Western dramatists, including Shakespeare, who emphasize complex psychological depth in character portrayal in the belief that the many-sided attributes of the subject help to round out their characters and make them seem real. Yet characterization in traditional Chinese drama has its own distinctive dramatic and aesthetic merit, considering that traditional Chinese drama and Shakespeare's plays belong to different modes of dramatic art. A similar example can be taken from the literary works of ancient Greece. The characterization found in Greek myth, drama, and epic seems to be simple in light of modern literary standards, but yet these works still fascinate us today. The main means of character portrayal of traditional Chinese drama can be compared to the skill of traditional Chinese brush painting. In traditional Chinese brush painting, simple strokes, black ink, and occasionally light colors are used, but vivid expressions and bold outlines result. Like dramatists, classical Chinese brush painters did not concentrate on the detail of what they depicted but tried to make everything in their pictures alike in spirit. As a rule, complex, ambiguous, grotesque, and very odd persons are excluded in traditional Chinese plays because they are distasteful to the ancient Chinese. Although the characters of both Shakespearean and traditional Chinese drama possess obvious social and cultural vestiges, Shakespeare's characters have a more comprehensive historical, social, and psychological context. Consequently his protagonists not only please us but also cause us to think, while on the other hand the characters of traditional Chinese drama mainly appealed to the ancient Chinese from a moral viewpoint and to us aesthetically.

In any comparison between Shakespeare and traditional Chinese drama one aspect constantly commands scholarly interest: both are examples of poetic drama and both show great richness in poetic presentation and the use of imagery. It is evident that Shakespeare's plays and traditional Chinese drama are not only expressed in poetry, but are actually conceived in terms of poetry. Both types would lose their artistic fascination if they did not possess such brilliant poetic qualities.

Shakespeare, like other Elizabethan dramatists, primarily used blank verse, which allows considerable variation and has been used by most major English poets to suit their different ends. He also used other forms of verse such as sonnets and couplets and prose, depending on the different characters or moods in his plays. For example, in A Midsummer Night's Dream, the Duke and the young lovers normally speak in blank verse and the fairies use couplets or other verse forms, but Bottom and his fellows use prose except when they assume their roles in the play-within-the-play.

Like Shakespeare's plays, the text of traditional Chinese drama consists of two parts, verse (qu) and prose (bai). Verse generally expresses emotion or depicts scenery while prose recounts stories or develops dialogue. Most classical Chinese playwrights concentrated on using verse, so that prose is frequently interspersed with short poems. Traditional Chinese drama epitomizes Chinese poetic tradition, for in it we can see almost every form of classical Chinese poetry: wu yan shi—five-character poems having five Chinese characters to each line and no strict tonal pattern or rhyme scheme; qi yan shi—seven-character poems with seven Chinese characters per line, again without strict tonal pattern or rhyme; jue ju—four-line poems, with each line containing five or seven Chinese characters and possessing a strict tonal pattern and rhyme scheme; pian wen—rhythmical prose similar to Shakespeare's blank verse and characterized by parallelism and ornateness; and finally ci—a poem written to certain songs and having a strict tonal pattern and rhyme scheme in fixed numbers of lines of unequal length.

All of the conventional poetic devices of the long Chinese literary tradition such as imagery, parallelism, and symbolism are used with ingenuity, endowing many traditional Chinese plays with an extraordinarily rich texture. The aesthetic values of Shakespeare's plays and traditional Chinese drama do not rely on their poetic forms but depend on their unique poetic flavors, which some say are the most beautiful poetic representations in world literature. Yet there is a striking difference between these two types of poetry, particularly in the use of poetic imagery.

Much has been written about the function of imagery in Shakespeare's plays. For example, Caroline F. E. Spurgeon, a pioneer in this field, points out that the poetic imagery in Shakespeare's plays can create atmosphere and underline themes or heighten and develop emotion in Shakespeare's tragedies.[12] The imagery in Shakespeare's plays is also used as a means of characterization, as Wolfgang Clemen says of *Richard II:*

> Imagery becomes the characteristic manner of expression of the chief character. To talk in similes, to make use of metaphors, is indeed a natural quality of the king's mind and temperament.[13]

Poetic imagery was also used frequently in traditional Chinese drama, playing a leading role in contributing to the brilliant richness of the poetry. Its function is similar to that in Shakespeare's plays, as Shih Chung Wen declares:

> Poetic eloquence is the strength of Yuan drama. . . . the dramatists used images not merely to add to the richness of poetic quality, but also to serve several other dramatic purposes: to create scenery, reflect and intensify emotions, strengthen characterization, and support the themes of the plays. In all these roles the poetic images function naturally and organically.[14]

Although poetic imagery may function similarly in both types of drama, the way it is employed is quite different, allowing us to see the apparent influences of the two literary and cultural traditions. The first and the most evident difference is that Shakespeare chose his images very comprehensively while classical Chinese dramatists selected theirs narrowly, making the range of imagery in Shakespeare's plays much wider than that of traditional Chinese drama. Shakespeare's universal mind could detect subtle interrelationships between things that were nearly invisible to everyone else. Everything in the world could be included in his vast kingdom of imagery, even those things that seemingly had no poetic value at all. In comparison, classical Chinese playwrights were so deeply steeped in traditional Chinese poetry that they only chose the images preferred by traditional poetic taste.

The animal images used in traditional Chinese drama and Shakespeare's plays are a good way to illustrate such a difference. Traditional Chinese plays have far fewer of these images than do Shakespeare's works. Usually only animals having conventional symbolic meaning could be used as poetic images in traditional Chinese plays. For instance, in many of the love tragedies and comedies, the playwrights used mandarin ducks to symbolize marital fidelity, as in *The Romance of the Western Chamber* and *The Sad Story of Lady Wang*. Similarly, the butterfly represents an affectionate couple in many traditional Chinese plays. The metaphor of fish and water describes the intimate relationship between lovers, as in *The Romance of the Western Chamber*. And traditionally, the wild goose, a migratory bird, is connected with lovesickness and homesickness, as in "Yan Ge Xing," the famous lyrical poem of the Jian An poet Cao Pi. It is also used very frequently in many traditional Chinese plays. For example, the full title of the well-known love-political tragedy *Autumn in the Han Palace* is *The Han Yuan Emperor Was Awakened by a Lonely Wild Goose on an Autumn Night in the Han Palace*. Another type of animal imagery used is that symbolizing a threat to society. Almost all the corrupt subjects in traditional Chinese drama are likened to tigers and wolves, as in *The Flag of Loyalty* and *The Story of the Honest Subjects*.

By contrast, Shakespeare used many more kinds of animals as poetic images than did classical Chinese dramatists. He seemed to be an animal expert, familiar with their habits and characteristics. Hence he can accommodate them properly into his metaphorical vision. Wild animals such as lions, bears, wolves, and foxes are frequently used in Shakespeare's plays as symbols of human vices, as we see in his early *Henry VI* plays, *King Lear,* and other tragedies. In *Timon of Athens,* a wild animal world becomes analogous to human society (4.3.327–45). When Shakespeare chooses poetic images, he shows a special interest in domestic animals such as sheep, horses, dogs, and pigs, which are rarely used by classical Chinese playwrights as poetical images. Shakespeare's England had a tradition of husbandry, so it is easy to understand his interest in these animals. In Shakespeare's plays they are also associated with particular qualities of human nature. For instance, a dog is often likened to a flatterer, as some critics have pointed out.[15] Many reptiles, amphibians, and poisonous insects are allowed to enter Shakespeare's poetic world, which would surprise classical Chinese dramatists. In *Timon,* we read:

That nature, being sick of man's unkindness,

. . . .

Engenders the black toad and adder blue,
The gilded newt and eyeless venom'd worm,
With all th' abhorred births below crisp heaven. . . .

(4.3.176, 181–84)

Richard II has similar images of "spiders, that suck up thy venom," "heavy-gaited toads," and "a lurking adder" (3.2.14, 15, 20). Shakespeare's animals not only serve as moral symbols, but they also describe the many emotions found in human nature. For example, we read in *As You Like It:*

I will be more jealous of thee than a Barbary cock-pigeon over his hen, more clamorous than a parrot against rain, more new-fangled than an ape, more giddy in my desires than a monkey. . . . I will laugh like a hyen, and that when thou art inclin'd to sleep.

(4.1.149–56)

Classical Chinese playwrights tend to choose beautiful and graceful subjects for poetic imagery in their works. Most of the images appeal to a sense of beauty worthy of painters. Many of the plays feature flowers, willows, poplars, grass, birds, butterflies, fish, pools, gardens, rivers, bridges, boats, mountains, the sun, the moon, stars, wind, rain, clouds—images pleasing to both the eye and the mind. Of course many of the poetic images in Shakespeare's plays are also beautiful, but Shakespeare is so large-minded that he frequently uses imagery that is antithetical to common poetic sense. In *Hamlet* he uses disgusting images such as "maggots" and "carrion" (2.2.181–82). Even the comedies contain images such as "worm's-meat" and "tar" (*As You Like It* 3.2.65, 68). It should be pointed out that in Shakespeare's plays this kind of imagery is indispensable in describing character and creating atmosphere, as in *1 Henry IV:*

. . . a tun of man is thy companion. Why dost thou converse with that trunk of humors, that bolting-hutch of beastliness, that swoll'n parcel of dropsies, that huge bombard of sack, that stuff'd cloak-bag of guts, that roasted Manningtree ox with the pudding in his belly. . . .

(2.4.448–53)

The tendency of classical Chinese playwrights to use beautiful and graceful poetic images was so strong that they could fill their descriptions with such images even when they wrote of intimate subjects such as sexual intercourse. For instance, in *The Romance of the Western Chamber* we read:

Spring is here and flowers flaunt their beauty;
Her willow-like waist is supple.
The heart of the flower is now gently plucked,
And the dewdrops make the peony unfold.
. . . .
I am like a fish delighting in water,
Or a butterfly gathering the sweet nectar of a bud.
Half-pushed back and half-welcomed,
I am filled with surprise and love.[16]
(Act 1, "Sheng Hu Lu," *Classical Chinese Comedies*, 126)

In comparison, Shakespeare used bold and straightforward images to describe this subject matter. Consider these lines from *Othello:*

Even now, now, very now, an old black ram
Is tupping your white ewe.

(1.1.88–89)

For that I do suspect the lusty Moor
Hath leap'd into my seat;

(2.1.295–96)

Traditionally Chinese writers used a very beautiful and explicit image of clouds and rain as a symbol of lovemaking; this figure of speech is employed in many traditional Chinese plays as well.

In general, then, classical Chinese dramatists normally favored soft, tender, and delicate poetic images, whereas Shakespeare used strong, vigorous, violent, and disruptive images in his works. In his tragedies many such images create a tragic atmosphere, and even in his historical plays and comedies, this type of imagery is not difficult to find. For example, *King John* has impressive images such as: "Neptune's arms," "earthquake of nobility," "tempest of the soul," "the vaulty top of heaven," "burning meteors," "storm," and "the giant world" (5.2.34–57).

Shakespeare's bias in favor of strong and vigorous images is evident even in his description of love affairs. Chinese playwrights use delicate and tender images such as mandarin ducks, fish and water, delicate flowers, supple willows, gentle sighs, and red tears, but *Twelfth Night* has "groans that thunder love," "sighs of fire" (1.5.256), and "as hungry as the sea" (2.4.100). In *Romeo and Juliet* we read:

My bounty is as boundless as the sea,
My love as deep; the more I give to thee,
The more I have, for both are infinite.

(2.2.133–35)

Shakespeare's plays have many symbolic images that vividly illustrate abstract concepts. For instance, to interpret the function and structure of a state, the playwright used "honey-bees" in *Henry V* (1.2.187), "belly" and other parts of the body in *Coriolanus* (1.1.96–164), and a garden in *Richard II* (3.4.29–66). In traditional Chinese plays, however, such an employment of imagery is hard to find because classical Chinese dramatists did not try to represent abstract philosophical concepts in their poetry. For instance, they were skilled in describing the sorrow and pleasure of lovers but seldom directly discussed the quality of love. Yet in Shakespeare's plays, such as *Romeo and Juliet*, a great many of these discussions utilize poetic images:

> Why then, O brawling love! O loving hate!
> O any thing, of nothing first create!
> O heavy lightness! serious vanity!
> Misshapen chaos of well-seeming forms,
> Feather of lead, bright smoke, cold fire, sick health,
> Still-waking sleep, that is not what it is!
> This love feel I, that feel no love in this.
>
> . . . .
>
> Love is a smoke made with the fume of sighs;
> Being purg'd, a fire sparkling in lovers' eyes,
> Being vex'd, a sea nourish'd with loving tears.
> What is it else? madness most discreet,
> A choking gall, and a preserving sweet.
>
> (1.1.176–82; 190–94)

Both the idea and the images in these passages would sound odd to the ancient Chinese, for they never understood love in such ambiguous and complex ways.

It is quite clear that the uses of poetic imagery in both Shakespeare's plays and traditional Chinese drama are deeply affected by their cultural heritage, as these selected examples show. In Shakespeare's plays the sea-ship-navigation image cluster is used quite often while traditional Chinese plays frequently employ the cluster of mountain-river-running water. The sea-ship-navigation trope not only depicts marine settings but is also associated with many symbolic meanings. I have previously pointed out that Shakespeare sometimes uses the sea as a symbol of passion or love, as in *Twelfth Night* (1.1.10–15). In *As You Like It*, Jaques says:

> Why, who cries out on pride
> That can therein tax any private party?

> Doth it not flow as hugely as the sea,
> Till that the wearer's very means do ebb?
>
> > (2.7.70–73)

Many more images connected with ships and navigation can be found in Shakespeare's plays, such as *The Merchant of Venice:*

> How like a younger or a prodigal
> The scarfed bark puts from her native bay,
> Hugg'd and embraced by the strumpet wind!
> How like the prodigal doth she return,
> With over-weather'd ribs and ragged sails,
> Lean, rent, and beggar'd by the strumpet wind!
>
> > (2.6.14–19)

In traditional Chinese plays, the images of mountain, river, or running water usually have fixed symbolic meanings. The mountain symbolizes an insurmountable barrier that separates two lovers or a person from his or her family. The river and running water stand for the endless sorrow of parting or separation of the characters from their spouses or families. Here is a passage from *The Romance of the Western Chamber:*

> How hard a separation is in our life,
> I lament that you have trudged, lonely,
> Over the mountains stretching thousands of miles.
> > (4.4, "Ze Gui Lling," *Classical Chinese Comedies,* 138)

In *The Sad Story of Lady Wang,* as they are separated by her parents the heroine says to her lover,

> It's hard to tell my sorrow of parting,
> I regret that we'll be separated by Heaven,
> With thousands of peaks and mountains.
> (Scene 15, "Zao Luo Pao," *Classical Chinese Tragedies,*
> > 387)

In the same play we find an image of running water:

> The torrent of Qu Tang Gorge surges forward,
> How much sorrow has gone with it since time immemorial.
> > (Scene 45, ibid., 469)

It is apparent that these two image clusters in Shakespeare's plays and traditional Chinese drama stem from different geographical cir-

cumstances and cultural backgrounds. England is a country noted
for its navigation tradition, so it is easy to understand why the sea,
ships, and sailing eventually became traditional poetic images in English literature and affected Shakespeare's use of imagery. By contrast, China is mainly a large landlocked and mountainous country.
Chinese civilization originated from the Yellow River Basin, thus
mountains and rivers were closely associated with the cultural thinking of the ancient Chinese. For example, because of the difficulty of
travel in ancient China, the mountain was regarded as a practical as
well as a symbolic barrier separating people from their homes and
families. Gradually it became a conventional poetic image in classical
Chinese poetry and drama, as the famous Tang poet Wang Bo writes
in "The Pavilion of Tengwang":

> The mountain is difficult to surmount.
> Who pities the traveller losing his way?
> Meeting by chance like patches of drifting duckweed,
> We are all strangers in this distant land.[17]

The image of the river or running water is also easily seen in classical
Chinese poetry. Consider, for example, two lines from the well-
known poem "Yu Mei Ren," written by Nan Tang emperor and poet
Li Yu:

> I wonder how you feel your sorrow?
> It's just like a spring river flowing east.[18]

In both Shakespeare's plays and traditional Chinese drama, two
opposing images are very obvious, the sun and the moon. This is
not merely because the image of the sun is frequently used in Shakespeare's plays while that of the moon is employed in traditional Chinese drama; it is mainly because these two images are profoundly
associated with Western and traditional Chinese cultures.

In Shakespeare's plays, the sun serves many functions as simile,
metaphor, and symbol. In the histories the sun is often likened to
the monarch. In *1 Henry IV*, when the King teaches the Prince of
Wales how to keep the true majesty of a king, he dismissively says
of Richard,

> So when he had occasion to be seen,
> He was but as the cuckoo is in June,
> Heard, not regarded, seen, but with such eyes
> As, sick and blunted with community,
> Afford no extraordinary gaze,

Such as is bent on sunlike majesty
When it shines seldom in admiring eyes;

(3.2.74–80)

And in *Richard II*:

See, see, King Richard doth himself appear,
As doth the blushing discontented sun
From out the fiery portal of the east,
When he perceives the envious clouds are bent
To dim his glory and to stain the track
Of his bright passage to the occident.

(3.3.62–67)

Besides serving as the symbol of power and authority, the sun is also used as a symbol of greatness and glory, as in *Henry VIII* when Cardinal Wolsey says,

I have touch'd the highest point of all my greatness,
And, from that full meridian of my glory,
I haste now to my setting. I shall fall
Like a bright exhalation in the evening,
And no man see me more.

(3.2 223–27)

Many other symbolic meanings of the sun are to be found in Shakespeare's plays; in fact, the sun is even associated with tender and emotional matters such as love and beauty, which I will discuss later.

By contrast, the moon has been often employed by classical Chinese dramatists as an important poetic image. In some of the plays, particularly in the love tragedies and comedies, the moon is used to create atmosphere. Many of the significant actions of these plays occur in moonlit scenes, as in *The Hall of Longevity, Autumn in the Han Palace, The Romance of the Western Chamber*, and *The Secluded Boudoir*. In some plays the moon serves as a recurrent image underlining the theme or mood of the plays, as in *The Hall of Longevity* and *The Romance of the Western Chamber*. The use of this device is most noticeable in this last play since references to the moon occur more than fifty times. Because of its power to evoke rich conventional associations, the moon diffuses a romantic atmosphere throughout this drama. Waiting anxiously for Ying Ying, Zhang Sheng sings,

Where are the colored clouds?
The watery moonlight floods the terrace

. . . .
The moon moves the shadows of flowers—
I wonder whether the lady of jade is coming.
(4.1, "Hun Jiang Long," *Classical Chinese Comedies*, 124)

In this play the moon is also connected with love and beauty. To express his affection to Ying Ying, Zhang Sheng recites,

This is a mellow moonlight night,
The shadows of flowers rest in the spring quiet;
Raising my head, I look at the bright moon
And hope I can meet the goddess in it soon.
(1.3, following "Xian Tao Hong," ibid., 79)

Here the goddess represents Chang E, the goddess of the moon. She is a heroine in Chinese legend who swallowed an elixir stolen from her husband and flew to the moon. Traditionally the Chinese compare beautiful women to the moon but rarely to the sun.

Shakespeare, on the other hand, often preferred the sun to the moon in dealing with love and beauty. In *King Henry V*, the King uses the sun rather than the moon to symbolize his love:

. . . but a good heart, Kate, is the sun and the moon, or rather the sun and not the moon; for it shines bright and never changes, but keeps his course truly.

(5.2.162–64)

And when describing the beauty of Juliet, Romeo also shows a preference for the sun:

But soft, what light through yonder window breaks?
It is the east, and Juliet is the sun.
Arise, fair sun, and kill the envious moon,
Who is already sick and pale with grief
That thou, her maid, art far more fair than she.
Be not her maid, since she is envious;
Her vestal livery is but sick and green,
And none but fools do wear it; cast it off.

(2.2.2–9)

A Midsummer Night's Dream, however, is an exception. Here the moon paradoxically creates a romantic atmosphere while at the same time serving as a symbol of chastity (and frigidity) (1.1.73–75).

Shakespeare's inclination to use the sun as a positive symbol can be connected with Western culture. Traditionally, Apollo is not only the god of sunlight, power, reason, and beauty, but he is also associated with medicine, the care of animals, the maintenance of society, and with prophecy, morality, music, and poetry. Through the centuries the spirit of Apollo has greatly influenced the creative inspirations of Western writers and artists, permeating many kinds of art. In comparison, the moon—while also an important symbol—is frequently associated with lunacy and inconstant love, although originally it represented virginity and childbirth.

The use of the moon as a positive poetic image in traditional Chinese drama directly stems from Chinese culture. In the earliest period of Chinese civilization primitive society also worshipped the sun, but gradually moon worship became more prevalent, along with the appearance of more folk legends associated with the moon. It has greatly influenced the spiritual activities and social customs of the Chinese. For example, the Midautumn Festival celebrates family reunions. All family members congregate, eat a special moon cake, and admire the full moon.

As a symbol of beauty, purity, solitude, and loftiness, the moon has been a favorite of classical Chinese poets. It is traditionally associated with all the major themes of classical Chinese poetry, particularly love, lovesickness, and homesickness. Moreover, the moon has also greatly affected other forms of Chinese art. For instance, much popular traditional Chinese music is associated with the moon, as is revealed by the titles of some favorite music of the Chinese: "The River on a Spring Moonlit Night" (*Chun Jiang Hua Yue Ye*), "The Moon Is Mirrored on the Two Springs" (*Er Quan Ying Yue*), "The Moon Floods the Han Palace in Autumn" (*Han Gong Qiu Yue*), "The Colored Clouds Run After the Moon" (*Cai Yun Zhui Yue*), "The Moon Is Mirrored on the Calm Lake in Autumn" (*Pin Hu Qiu Yue*), and many others.

I have attempted here, as other Chinese scholars have,[19] to summarize the essential characteristics of Western and Chinese cultures through the symbolism of the sun and the moon. It is possible that I have made some assumptions too broad to be rigorously applied and incapable of withstanding close scrutiny. But to some extent the spirits of the sun and the moon indeed represent many obvious and important features of the two cultures, particularly their literature, art, and national identities. For instance, the bold, enthusiastic, and aggressive tendency of Western culture contrasts with the restrained, passive, and conservative tendency of Chinese culture. The differences in the cultures are given weight by the imagery used in both Shakespeare's plays and traditional Chinese drama.

This brief survey of the use of poetic imagery in Shakespeare's drama and traditional Chinese drama shows that there are some obvious differences in poetic presentation between the two dramas. First, the poetic language in traditional Chinese drama usually describes scenery and expresses emotion while in Shakespeare's plays it is also used to portray character, to represent thoughts, and to embody abstract concepts. Second, poetic representation in traditional Chinese drama is implicit, refined, and restrained, whereas it is explicit and straightforward in Shakespeare's plays. The figurative language in traditional Chinese drama often produces a feeling of gentleness, delicacy, and gracefulness in the audience, and in Shakespeare's plays it makes us feel strong, forceful, vigorous, and impassioned. In addition to the poetic flavor, there are other differences in the language of Shakespeare's plays and traditional Chinese drama. For instance, Shakespeare's plays are interspersed everywhere with philosophical ideas and "golden sayings" that one seldom sees in traditional Chinese plays. The humorous style of Shakespeare's language is also unique and is completely lacking in traditional Chinese drama.

Thus far I have compared the general artistic characteristics between Shakespeare's drama and traditional Chinese drama. To understand fully the aesthetic qualities of the two dramas, one needs to draw some conclusions. Yet it is difficult to categorize the two dramas in any fixed style because Shakespeare's works mix many artistic styles, making it inappropriate and confining to classify him by a single style. Also, the differing literary terms of the West and the East make it hard to find common ground for defining the principal aesthetic qualities of both types of drama. My purpose here, then, is not to precisely classify each tradition but to limit myself to a brief discussion of their primary aesthetic tendencies.

An examination of Shakespeare's plays and traditional Chinese drama shows that the former tends toward romanticism and the latter toward classicism. Since the two terms should be understood in the light of Western literary theory and the definitions commonly accepted by Western critics, by *classicism* I mean the principles, ideas, and styles shared by traditional Chinese dramatists and writers with writers in ancient Greece and Rome and the seventeenth and eighteenth centuries in Europe and England.

Romantic writers in general showed a freedom from the constraints of reason, literary rules, or social conventions, and fully expressed their feelings and emotions. Classical authors, on the other hand, showed an inclination towards emotional restraint and tried to keep a balance between emotion and reason in their works. There is no doubt that these two terms can be applied to Shakespearean and traditional Chinese drama, particularly in light of my previous discussion concerning characterization and poetic treatment in the two dramas.

Many romantic writers tended to create complex and sometimes morally imperfect characters, which was one of the principal means of character portrayal in Shakespeare's plays. By contrast, classical writers favored one-sided or "single passion" characters. The protagonists in their works are usually upright persons of strong moral fiber, similar to the characters in traditional Chinese plays, especially the tragedies. Character portrayal in the romantic period was also typified by the exploration of the inner world and by the revelation of psychological conflict. Classical writers, however, tried to create characters that would be balanced between reason and emotion, personal will and social responsibility. These differing methods can apply to Shakespeare and traditional Chinese drama respectively, as is clear from my earlier discussion on characterization.

It is well known that Shakespeare focused on individuality, which was a prevailing tendency of romanticism. In classicism, however, emphasis was placed on the qualities that people possess in common, particularly their moral sense and consciousness of personal limitations. In discussing these two principles T. E. Hulme says,

> The root of all romanticism is that man feels the individual is an infinite reservoir; and if you can so rearrange society by the destruction of oppressive order then these possibilities will have a chance and you will get progress. . . . One can define the classical quite clearly as the exact opposite to this. Man is an extraordinarily fixed and limited animal whose nature is absolutely constant. It is only by tradition and organization that anything decent can be got out of him.[20]

Judging from this statement, traditional Chinese drama appears to be an exact copy of classicism in this aspect because Chinese dramatists have always viewed humanity in the light of society and not as individuals. In their works, as I pointed out before, characters often must reconcile their personal will with the moral order. This principle stems from the collectivism of Confucianism.

Antithesis was commonly used by romantic writers, Shakespeare among them, as Schlegel points out:

> [Romantic drama] delights in indissoluble mixtures; all contrarieties: nature and art, poetry and prose, seriousness and mirth, recollection and anticipation, spirituality and sensuality, terrestrial and celestial, life and death, are by it blended together in the most intimate combination.[21]

Classical writers normally did not employ such a method. Traditional Chinese drama shows no use of it, particularly in character portrayal. Like European classical authors, traditional Chinese dramatists did not intend to create opposition between beauty and ugliness and good and evil. The classical ideal demands impeccable finish, stylistic decorum, graceful expression, and harmony and balance of form. These are also the principles and ideals that traditional Chinese dramatists tried to achieve, particularly in the use of poetic imagery. By contrast, the romantic ideal is that of literary geniuses, demanding innovation instead of traditionalism and disregarding classical precedent and rules. This is so obvious in Shakespeare's case that it needs no further discussion.

Having demonstrated that Shakespeare frequently displays a romantic tendency and that traditional Chinese drama manifests a classical style, I must add that other features steer the two dramatic traditions away from becoming "pure" romanticism and classicism. Shakespeare also demonstrates a realistic vein, as a critic points out: "Shakespeare achieves through realism the effect of the Romantic sublime, as described specifically by Kant."[22] Traditional Chinese drama also manifests a deep and strong inclination toward sentimentalism.

The foregoing discussion of the general aesthetic qualities of Shakespeare's plays and traditional Chinese drama is crucial to an understanding of the impact of Shakespeare's works upon traditional Chinese drama in modern China, which I shall undertake in the next chapter.

Part II

3

The Impact of Shakespeare
on Traditional Chinese Drama:
Shakespeare in Modern China

IN the last two chapters I have compared Shakespeare with traditional Chinese drama. In the next two chapters, however, I will study the influence of the two types of drama. It is a pity that Shakespeare's plays and traditional Chinese drama had no opportunity to influence each other four hundred years ago, owing to the difficulty of communication. The golden age of classical Chinese drama (the Yuan dynasty) had occurred three hundred years before the Elizabethan age, and many important classical Chinese playwrights were contemporaries of Shakespeare. Yet ever since Shakespeare was introduced into China at the beginning of the twentieth century, his works have had a great impact upon traditional Chinese drama, modern Chinese theater, and the whole of cultural life in modern (1900–1980) and contemporary (1980–95) China. At the same time the dramatic techniques of traditional Chinese drama have greatly affected the stage presentation of Shakespeare in twentieth-century China. Thus this chapter will concentrate on the interaction of Shakespeare's plays with traditional Chinese drama in the twentieth century.

The introduction of Shakespeare into China occurred at the same time of a great change in social and political circumstances in modern China, at the beginning of the twentieth century. Although a trade exchange between China and Western countries took place two thousand years ago through the famous Silk Road, a formal cultural interchange did not occur until the trade wars between China and several Western countries in the middle of nineteenth century. The wars ended with the establishment of a series of concessions to coastal cities of China such as Hong Kong, Shanghai, Tianjing, and Qingdao. In the meantime many missionary schools were established in the larger cities of China. All of this served as a way to introduce Western civilization into China. During this period and afterwards,

97

particularly at the end of nineteenth century and the beginning of the twentieth, the Chinese elite, recognizing the backwardness of their country, inaugurated several initiatives to import modern science and technology, as well as social ideology, from the West. The earliest effort was started by officials in the Qing government. This Westernization movement (called *yang wu yun dong*, 1860–90) aimed mainly at improving Chinese industry by introducing Western technology and science. Since then increasing numbers of Chinese students and scholars have traveled to Western countries and brought back new knowledge and Western culture. The interest of the Chinese in the West gradually extended to social and political ideas, which accelerated the overthrow of the last feudal empire in 1911. After that, in 1919, a great upsurge was initiated by Chinese intellectuals. They had a more radical goal: the criticism of traditional Chinese culture centered on Confucianism on the assumption that it served as a vehicle for feudalistic ideology and had become a barrier to the development of a modern China. This movement also advocated the study and acceptance of Western culture, which was regarded as a powerful ideological weapon capable of destroying the deep-rooted feudalism of China and building a new democratic and prosperous China. This important movement was called the May Fourth New Culture Movement. Considering the historical background, one can understand why Western culture was introduced into China during this period. It was through these initiatives that Shakespeare came, step by step, to Chinese scholars, readers, and audiences.

In chapter 1 I pointed out that literary traditions are emphasized in Chinese culture because literature in ancient China served not only as a sort of entertainment or personal accomplishment but also as a means for an individual to achieve high social status. It was therefore natural for the Chinese to pay particular attention to Western literature along with the many other aspects of Western culture that were being introduced into China. Shakespeare is commonly considered one of the first Western writers brought to modern China. At the outset, because of the language barrier and the difficulty of translation, Shakespeare was known to the Chinese not through his works but through allusions and brief remarks in books and writings by foreigners and Chinese scholars.

It is not surprising that the earliest introduction of Shakespeare was undertaken by English and American missionaries. In 1856, Shanghai Mohai Academy published Thomas Milner's *The History of Great Britain,* translated by an English missionary, William Muirhead. The book included a brief reference to Shakespeare:

Shakespeare was a well-known public figure in the Elizabethan age. His brilliant works represent both beauty and virtue. No one has outshone him so far.[1]

An American missionary, Chevalier, published *The History of the World* in 1882, which also mentioned Shakespeare. Another reference to Shakespeare came in a later book, *The Highlights of Western History*, edited and translated by an English missionary, A. Joseph. He writes:

The most famous English poet was Shakespeare. In his poems and plays, he vividly depicts man's joy and sorrow. He has seen much of the world and been steeped in literary and dramatic techniques. So he is good at portraying the wide variety of personality: good and evil, great and mean.[2]

By the beginning of the twentieth century Shakespeare was mentioned more frequently in the books edited and translated by foreign missionaries or scholars and published in China. A typical reference is a passage in *The Concise Encyclopedia*, edited by the English missionary Timothy Lee in 1903: "Shakespeare . . . has been called the king of poetry. He was also a famous dramatist."[3] Another book, *The Famous Foreign Personages of Past Ages*, published in Shanghai, says: "Shakespeare, the English playwright, often mocked and criticized the monarch and ministers. Thus he can be called a foreign Player Meng" (516).[4] In 1940, the English missionary John Leith published *The Short History of the World*, which includes a reference to Shakespeare that echoes Milner's of 1856: "Shakespeare was a celebrated poet. His poems are beautiful and brilliant. His works have been read with admiration by people and no other English writers can outshine him" (517). Over the years, many biographical books appeared. Shakespeare was included in all of them, as for example in *Sixty Famous Figures in the Modern World*, 1907, and *A Biography of Celebrated Personages in the World*, 1908 (517).

The first Chinese who mentioned Shakespeare was a minister to Great Britain in the 1870s, Guo Song Tao. During his tenure he not only investigated Western science and technology but also acquainted himself with Western literature. In his diary he mentioned Shakespeare three times. On 11 August 1877 Guo was invited to visit an exhibition of English printing machines. Many well-known literary works were on display at the exhibition, including Shakespeare's works. His diary says,

Among all the books on display, Shakespeare's was the most well known. He was an outstanding English playwright about two hundred years ago, enjoying equal popularity with the Greek writer Homer.[5]

One year later Guo mentioned Shakespeare again in his diary. It was on 26 September 1878, when he met and talked with German and Japanese diplomats and an English official. The English official, joking with the German diplomat, used the sentence "Sorrow makes fat," which he said came from Shakespeare's plays.[6] In fact, the sentence was paraphrased from a passage spoken by Falstaff in *1 Henry IV:* "A plague of sighing and grief, it blows a man up like a bladder" (2.4.330–32). The third time Guo mentioned Shakespeare in his diary was on 18 January 1879, when he was invited to see a Shakespeare production:

> In the evening, I was invited to go to London Lyceum Theatre to see a Shakespeare production. Emphasis was placed on the lively and attractive plot design of the play, and not on florid language and ornate style.[7]

Guo unfortunately did not give details on the play, a production of *Hamlet* with Henry Irving in the leading role.

At the end of the nineteenth century and at the very beginning of the twentieth, Shakespeare's works began to attract the attention of increasing numbers of Chinese scholars. In 1894, in *The Evolution of Nature,* the influential Chinese scholar Yan Fu wrote; ". . . Shakespeare, the English poet and playwright whose works are spread far and wide among readers all over the world."[8] Yan Fu also noticed particular characteristics of Shakespeare's works such as his common humanity:

> Shakespeare's characters look very similar to people living today. We can identify ourselves with his characters not only in appearance and manner, but also in thought and emotion.[9]

Fourteen years later Yan mentioned Shakespeare again in another book. This time his purpose was not to comment on Shakespeare directly: instead he took Antony's speech in *Julius Caesar* (3.2. 73–107) as a way to explain the function of logic in argument:

> Shakespeare wrote a play recounting the murder of Caesar. When Antony delivers a speech to the citizens while showing the body of Caesar to the public, he uses logic to stir up the citizens cleverly because Brutus warned him that he would not be allowed to redress a grievance for Caesar and blame the murderers. The citizens are greatly agitated by the speech and

their resentment against Brutus and his comrades is running high. We should attribute Antony's success to the function of logic![10]

In 1902 a leading Chinese politician and scholar, Liang Qi Chao, wrote an article for a literary column in the monthly journal *Xin Min*. In it he mentioned Shakespeare and other Western writers:

> Homer, the Greek poet, was the greatest poet in ancient times . . . as for later poets, such as Shakespeare, Milton, Tennyson, their poems usually contain several thousand lines. How wonderful! Just the sublime style is brilliant enough to overwhelm you, so you no longer need to comment on the language of their poems.[11]

The characters that he chose to write Shakespeare's name have since then been commonly used in China, although the translations of others are superior for pronunciation. The adoption of Liang's translation may be partly due to his fame in both the political arena and academic circles. In 1898 he was one of the leaders of a famous political group, the Reform Movement. Similar to the Glorious Revolution of England, this movement tried to change China into a combined monarchy and parliamentary democracy. It failed to fulfill its goal, however, because of the powerful resistance of the monarchy.

A very effective introduction of Shakespeare into China was undertaken by China's greatest modern writer, Lu Xun. Early in 1907, when Lu Xun was a student in Japan, he wrote three influential articles on science, literature, and culture. In all of them he mentioned Shakespeare briefly. In "On the Function of Poetry" (*Mo Luo Shi Li Shuo*), Lu paid high tribute to Shakespeare. After quoting some passages of Thomas Carlyle discussing Dante and Shakespeare in *On Heroes, Hero-worship and the Heroic in History*, Lu said that both Dante and Shakespeare were indeed heroes because as poets they conveyed the voice of a nation. The thoughts and feelings they represented in their works would help to unite a nation and unify a country. Then Lu concluded that a nation must have great writers like Dante and Shakespeare if it wanted to survive in the modern world.[12] In his article "The History of Science," Lu discussed the different functions of scientific knowledge and emotion as conveyed by literary works. He maintained that people must not have so much esteem for knowledge that they look down on emotion because that would damage the meaning of science. He says:

> Therefore, what a society needs is not only Newton but also Shakespeare . . . a writer like Shakespeare can make people have a sound and perfect

human nature and avoid an odd and partial humanity, making them the very people a modern civilized society needs.[13]

In the third article, "On Cultural Bias," Lu Xun used Antony's speech in *Julius Caesar* to support his philosophical viewpoint. During this period, Lun was so greatly influenced by Nietzsche's theory of the "will to power" and "superman" that he believed that the peace of the world depended entirely on political supermen. In his article he regretted that the Roman citizens were very unreliable because they were always changing. In the light of his beliefs, Lu maintained that one should "Never tell truth to the masses and never tell state affairs to the masses."[14]

In this early stage the references to Shakespeare by both foreigners and Chinese scholars served as an effective means of making Shakespeare known to the Chinese, although these simple introductions did not describe Shakespeare's works in detail. Gradually Shakespeare became known to more Chinese people, resulting in an increasing demand to read his works. A few Chinese scholars began to try to translate Shakespeare's works into Chinese.

The first Chinese translation of Shakespeare was of none of the various editions but rather Charles and Mary Lamb's *Tales from Shakespeare*. It was published by Shanghai's Da Wen Press in 1903 with the title *Strange Tales from Overseas*, but with no acknowledged translator. The book was translated into classical Chinese and included ten stories from the Lambs' book. As in a classical Chinese novel, each story was given a title and the names of the characters were changed to quasi-Chinese names. The titles of the ten stories are: "To Avenge His Father, Hamlet Kills His Uncle" (*Hamlet*); "Proteus Is Being Lecherous in Betraying His Honest Friend" (*Two Gentlemen of Verona*); "Antonio Contracts a Loan with His Flesh" (*Merchant of Venice*); "Olivia Has Made a Mistake in Loving a Twin Sister" (*Twelfth Night*); "Petruchio Tames the Lady with a Bad Temper" (*Taming of the Shrew*); "Error Compounds Error: There Is a Fantastic Story in Ephesus" (*Comedy of Errors*); "Trick after Trick, the Wife Gets the Ring" (*All's Well That Ends Well*); "She Takes a Risk in Looking for Her Husband and the Couple Reunites at Last" (*Cymbeline*); "Takes Pains to Save Her Brother and Still Maintains Her Virginity" (*Measure for Measure*); and "Jealous Leontes Wrongs His Wife" (*The Winter's Tale*). In the preface of the book a brief statement introduces Shakespeare:

This book was written by the English writer Shakespeare. Shakespeare was an unrivaled dramatist in the world. He was good at writing poetry.

His dramatic stories are very popular and he has been regarded as the world's greatest English writer. His works have been translated into many languages such as French, German, Russian, and Italian, and have been well received by numerous readers. As for the academic and literary circles in our country, there are also many poetic and fictional critics who highly praise Shakespeare. But it is a pity that we have not read his works before now. Therefore I have translated his works into Chinese and offer it to our readers. In the meantime, it will be added to our literary circles as a wonder with radiant splendor.[15]

In the next year a complete translation of the Lambs' book was published by the famous Commercial Press in Shanghai, under the title *The Mysterious Stories of the English Poet*. The translators were the well-known scholar Lin Shu and his collaborator, Wei Yi. It is interesting that Lin Shu did not know English at all. His collaborator interpreted the stories first, then Lin Shu wrote and polished them. By this unusual method he published more than 170 "translations" of European and American novels, all of them very influential in Chinese literary circles. *The Mysterious Stories of the English Poet* contained twenty stories. Lin Shu called it "a novel of gods and spirits." He gave each story a title in the style of classical Chinese short stories. For instance, the title of *The Merchant of Venice* was "The Bond of Flesh." *Romeo and Juliet* was "Everlasting Love," and the title of *Hamlet* was "The Instruction of the Ghost." In the preface of the book the translators briefly stated the significance of Shakespeare to world culture:

Shakespearean poetic works have been read by numerous families in the world. When they are presented in the theater to gentlemen and ladies, the audience is always deeply moved.[16]

These two translations of the Lambs' *Tales from Shakespeare* can be seen as the first phase by which Shakespeare's works came to be known to the Chinese. At this time, what the Chinese knew about Shakespeare's works was not their characteristics as drama and poetry, but rather their features as narrative literature because the translations gave only a broad outline of the plot, characters, and themes of the chosen plays. Simple as these translations were, they made a great contribution to the initial reputation of Shakespeare in China. Of the two translations Lin Shu's book was more influential. Many famous modern Chinese dramatists first knew Shakespeare through Lin's translation. The great master of modern Chinese literature, Guo Mo Ruo, looked back at the deep impression made by *The Mysterious Stories of the English Poet* in his book *My Childhood*:

The fictions translated by Lin Shu were very popular at that time. I liked to read them too. . . . Lamb's *Tales from Shakespeare* was translated by Lin Shu with the title *The Mysterious Stories from the English Poet*. It gave me great pleasure and influenced me a lot.[17]

Lin Shu's translation not only influenced many modern Chinese writers, but it also served as the stage script for the first Shakespeare productions in China before the May Fourth Movement (1913–18). I shall discuss Lin Shu's translation further later in this chapter.

The translations of Shakespeare's plays themselves did not appear until the occurrence of the May Fourth New Culture Movement, which also introduced a large quantity of Western and Russian literary works to Chinese readers. The demand of the Chinese to see Shakespeare's works in dramatic form became much stronger at that time. Eventually the first Chinese translation of Shakespeare, that of *Hamlet*, was published by the Chinese Publishing House in 1922. The translator was the celebrated modern Chinese playwright Tian Han, an ardent admirer of Shakespeare. The translation was of great importance because it was written not only in the complete dramatic form that Shakespeare used, but also in modern Chinese, which was a very convenient way for Chinese people to read Shakespeare's works and grasp the aesthetic charm of the playwright. At that time the classical Chinese language had not been suitable for modern social communication, so one of the main goals of the May Fourth New Culture Movement was to replace classical Chinese with modern Chinese (the vernacular). Two years later Tian Han finished his translation of *Romeo and Juliet*, which was also published by the Chinese Publishing House.

In the 1920s, following the translations of Tian Han, seven other translations of Shakespearean plays were published in China. These were Cheng Kou Yi's *The Taming of the Shrew* in 1923, Zeng Guang Xun's *The Merchant of the Venice* and Shao Ting's *Hamlet* in 1924, a translation of *Julius Caesar* by Shao Ting and Xu Shao Shan in 1925, Zhang Cai Zhen's *As You Like It* in 1927, Zheng Yi Zhe's *Romeo and Juliet* in 1928, and Liao Lan Hui's *The Merry Wives of Windsor* in 1929.

In the 1930s more translations of Shakespeare's plays were published in China, now including the tragedies: *Macbeth* (three versions), *King Lear, Othello, Hamlet, Julius Caesar;* the comedies: *The Merchant of Venice* (three versions), *Twelfth Night* (two versions); and the romances: *The Tempest* (two versions). The translators evidently worked separately, without a unified arrangement, and always chose plays that they personally liked. This is why some of the most popular of Shakespeare's plays could be found in several Chinese versions at the same time. Each of these versions has its own features, with the choices of the translators obviously affected by the social background and popular taste of that time. For instance, the themes of *Macbeth* attracted attention more than those of *King Lear* and *Othello* because during the 1920s and 1930s there were many conflicts among Chinese warlords, with each one trying to usurp state power and become a new emperor. The quality of the translations in the 1930s was generally higher than the earlier ones, mainly because of the increasing demand for stage presentations of Shakespeare during this period. Most of these translations were written for drama companies that intended to present Shakespeare's plays. For instance, Gu Zhong Yi's translation of *The Merchant of Venice* was completed for performance by the Shanghai Drama Association in May 1930.

During 1940s and 1950s even more sophisticated translations of Shakespeare's plays were published in China, such as a version of *Romeo and Juliet* (1944) translated by Cao Yu, the leading figure in modern Chinese theatrical circles; a version of *Timon of Athens* (1944) translated by Yang Hui; Liu Wu Ji's translation of *Julius Caesar* (1944); Sun Da Yu's translation of *King Lear* (1948); Fang Ping's translations of *Much Ado About Nothing* (1953) and *Henry the Fifth* (1955); Bian Zhi Lin's translation of *Hamlet* (1956); Wu Xing Hua's translation of *Henry the Fourth* (1957); and Fang Zhong's translation of *Richard the Third* (1959).

Shakespeare's dramatic achievement could not be fully appreciated by the Chinese until his complete works had been translated. So early in the 1930s a special translating association, founded by the Chinese Education and Culture Trust, planned to translate and publish the complete works of Shakespeare. Some well-known Chinese scholars were invited to undertake this task, but the association failed to achieve its goal at that time due to social and financial problems. However, three noted Chinese translators are worth mentioning since they made important contributions to the eventual translation of Shakespeare's complete works.

The first translator was Cao Wei Feng. He began his work in 1930 and planned to translate all the works of Shakespeare. But his work advanced at a slow pace because of the hard living and working conditions then prevalent. He finished translating only eleven Shakespearean plays. In 1943 his translations were published by the Gui Yang Wen Tong Press with the title *The Complete Works of Shakespeare*. Three years later the Shanghai Cultural Cooperation reprinted nine of Cao's translations and published, together with a new translation by Cao, another book with the same title. It should be pointed out that although Cao did not actually achieve his goal of translating all the plays of Shakespeare, his work was influential in China.

The second translator who tried to complete all of Shakespeare's plays was the famous scholar Professor Liang Shi Qiu. He was the chief translator invited by the association to undertake the translation of the complete works in the 1930s and was the only one who finished, a task that took almost thirty years. During the 1930s he translated only eight plays, and he did not finish the rest until 1967, eighteen years after he moved to Taiwan with the defeated National Party. His translation of the complete works was published by the Far East Publishing Company in Taiwan. Unfortunately, because of the political and cultural separation of Taiwan from mainland China for forty years, Professor Liang's translation has been unknown to the people of his homeland.

Zhu Sheng Hao, the third person to undertake the translation of the complete works of Shakespeare, is considered by the Chinese to be the greatest Chinese translator of Shakespeare. In his early years, as a high school student, he was very fond of Shakespeare. After becoming an editor at the Shanghai World Bookshop, a publishing company, he became even more interested in Shakespeare's works. Encouraged by his colleagues and his brother, he worked out a schedule to translate all the plays of Shakespeare. He started his work in 1935 and kept up a plan of completing about three plays each year until 1944, when he died of illness and overwork, leaving only six and a half plays unfinished. In 1947 the greater part of his translations, twenty-seven plays, was published by the Shanghai World Bookshop in three volumes under the title of *The Complete Works of Shakespeare*. In 1954 all of his translations were published by the Beijing Writers' Press in twelve volumes, which included thirty-one plays. Zhu Sheng Hao's translations of Shakespeare's plays were commonly accepted as the best Chinese versions of Shakespeare's plays by both academic circles and the reading public of China because the translator worked hard to convey the spirit and charm of Shakespeare in easy and smooth Chinese. Zhu took his translating work very seriously. Sometimes, in order to find a suitable word, he wracked his brain for several days. His excellent mastery of both English and Chinese, profound literary accomplishment, and hard work brought about his success. It is not an exaggeration to conclude that the popularity of Shakespeare in China should be largely attributed to the contribution of Zhu Sheng Hao.

The translating work of Zhu Sheng Hao laid a foundation for the publication of the first truly complete Chinese version of Shakespeare's works. An opportunity for this to happen came in 1964 when Chinese Shakespearean scholars and translators enthusiastically celebrated the four hundredth anniversary of the birth of Shakespeare. To show their great respect for the English playwright, the editors of the People's Literature Press in Beijing planned to publish a complete version of Shakespeare's plays and poems, based on Zhu Sheng Hao's translations. The press asked well-known Shakespeare scholars and translators to check Zhu's translations against the old and new Oxford editions and to translate the six historical plays and the poems that Zhu had not been able to complete before his death. The plan, however, was disrupted by the great turbulence brought about by the Cultural Revolution, during which both Western and Chinese cultural heritages were condemned as bourgeois and feudal rubbish. The desire of the Chinese to have a Chinese translation of the complete works at last came true in 1978, after the disaster of the Cultural Revolution had ended. The People's Literature Press eventually fulfilled its 1964 plan and published a brilliant translation of the complete works in eleven volumes, including all thirty-seven plays and the poems. It was well received by Chinese readers and has been regarded as the most authoritative Chinese version of Shakespeare's works. This was the first time that the Chinese had a translation of a foreign writer's complete works.

The extent to which literary works are accessible to foreign readers largely depends on the quality of the translation available. Because of the differences between two languages, it is very easy for a literary work to lose its artistic charm during translation. For example, when classical Chinese poems are translated into English, we can no longer see the subtle aesthetic effect produced by the uniqueness of the Chinese language, although the general meaning and emotion can be conveyed. Shakespeare's plays are probably some of the most difficult Western literary works for the Chinese to translate. Most of the early Chinese translations of Shakespeare's plays were done word-for-word, which emphasized the correctness of particular words but neglected the unique style of Shakespearean language. The most successful translations of Shakespeare's plays, such as Zhu Sheng Hao's translations, were based on the goal of expressing the spirit of the original. These translations were the first to fully represent the spirit and charm of Shakespeare. One of the difficult points in the translation of Shakespeare's works was his "golden apple"—the pun. It not only vexed Dr. Johnson but also frustrated many Chinese translators. In traditional Chinese drama, although there are examples of witty dialogue—for example, the dialogue between Jiang Shi Long and the waiter in the Zhao Shang Public House in *The Secluded Boudoir*—

one seldom sees the use of puns except in the poems of some comedies, in which the lover expresses affection for his beloved. However,
some Chinese translators, especially Zhu Sheng Hao, solved this
problem competently, thereby helping Chinese readers to appreciate
the humorous style of Shakespearean language. For instance, in *The
Merry Wives of Windsor*, Falstaff uses a pun to complain about his
bad luck:

> Mistress Ford? I have had ford enough. I was thrown into the ford; I
> have my belly full of ford.

> (3.5.35–36)

It is very difficult to find a double-meaning word to render this pun
into Chinese, yet Zhu cleverly used homophones instead. For the
name "Ford" Zhu used the Chinese word *fu de;* for "ford" in the
next three sentences he used another Chinese word that has the same
sound but is different in written form. Interestingly, the first *fu de*
correctly represents the sound of the English name "Ford" and the
second *fu de* means 'to float on water or to steep in water.' This
translation, therefore, is instantly recognized by the Chinese as an
amusing pun.

The most difficult aspect of the translation of Shakespeare's plays
is representing Shakespeare's blank verse in Chinese, an issue ener-
getically argued by Chinese scholars and translators. The key problem is that we cannot find an exact corresponding form in either
traditional Chinese drama or classical Chinese poetry, although there
is a similar poetic form, *pian wen*, in classical Chinese poetry, as I
mentioned in the last chapter. *Pian wen* can be seen as a type of
unrhymed verse, but it is not the correct form for presenting blank
verse in the Chinese translation because it uses parallelism and ornateness and usually contains not more than seven Chinese characters
in each line (roughly equal to three and a half beats in English verse).
If each translated line must have five beats, then ten Chinese characters are needed. Reading great numbers of ten-character lines would
be véry tedious for Chinese readers since they are accustomed to
traditional poetic rhythm patterns of five or seven characters per line.

There are two approaches to this problem. One emphasizes poetic
flavor in translation and the other advocates poetic form. Translators
representing the first method are Professor Liang Shi Qiu and Zhu
Sheng Hao. Professor Liang maintains that to translate Shakespearean blank verse, one should use smooth prose because it is very
difficult or almost impossible to find an alternate poetic form.[18] A
typical translator using the second method is Professor Sun Da Yu.

He insisted that since Shakespeare's works were poetic drama, it was a pity to translate blank verse with prose because readers would lose the beauty of the plays as poetic drama.[19] In his translation of *King Lear* he tried to use a syllabic unit that he created to produce the effect of a beat in Shakespeare's blank verse. Each unit contains two or three Chinese characters, and the number of characters in each line varies from twelve to fourteen. Professor Sun's method is a valuable contribution in the translating of Shakespeare's blank verse into Chinese.

Each of the two approaches has its own advantage. In practice the Chinese reader prefers the first to the second because the prose mode, particularly that of Zhu's translation, can fully represent the poetic flavor of Shakespeare's plays even though it does not comply with the rhythmical pattern of the blank verse. In fact, in a broad sense, Zhu Sheng Hao's prose should be regarded as prose poetry, for it still has a free tonal and rhythmical pattern and is suitable for recitation on stage. So far, however, the poetic mode has not proved very successful in imitating Shakespeare's blank verse. Most of such "Chinese blank verse" seems to suit neither the aesthetic taste of the Chinese nor the free, bold, and smooth style of Shakespearean language. Recently some Chinese Shakespearean scholars have appealed to colleagues to carry on the effort to translate Shakespeare's blank verse using a poetic form. Professor Qiu Ke An holds that Chinese Shakespeare scholars, translators, and readers should not be satisfied with prose versions of Shakespeare's plays. It would be better, he believes, for the Chinese people to have another translation of the complete works of Shakespeare entirely in a poetic form.[20]

It is quite clear that the problem of how to treat Shakespeare's blank verse has been caused by a cultural gap. Nevertheless the appreciation and reception of Shakespeare in China will not be affected because Zhu Sheng Hao's translation is brilliant enough to convey fully the subtlety and fascination of Shakespeare's works. Zhu's translation is so well suited to the taste of the Chinese that many Chinese readers and audiences say that he has polished Shakespeare's plays into Chinese literature.

During the process of translation, Shakespeare's works were affected, more or less, by traditional Chinese drama and other literary genres. For instance, when Yang Lie translated *Macbeth*, he used a form of verse, *chang duan ju*, that was most often employed in traditional Chinese drama. Zhu Sheng Hao's translation also has many forms borrowed from traditional Chinese drama. For example, he translated the two songs in *As You Like It* (4.2 and 5.3) in the form of *qi yan shi* (seven-character poems), one of the main poetic forms in traditional Chinese drama. Also, as mentioned previously, in the early translation of Shakespeare's works, especially the translation of the Lambs' *Tales from Shakespeare*, the translators used the form of the classical Chinese novel.

As a great dramatist Shakespeare is eternal not only in written literature but also on the stage. Consequently the stage presentations of Shakespeare have been another way for the Chinese to become acquainted with the playwright. They have also served as an important medium through which Shakespeare strongly influenced traditional Chinese drama and theatrical practices in modern China. The staging of Shakespeare in modern China so far can be roughly divided into four periods. The first period (1913–29) was characterized by little activity, but the second period (1930–49) had formal and serious attempts at presenting Shakespeare's plays. In the third period (1949–66) all of the performances of Shakespeare in China were greatly influenced by the Stanislavsky acting method. The fourth period (1978–90) has marked the greatest maturity to date of the theatrical technique of Chinese actors in presenting Shakespearean plays.

The earliest Shakespeare production with Chinese actors was held in 1902. It was a production of *The Merchant of Venice*, performed in English by the students of the Foreign Language Department, Shanghai St. John College. The main purpose of the performance was to promote the English study of the students, so it cannot be regarded as the first Shakespeare production in Chinese. The first one in Chinese was presented in 1913 by the New People's Society (Xin Min She), a dramatic organization in Shanghai. The production had an alternative title, *The Bond of Flesh*, because it was based on the story from Lin Shu's translation of *Tales from Shakespeare*. In 1914 and 1915, another drama company, the Spring Willow Association, presented two tragedies, *Othello* and *Falling in Love (Romeo and Juliet)* and one comedy, *The Taming of the Shrew*. There were two Shakespearean productions in 1916: an adaptation of *Macbeth* performed by the Yao Feng New Drama Troupe under the title *The Usurper of State Power*, and an adaptation of *Hamlet* called *The Instruction of the Ghost*, presented by the Spring Willow Association.

Before and during the May Fourth New Cultural Movement (1917–29), more Shakespeare productions appeared on the Chinese stage. As all of them used the stories from Lin Shu's translation of the Lambs' *Tales from Shakespeare*, they often had alternative titles to suit the taste of Chinese audiences: *Filial Piety in Mind and in*

Words (*King Lear*); *A Hatred for Gold* (*Timon of Athens*); *The Twin Brother and Sister* (*Twelfth Night*); *The Opposed Mates Become a Happy Couple* (*Much Ado About Nothing*); *The Cousins* (*As You Like It*); *The Daughter of the Doctor* (*All's Well That Ends Well*); *The Confusion Caused by Twins* (*Comedy of Errors*); *The Duke of Vienna* (*Measure for Measure*); *A Dream of a Summer's Night* (*A Midsummer Night's Dream*); *The Seduction of Love* (*Two Gentlemen of Verona*); *The Story of a Statue* (*The Winter's Tale*); *The Favor and Enmity Caused by a Ring* (*Cymbeline*); *Tempest the Matchmaker* (*The Tempest*); and *The Story of a Sunken Pearl* (*Pericles, Prince of Tyre*).[21]

It is evident that the early Chinese stage presentations of stories from Shakespeare's plays cannot, in a strict sense, be seen as real performances of Shakespeare's plays. In fact, they were really just tentative rehearsals. The simple and informal style of the performances during this period was partly due to the lack of genuine Chinese versions of Shakespeare's plays and to the unformed method of modern Chinese drama. Modern drama was new and exotic in China and was based on Western spoken drama. During its early stage it was called "civilized drama" by the Chinese and apparently included some elements of traditional Chinese drama, as, for instance, stereotyped roles and stylized movement. To attract more audiences, the theater that presented "civilized drama" had to change its program every day. There was no time for the troupe to ask a playwright to write a script for the performance and there was no time even to rehearse. Consequently a very simple performing method was commonly used. Before the performance the actors made copies of the play's plot outline and then gave an impromptu performance based on it. All the "Shakespeare" productions during this period were given in this way. It is a pity that the audiences saw only the rough plots of Shakespeare's plays and had no opportunity to enjoy their beautiful lines. Nevertheless these productions still made their contribution to the popularity of Shakespeare in China.

The first genuine Shakespeare production on the Chinese stage did not appear until 1930. In that year a production of *The Merchant of Venice* was presented by the Shanghai Theatre Society in Shanghai Central Hall. The play was directed by Yang Yun Wei, Yu You Yun took the role of Portia, Cheng Xiao Mo was Antonio, and Shen Tong acted the part of Shylock. It was the first time that the Chinese saw a real stage representation of a Shakespearean play given in a mature form of modern spoken drama and with Shakespeare's original text. Professor Gu Zhong Yi of Fudan University translated the play into Chinese for the performance.[22] The second Shakespeare production formally presented in China was the successful *Romeo and Juliet* in 1937. It was performed by the Shanghai Practical Drama Company in the Carlton Theatre under the direction of Zhang Min. The well-known actor Zhao Dan played the part of Romeo and the famous actress Yu Pei Shan played Juliet.[23] The production used a Chinese version of *Romeo and Juliet,* translated by the celebrated dramatist Tian Han. In the 1940s and in later years other serious performances of Shakespeare's plays appeared on the Chinese stage, although cultural life in China was completely disrupted by the war with Japan. Some of these productions were very influential, particularly three plays presented by the State Drama School. These plays were a production of *The Merchant of Venice* in 1937 in Nanjing, the capital of China at that time, a 1938 production of *Othello* in Chongching, where the school moved because of the war, and a production of *Hamlet* in 1942, which toured some cities in Sichuan province. In 1944 a production of *Romeo and Juliet* caused a sensation in Chongching, the rear bastion during the war. The play was presented by the Divine Eagle Drama Company and directed by Zhang Jun Xiang, an important figure in modern Chinese theatrical circles. The well-known actor Jin Yan, who was called "the movie emperor," was cast for the part of Romeo, and the famous actress Bai Yang was Juliet. The production used a poetic version translated by Cao Yu, the leading dramatist in modern China. The performance was praised as the best stage representation of Shakespeare's plays in China to that time.[24]

Affected by the general trend of modern Chinese drama in the 1930s and 1940s, the staging of Shakespeare in this period tended to play down the influence of the stylized performance common in traditional Chinese drama and to become more realistic. Most of the Shakespeare productions tried to create a visual reality on the stage, with the performers acting as they would in real life. For example, in preparation for a *Romeo and Juliet* in 1937, the actors and actresses of the Shanghai Practical Drama Company rehearsed many times. To make the fight scenes true to life, the company engaged a Russian fencing master for two months to teach the actors how to fight with swords. When the play was performed, the audience was surprised at the fencing skills of the actors and observed that the fight seemed very real. The set designs, which included houses, streets, gardens, and fountains, also tried to produce an illusion of a real environment on the stage. Another trend focused on the use of costume. The players were often elaborately dressed and richly ornamented. Some dramatic critics felt that the directors of the productions overemphasized the showiness of the settings and costumes and neglected acting technique because the acting of the performers often was unsatisfactory.[25] Since most of the actors and actresses lacked formal training and performance experience, they often just read their lines in unemotional monotones.

The staging of Shakespeare in China in the third period (1949–66) was related to the prosperity of modern Chinese drama after the founding of the People's Republic of China. Because of the stable social order, the country's cultural life and literary creativity were greatly improved, in spite of the strong influence of the Chinese Communist party. In addition to traditional drama, exotic Western spoken drama, called "modern drama" in China, was commonly accepted as an important dramatic form. At that time almost every province and big city set up a modern drama company to supplement the troupe already performing traditional Chinese drama. By 1966 there were about 160 modern drama companies and twenty thousand theater professionals in China.[26]

Shakespeare's plays were frequently staged during this period, particularly in Beijing and Shanghai, the two cultural centers of modern China. Some of these productions are worth mentioning. In 1956 the Chinese Central Drama Academy presented *Romeo and Juliet*. The play was directed by two dramatic experts from the Soviet Union, Lekov and Danny. Ji Qi Ming was cast for the part of Romeo and Tian Hua for Juliet. Zhu Sheng Hao's translation was used for the performance, which was the first time a Beijing audience, which included Premier Chou En-lai, saw a Shakespeare production on stage. In the same year the Shanghai Drama Institute presented *Much Ado About Nothing*, directed by another stage expert from the Soviet Union, Y. K. Lepkovskaya. *Twelfth Night* must have been a favorite with Chinese drama companies because there were four productions of the play in the 1950s and 1960s, separately presented by the Beijing Film Institute in 1957, the Shanghai Drama Company of Film Actors in 1957, the Shanghai Film Drama Troupe in 1959, and the Shanghai Film School in 1962.[27]

The performance of Shakespeare's plays in this period was evidently influenced by Stanislavsky's innovative style of naturalistic production, owing to the close relationship between China and the Soviet Union at that time. Soviet drama coaches were invited to instruct Chinese actors, and likewise many Chinese drama professionals were sent to the Soviet Union to study modern drama. In nearly all the performances of Shakespeare's plays on the Chinese stage during this period, Stanislavsky's acting method was followed.[28] The Chinese directors wanted to transcend the limitations of a more visual reality and to seek a greater reality of character and psychology. The actor needed to understand and identify fully with the thought and emotion of the character he or she played. This method helped the actor not only to imitate the outer manner of the character, but also to recreate personality. A typical example is the 1961 performance of the famous actress Zhu Xi Juan when she played the part of Beatrice in *Much Ado About Nothing* in Shanghai. In following the method of Stanislavsky, she intended to "become" Beatrice both on stage and in daily life. In the church scene she was shocked when Claudio blamed Hero for her lack of chastity and then became very angry because she felt that somebody was plotting against Hero. Seeing that Benedick looked blank, she believed that he had had no hand in the plot. So when Hero fainted, she could not help but stretch out her hand toward Benedick and cry, "Help her! Benedick!" Here Zhu Xi Juan identified so closely with Beatrice that she acted by the logic of Beatrice's personality and did not follow the lines.[29]

For thirteen years the Great Cultural Revolution, a nightmare for most Chinese, made China a cultural wasteland and kept the stage nearly empty except for the performance of the eight "Revolutionary Model Plays," which served the political ambition of Mao's wife. The death of Chairman Mao and the fall of the Gang of Four indicated the beginning of a new era, marked by comparative political and ideological tolerance and a cultural renaissance. The period from 1978 to 1988 can be seen as a golden age for the stage presentation of Shakespeare, during which time drama professionals gradually evolved a style of their own and successfully created a Chinese Shakespeare on the stage. There were so many Shakespeare productions in this period that it is difficult to discuss all of them in detail. From 1980 to 1985, however, approximately ten Shakespeare productions in China were especially well received by Chinese audiences and praised by the dramatic critics. They were:

—*The Merchant of Venice*, Chinese Youth Arts Troupe, 3–13 September 1980
—*Macbeth*, Central Drama Academy, 3–8 January 1980
—*Measure for Measure*, Beijing People's Arts Theatre, directed by Toby Robertson, 2 April–30 May 1981
—*Romeo and Juliet*, Shanghai Drama Institute, 5–15 April 1981
—*The Tempest*, Shanghai Drama Institute, 5–12 January 1982
—*Antony and Cleopatra*, Shanghai Youth Spoken Drama Troupe, 27 April–27 May 1984
—*The Winter's Tale*, Shanghai Drama Institute, 1–7 December 1984

—*Othello*, Guangdong People's Arts Company, 25–27 September 1984

All of these productions achieved remarkable dramatic effects and attracted much larger audiences than before. During this time productions of Shakespeare's plays were no longer limited to Beijing and Shanghai: they rapidly expanded to other provinces, even to very remote areas. For example, in January 1982 the Tibetan Drama Troupe presented *Romeo and Juliet* in Tibet. Because Tibet has been called "the roof of the world," this was the highest stage in the world upon which Shakespeare's plays had ever been performed.

The Inaugural Chinese Shakespeare Festival, which was held in April 1986, represented a peak for Shakespearean drama on the Chinese stage. The festival was an exceptionally grand occasion for the Chinese, remarkable not only for its scale and variety, but also for the achievement of dramatists in creating a distinctively Chinese Shakespeare on the stage. The festival began simultaneously in Beijing and Shanghai on the tenth of April and ended on the twenty-third, which might have made it difficult for any passionate theater-goer to see all twenty-eight productions: sixteen were in Shanghai and twelve were in Beijing, with a total of 102 performances altogether. Twenty-three different companies at a dozen theaters performed eighteen different plays of Shakespeare, attracting an audience of more than one hundred thousand. I can find no precedent for such activity in the history of Shakespeare production, which was the reason why the late Professor Philip Brockbank called it "a Shakespeare Renaissance in China."[30]

The twenty-eight productions included:

—*Othello*, three productions (by China Railway Drama Troupe, Experimental Beijing Opera Troupe, and Mongolia class of Shanghai Drama Institute)

—*King Lear*, three productions (by Central Drama Academy, Tianjing People's Arts Theater, and Liaoning People's Arts Theater)

—*Macbeth*, one production (by Shanghai Kunju Troupe)

—*Timon of Athens*, two productions (by North China Drama Society of Beijing Teacher's University and Second Foreign Language Institute of Beijing, in English)

—*Titus Andronicus*, one production (by Shanghai Drama Institute)

—*Antony and Cleopatra*, one production (by Shanghai Youth Spoken Drama Troupe)

—*The Merchant of Venice*, two productions (by China Youth Arts Theater and the Arts Academy of the Chinese People's Army, in English)

—*The Merry Wives of Windsor*, two productions (by the Central Experimental Theatre and Wuhan Spoken Drama Troupe)

—*The Taming of the Shrew*, two productions (by Shanghai People's Arts Theater and Shanxi Spoken Drama Troupe)

—*Twelfth Night*, two productions (by North China Drama Society of Beijing Teacher's University and Shanghai Shaoxing Opera Troupe)

—*Love's Labor's Lost*, one production (by Jiangsu Drama Troupe)

—*All's Well That Ends Well*, one production (by Xian Drama Troupe)

—*Much Ado About Nothing*, one production (by Anhui Huangmeixi Troupe)

—*A Midsummer Night's Dream*, one production (by China Coal Miners' Drama Troupe)

—*Richard III*, two productions (by China Children's Arts Theatre and Shandong Spoken Drama Troupe)

—*The Winter's Tale*, one production (by Zhejiang Shaoxing Opera Troupe).

By 1986, then, twenty-three Shakespeare plays had been staged in China. Only fourteen plays did not appear on the stage, including two tragedies (*Julius Caesar* and *Coriolanus*), two comedies (*Two Gentlemen of Verona* and *Troilus and Cressida*), one romance (*Pericles*), and nine historical plays (all except *Richard III*).

The Inaugural Chinese Shakespeare Festival was a milestone in the history of Shakespeare production in China. The maturity of the Chinese actors was evident in their individual interpretations of their roles. Moreover, the staging of some unusual plays, such as *Titus Andronicus* and *Timon of Athens*, which are rarely presented on the Western stage, revealed the ambition of Chinese directors. For example, Xu Qi Pin, the director of *Titus Andronicus* by the Shanghai Drama Institute, interpreted this bloody revenge tragedy as a political tragedy from the perspective of Chinese culture. The two productions of *Timon of Athens* were deliberately designed to represent conventional moral concepts and a serious social problem in contemporary China—the prevalent worship of money since the beginning of the economic reform. I will discuss the significance of these three productions in detail in chapter 6.

When I attended the festival I felt that some of the directors, such as Xu Qi Pin, intended to interpret the themes and characters from a new angle. For example, Cheng Ping, the director of the China Railway Art Drama Troupe, gave a feminist interpretation of the protagonists in *Othello*. Some productions were designed to heighten Shakespeare's romantic atmosphere with Asian aesthetic qualities.

The festival demonstrated that the Chinese stage representation of Shakespeare had entered a period having a variety of artistic styles. It seemed to me that the Stanislavsky method was no longer dominating Chinese directors and actors. They used instead many acting styles to give full range to their talents. For example, some of the productions were evidently influenced by the principles of Brecht, particularly his "distancing" technique; some of them showed a "modernization" theme with trendy costumes, props, and language to attract young people and convey up-to-date ideas; and more important, some of the productions were presented in the form of traditional Chinese drama, brilliantly combining the beauty of the two types of drama. I shall discuss this in detail in the next chapter.

These pages have shown how Shakespeare has survived transplantation into Chinese culture, how his reputation has grown in modern China, and how his works have impacted traditional Chinese drama. Since Shakespeare was introduced into China, traditional Chinese drama has been dealt a hard blow by the great English playwright and other Western dramatists such as Ibsen. Shakespeare has greatly influenced the conventional dramatic concepts of the Chinese, helping to infuse new ideas. It was Shakespeare, together with other Western dramatists, who ended traditional Chinese drama's thousand-year monopolization of the Chinese stage. In theatrical and academic circles, and among educated Chinese people, Shakespeare has been crowned the king of drama and the most prestigious representative of Western culture.

The initial impact of Shakespeare on traditional Chinese drama occurred when the May Fourth New Cultural Movement was in full swing in 1919. During this movement Western culture was used as a powerful weapon to criticize the outworn Chinese feudalistic culture. Most of the traditional literary genres were attacked, particularly traditional Chinese drama, which was seen as an important vehicle for spreading feudal poison. The magazine New Youth, which was the main propaganda instrument of the radical side of the movement, published special issues to initiate a debate on the reform of conventional Chinese theater. After comparing traditional Chinese drama with the works of Shakespeare and other Western playwrights, many proponents of the movement held that traditional Chinese drama was backward and outmoded and no longer suited the taste and needs of modern China. By contrasting it with Shakespeare, Chinese scholars in effect criticized many aspects of traditional Chinese drama.

Chinese critics maintained that Shakespeare reflected reality in his works even though the atmosphere and plots of his plays looked more romantic than life really was. While Shakespeare used old tales and chronicles as plots, he nevertheless represented the thought and emotion of his contemporaries and modern Europe. By contrast, Chinese critics complained that traditional Chinese drama failed to depict the reality of modern Chinese society. Traditional Chinese drama recounted very old stories and events in ancient China that were greatly idealized to serve feudal politics. The philosophy of these characters was quite different from that of modern Chinese people, making it difficult for audiences to find common ground. The critics were most disgusted with the strong moralizing tone of traditional Chinese drama. As I have discussed in an earlier chapter, traditional Chinese drama was inclined to teach the Confucian ethical code, which was regarded as repressive by modern Chinese people. By comparison, Shakespeare represented the ideal of humanism, as the great modern Chinese dramatist Cao Yu says:

> In his works, Shakespeare sings the praise of the universe and humanity. He delineates subtly the mystery of human nature and eternal philosophy of life and represents the essence of humanism.[31]

In contrast to Confucianism, humanism was associated by Chinese scholars with individual liberty and the prosperity of Western countries in modern times. The failure of traditional Chinese drama to depict a generalized human nature was considered by the critics to be one of the main causes of its backwardness. In fully representing all of humanity in his works, Shakespeare's plays had great universal appeal, as the influential Shakespeare critic and translator Professor Liang Shi Qiu said in 1929:

> People always wonder why nowadays the *Iliad* is still commonly read and most of Shakespeare's plays are still being staged. The reason is that both of them represent general humanity, which serves as the foundation of all great literary works.[32]

Another characteristic element that Chinese scholars disliked in traditional Chinese drama was the "fraudulent nature" of the drama. The scholars held that Shakespeare and other Western dramatists— Ibsen and Bernard Shaw, for example—revealed conflicts between different social forces and exposed social problems and contradictions in their works. But traditional Chinese drama was supposed to present in the end a false picture of peace and harmony that concealed serious social difficulties. Traditional Chinese drama, therefore, belonged to a literature of deception. The great modern writer Lu Xun once criticized traditional Chinese drama for covering up the serious marriage problems of ancient and modern China. He maintained that, bound by the feudal ethical code, young people in China had no freedom to find their mates by themselves. All marriages were arranged by parents and matchmakers, ruining the happiness and lives of numerous young people. Yet traditional Chinese drama ignored this problem and tried to conceal it. Lu says:

> As everyone knows, although the action of the lovers to become engaged on their own has been praised in conventional drama and novels (the action is of course only limited to the young men who can pass the imperial examination and win the title of Zhuang Yuan), the fact is that it cannot be tolerated by people in real life and the marriage is bound to be ruined. . . . Traditional drama often uses a pattern where the gifted scholar passes the imperial examination and his marriage is arranged by the emperor, who is used to compromise on the problem caused by the principle of the parents' decision. Then seemingly the unreasonable marriage system is no longer problematic, and the key point to solve the problem now becomes whether the young man can pass the imperial examination, but not whether the marriage system itself is reasonable or not.[33]

Thus Lu Xun thought that changing status was a false solution for the problem and would not work in reality:

> This pattern of traditional drama is designed to deceive readers and audiences and to make them believe that society is basically optimistic and that if misfortune happens to someone, it is his own fault.[34]

In the first chapter I pointed out that the tragic concept of traditional Chinese drama differs from that of Shakespeare. Chinese tragedy always ends with a happy event that serves the purpose of comic relief but damages, more or less, the tragic effect of the play. This too was another characteristic of traditional Chinese drama that modern Chinese critics lamented. Compared with Shakespeare's tragedy, Chinese drama displays no real tragic ideals, as the leading figure of the May Fourth New Cultural Movement, Dr. Hu Shi Zhi, writes:

> What traditional Chinese literature lacks most is a tragic concept. In the works of conventional drama, as well as fiction, we always see a happy ending. . . . Yet Western literature has had very profound tragic ideas since ancient Greece.[35]

The famous modern Chinese playwright and Shakespeare translator Tian Han also held that Shakespeare's tragedy was genuine and could arouse sympathy particularly in Chinese readers and audiences. He thought that Shakespeare provided a better model for tragedy than did traditional Chinese drama, one that would allow Chinese writers to represent the sharp contradiction between Chinese people and the dying feudal system. In the preface to his translation of *Hamlet*, he writes:

> *Hamlet* is one of Shakespeare's most stirring and moving tragedies. Today we have a lot of young people of the Hamlet type. What will they think about their society after reading this great tragedy?[36]

The performance of Shakespearean drama uses a basically realistic style, although the playwright has employed poetic language and techniques that appeal to the imagination of an audience. By contrast, traditional Chinese drama is characterized by stylized movements, symbolic gestures, and performances that include speeches, acting, singing, dancing, acrobatics, and so forth. For this reason traditional Chinese drama was often called "opera" by foreigners, although it is quite different from Western opera and should be classified as a type of drama. As time has passed, greater emphasis has been placed on the stage techniques of traditional Chinese drama, causing the performers to neglect improvement of its literary content. Rather than attracting an audience through literary qualities such as profound themes, exciting plots, vivid characterizations, passionate emotions, and special effects—the main source of artistic fascination with Shakespeare's works—traditional Chinese drama uses performance techniques. Thus during the May Fourth New Cultural Movement several scholars criticized traditional Chinese drama for its lack of literary merit and realistic orientation, particularly when compared to Shakespeare's plays. Qian Xuan Tong, one of the leaders of the movement, singled out the Beijing opera (a major type of traditional Chinese drama):

> Referring to Beijing opera, we can hardly find any social ideals in the plays and the texts are often badly written. Do not take it for granted that because Beijing opera is a type of drama it has literary value. As for traditional Chinese drama, it just emphasizes singing skills and the audience often does not care about the libretto at all. In addition, the types of facial makeup look absurd and the stage equipment is very simple, and neither of them is good enough to move an audience. The production on the stage should imitate real men and events. From the old saying "the costume of player Meng"[37] we understand that when an actor plays the ancients, he should do it as well as player Meng did when he vividly imitated the appearance and manner of the late Prime Minister Sun Shu

Ao. An actor not caring about the fidelity of his performance would go against the purpose of theater. But why do today's actors pay no attention to this principle?[38]

Other critics also complained about the formulistic and stereotyped nature of traditional Chinese drama. For instance, the themes of lovers becoming secretly engaged to each other in a garden and a poor scholar finally passing the imperial examination were used so indiscriminately in so many plays that audiences became quite fed up.

The initial impact of Shakespeare upon traditional Chinese drama during the May Fourth New Cultural Movement and afterwards resulted in the gradual decline of traditional drama in Chinese academic and theatrical circles. Most of the critics held that Shakespeare was superior to traditional Chinese drama in both literary and theatrical merits. Shakespearean drama was still regarded as an elite form, however, owing to the scarcity of performances in this period and the lack of excellent translations available for the reading public, while Chinese drama continued to attract the majority of Chinese audiences and served as the main entertainment for ordinary people. The bias of the early-twentieth-century Chinese scholars criticizing traditional drama after comparing it with the works of Shakespeare and other Western playwrights was caused by a readiness to abandon conventional Chinese culture and accept Western society entirely and uncritically. In relating traditional Chinese drama to Shakespeare's plays they paid special attention to the social function of drama as a means of reflecting community problems and impelling people to improve society. But they neglected to evaluate the two types of drama from an objectively aesthetic point of view, which in fact hindered a comprehensive understanding of Shakespeare. For instance, some left-wing critics preferred Ibsen and Chekhov to Shakespeare because these nineteenth-century realistic dramatists more directly served the purpose of using drama as a powerful weapon for social struggle. Nonetheless, the initial impact of Shakespeare upon traditional Chinese drama indeed demonstrated basic differences between the two forms and helped the Chinese to see clearly the weak points of traditional Chinese drama from the standpoint of modern theater.

In the 1930s and 1940s traditional Chinese drama continued to take a pounding as more Shakespeare productions appeared on the Chinese stage and better translations of Shakespeare's plays were published. The Chinese Communists saw literature and art as a way to mix political propaganda with puritanism, which might have become a barrier to the further spread of Shakespeare's reputation in

China. Fortunately, the favor Marx himself showed towards Shakespeare and the preference of the Soviet Union for the playwright made Shakespeare legitimate drama in the proletarian culture of China after the establishment of the People's Republic of China. Even the top leaders of the party and government showed their interest in Shakespeare: Premier Chou En-lai, for example, attended a performance of *Romeo and Juliet* presented by the Central Drama Academy in 1956. Ironically, party leaders were as disgusted with the feudal ideology espoused in traditional Chinese drama as were the scholars. In the 1950s performances of some Chinese plays representing horror, superstition, or pornography (such as *The Chopped-up Coffin*, *The Man Who Killed His Son*, and *Lady Huang Travels to Hell*), were banned from performance by the government. Even in this politically austere period Shakespeare still had a higher standing in Chinese cultural circles than did traditional drama.

The greatest impact of Shakespeare on established Chinese drama occurred at the end of the 1970s, when China at last extricated herself from the crisis of the Cultural Revolution, and throughout the 1980s, during which great changes took place in many aspects of Chinese society. Casting off Stalinism and the ultra-left trend in the Chinese Communist party, China reopened its gate to the West. The Chinese set up a new initiative by studying Western culture thoroughly, without political prejudice caused by modern antagonism between China and Western capitalistic countries. As an icon of Western culture, Shakespeare naturally once more attracted special attention from the Chinese. The social and aesthetic value of his works was even more fully appreciated by Chinese audiences and readers. Since then the playwright has been regarded as the highest authority in dramatic art. During this period many kinds of traditional Chinese art lost their allure, especially for young people. A decline in traditional Chinese drama is also obvious: audiences have become markedly smaller and the average age of a patron has become increasingly older. It is evident that the impact of Shakespeare is one of the main causes of the decline of traditional Chinese drama in academic, theatrical, and literary circles during the 1980s.

Since the beginning of the Reform of China in 1978, Shakespearean studies have flourished rapidly in Chinese academic circles. The number of published writings on Shakespeare has increased sharply. About 1,115 articles dealing with various aspects of Shakespeare were published in China from 1978 to 1988, which is almost four times as many as in the period from 1918 to 1978.[40] Some of the articles compare Shakespeare with traditional Chinese drama. Like their predecessors in the May Fourth New Cultural Movement, the more the writers appreciate the dramatic merits of Shakespeare's plays, the more they disparage traditional Chinese drama. But unlike the critics of sixty years ago, the new generation approaches the two dramas not only politically but also aesthetically. While affirming the distinction of traditional Chinese drama, they maintain that because the aesthetic taste of contemporary Chinese has changed, traditional drama no longer satisfies audiences. Shakespeare's works, with their unique charm and universal appeal, are received much more enthusiastically.

In his book the young critic Zhang Fa points out that the main purpose of Shakespearean tragedy, as well as other Western tragedies, is to expose the social problems of the existing system or to show human weaknesses. The failure and destruction of the protagonist in Shakespearean tragedy derive from a strong will trying to uncover the truth of the situation:

> Hamlet intends to clarify the truth of his father's death. Yet he demonstrates his own weakness when he undertakes the task to avenge his father. . . . He also realizes the contradiction between his duty for vengeance and his character and is baffled by the attitude of man towards this reversed world. All of these factors bring about his destruction. . . . the tragic protagonist clearly exhibits a complex ability to transcend the simple division of good and evil, to transcend the provisional social institution or even to transcend culture itself.[41]

In comparing Shakespeare's plays with traditional Chinese drama, however, Zhang Fa holds that traditional Chinese drama, particularly political tragedy, represents an opposite tragic idea:

> The presentation of the faithful ministers who fight with treacherous ministers has been based on the qualities of stability, patience, and preservation of Chinese culture. It aims to neither thoroughly examine the existing social system and ideology nor show a transcending spirit through the complexity of the protagonist. It is designed mainly to sacramentalize the existing system and ideology and to portray the characters by the simple division of good and evil. . . . One cannot say that the classical Chinese playwrights do not see the serious problem in reality. But they always tend to reassure themselves and the people with conventionally political ideas and the strong rationalism of Chinese culture.[42]

Here Zhang Fa has expressed a common feeling of many Chinese audiences and readers who have grown weary of the stereotyped pattern of traditional Chinese drama while being strongly attracted by the variety and complexity of Shakespeare's plays.

The reasons for the increasing popularity of Shakespeare and the decline of traditional Chinese drama in contemporary China have been the focus for various writers' comparisons of Shakespeare with traditional Chinese drama. Critics have dealt with it in many aspects such as theme, characterization, and stage technique. After attending the Inaugural Chinese Shakespeare Festival, for example, one critic wrote an article discussing the impact of Shakespeare upon traditional Chinese drama. He believed that one of the principal causes of the rise of Shakespeare and the fall of traditional Chinese drama was that the rich and colorful presentation of individuality in Shakespeare's plays appealed to Chinese audiences and readers more than the stereotyped characterization of traditional Chinese drama. He writes:

> One of the important characteristics of Shakespeare's plays is that the portrayal of individuality is greatly emphasized, which would provide a vast field for using the actor's talent to play the role. We rarely see stereotyped characters in Shakespeare's plays. Every actor can have a different interpretation of Hamlet, Othello, and Shylock. . . . By contrast, the fatal weakness of traditional Chinese drama is to neglect the portrayal of individuality. The actors lack the consciousness to "recreate" the roles they play. All they do on the stage is present the plot, not to represent the personality of the characters. They usually treat the roles with the same method, which inevitably leads to a stereotyped orientation. That is strikingly contrasted with the variety and richness of the portrayal of personality in Shakespeare's plays. So we have drawn a good lesson from the impact of Shakespeare upon traditional Chinese drama.[43]

The discussion in Chinese academic circles, as we can see from the above excerpts, clearly shows the trend of contemporary China to replace traditional Chinese dramatic concepts with those of Shakespeare.

The impact of Shakespeare upon traditional drama can be seen even more distinctly in Chinese theatrical circles than in academe, for in the 1980s the staging of traditional Chinese drama rapidly declined as the performance of Shakespeare's plays flourished. It is true that other reasons such as the popularity of television also affected the staging of traditional Chinese drama, yet there is no doubt, as I stated earlier, that the sharply growing number of Shakespeare productions on the Chinese stage have proved an important factor in bringing about the decline of traditional Chinese drama. In the past theaters staging traditional Chinese drama were always filled to capacity. But in the 1980s a performance of a traditional Chinese play would find numerous seats unoccupied and the average age of the audience approaching sixty. The performers of traditional Chinese drama, especially in big cities, have frequently complained that they lose money from the performances. Certain plays cannot maintain even a short run now: after three or four days, there is no audience at all.[44] In January 1986, for example, a well-known actress of the Beijing Opera was on tour in Shanghai. She gave a total of fifteen performances from several different productions, at which the average seat occupancy was only thirty percent.[45] In China, drama companies at all levels are subsidized by the government. In fact, in the 1950s and 1960s the performance of traditional Chinese drama always made a great deal of profit. In the 1980s, however, most troupes of traditional Chinese drama had to depend totally on government subsidies. Sometimes the subsidy was not enough to maintain regular performances, so recently some troupes have tried to get commercial sponsors as well.

In contrast to the depressing state of traditional Chinese drama, Shakespearean plays always draw large audiences for extended runs. For instance, when the Beijing People's Art Theater presented *Measure for Measure* in April 1980, the play ran for forty-seven performances to capacity audiences. The production of *The Merchant of Venice*, presented by the Chinese Youth Art Theater, ran almost for two years, from 3 September 1980 to 13 August 1982, with a rare record of two hundred performances. When the Inaugural Chinese Shakespeare Festival was held in April 1986, people could always be found standing in the front of the theater before each performance, anxiously waiting for returned tickets. In March 1986 I attended a production of *The Merry Wives of Windsor* at Beijing Haidan Theater, performed by the Central Experimental Theater. The theater was filled to capacity, with many of the audience appearing to be students. After the performance I talked with several students of Qinghua University, a respected university specializing in science and technology. They told me that they enjoyed the play very much because they liked Western literature, particularly Shakespeare. The reason they gave was that Shakespeare vividly delineated the beauty of life and humanity, even though his plays were set in a totally alien culture. They said that they were very excited when they knew the play was to be performed in public, so they booked group tickets because all the students in their department were eager to see the play. When I asked them whether they often went to see traditional Chinese theater, especially Beijing opera since it was often performed in the capital, the students shook their heads. A tall young man smiled and said,

Yes, I know it is a cultural treasure, but it does not suit our taste. I once went to the theater and tried to appreciate traditional drama. But I only stayed for twenty minutes and then left because I could not understand what the players sang and said. The stereotyped characters were boring and I was unable to find anything exciting, which I strongly feel from Shakespeare's characterization. Besides, the tempo of traditional drama is too slow to suit the fast pace of contemporary life.[45]

In the past Shakespeare's plays were believed to attract a highly educated elite audience in China. Today, however, it is quite clear that they increasingly appeal to middle-class or semieducated urban audiences, even poorly educated peasant audiences. During the Inaugural Chinese Shakespeare Festival, while waiting outside the Cultural Palace of the Nationalities for the performance of *The Merchant of Venice* by China Youth Art Theater to begin, I saw a young man looking carefully at the poster of the play. I went over to talk to him. He told me that he was a farmer in a village of Anhui province and had traveled a long way to Beijing especially to attend the festival. I was surprised at his interest on Shakespeare because at that time it was very difficult for a person living in the country to travel several thousand kilometers to the capital, considering the low income earned by most Chinese peasants and the high cost of transportation and accommodations in Beijing. But my surprise also stemmed from the fact that a poorly educated farmer could show such interest in an English playwright. He told me that after graduation from elementary school he had gone to work in the fields. Two years previously he had an opportunity to read Shakespeare's plays and was immediately attracted to them. Since then he had yearned to see performances of the plays. "The Inaugural Chinese Shakespeare Festival is a rare chance for me," he said, "because you can see so many productions in just two weeks. It's worth spending my savings to see these fantastic plays." He admitted that he liked traditional Chinese drama but preferred Shakespeare. "I am greatly attracted to Shakespeare's rich and colorful characterizations and 'golden sayings' on the philosophy of life, which you rarely find in traditional Chinese drama."

The assumption that Shakespeare has won over increasing numbers of lower- and middle-class audiences has been supported many times. For example, in a discussion about Shakespeare in China during the festival the speech of a Mr. Tong, the official of a cultural center in Liangshan prefecture, Sichuan province, evoked strong responses among the participants. Tong told how Shakespeare was well received by the people in Liangshan, which is a very remote mountainous area in southwest China. He said that a few years ago the library of the cultural center bought some copies of Shakespeare's plays, which were frequently borrowed by the local residents, most of them farmers. Inspired by the increasing interest in Shakespeare, an amateur troupe organized by the cultural center performed a production of *Much Ado About Nothing* that drew large audiences. Tong said that he was very pleased to let the Shakespeare scholars know that Shakespeare's plays were not only highly appreciated by audiences and readers in big cities, but were also well received by the people living in remote areas. When Professor Zhang Si Yang, the vice-chairman of the Shakespeare Association of China, asked Tong whether the local residents of Liangshan had any difficulty in understanding Shakespeare's plays, Tong said:

> Not at all! When the play was performed, many of the audience were poorly educated and even illiterate farmers. But it seemed that all of them understood the production very well. After the performance some young men told me that the exotic atmosphere of the play struck them as new. Yet they liked it very much. There were no strange customs or moral doctrines in the play, so they were able to identify with the characters. For them, Shakespeare's plays sometimes were even easier to understand than traditional Chinese drama. For example, a young man told me that when he saw the famous classical Chinese tragedy *The Injustice to Dou E*, he could not understand why Dou E had to be loyal to her dead husband and not remarry although she was only seventeen years old.[46]

It is not difficult to understand why Shakespeare's works appeal to lower-class Chinese audiences, considering that in the Elizabethan age Shakespeare's plays were written for both aristocracy and townspeople. In his plays Shakespeare represents common humanity, which is easily accepted by people at all educational and cultural levels, even though it has been assumed that people with little education, particularly peasants, tend to be conservative and prefer conventional institutions and culture.

Shakespeare's great impact on traditional Chinese drama has also affected China's literary world since the plays serve as high-value material for the country's vast reading public. There can be no doubt that in contemporary China Shakespeare has more readers than audiences, for theatrical activity is often limited by finances and facilities. In the past decade Shakespeare's complete works and most of his plays and poems have been published in China. The number of copies published has reached three million, which is almost five times as much as that produced from 1949 to 1977. Certain editions were often published in incredibly large numbers. For example, the print run of the second edition of Zhu Sheng Hao's *Complete Works of Shakespeare* in 1988 amounted to one million copies. Fang Ping's translation entitled *Five Comedies of Shakespeare* totaled one hundred thousand and Tu An's *Shakespeare's Sonnets* three hundred and fifty thousand.[47] On the other hand, traditional Chinese plays were published in much smaller numbers during the same period, only about two hundred thousand copies.[48]

As the sharply increasing publication of Shakespeare's works in China might indicate, there has been a "Shakespeare craze" in contemporary China since 1986, when the Chinese Shakespeare Festival took place. Since then his works have been so commonly read by all people that reading his works has become fashionable. In recent years numerous "literary salons" have been established throughout China in which Shakespeare has been one of the major topics. There are also many groups reading Shakespeare's works in Chinese universities and colleges. The students meet to discuss particular Shakespeare plays or to recite lines chosen from the plays. A friend living in Changchun city in northeast China wrote to me in 1988 to relate that a long line had formed at the door of the city's main bookshop at five o'clock one morning because a new edition of Zhu Sheng Hao's *Complete Works of Shakespeare* would be sold on that day. Among these ardent Shakespeare enthusiasts were students, clerks, workers, engineers, and soldiers. My friend was very disappointed, he wrote, for the copies were already sold out when he came to the counter. Fortunately he was able to buy a copy through the "back door" (an unsafe way to purchase an item). The shop often held back a small number of best sellers for friends and relatives of employees.

In contrast to the mania among the Chinese public for reading Shakespeare's works, traditional Chinese plays have been given the cold shoulder. Fewer Chinese people read these plays in recent years, except for the scholars and students who study the drama as a research field. Most of the devotees of traditional Chinese drama are old people who usually appreciate the plays by attending performances to enjoy the stage techniques and not by reading them for their literary merits. Most other people, particularly the young, believe that the literary value of Shakespeare's plays is much higher than that of the established drama. As I pointed out in the second chapter, the major distinction of traditional Chinese drama is its poetical quality, which is different from that of Shakespeare. Yet most Chinese readers prefer Shakespeare's poetry to that of traditional drama because his vigorous and impassioned presentation better suits the taste of contemporary Chinese than the sentimental and restrained poetic style of traditional drama. It is no exaggeration that Shakespeare helps many young men win the affections of their girlfriends when they recite beautiful lines that they believe express their own passions as well. In addition, the "golden sayings" in Shakespeare's plays also attract the attention of readers, while traditional drama has only some outmoded epigrams suitable for feudal Chinese society. The humor found in Shakespeare's plays is another aspect of his art that causes readers to prefer this drama.

The consequences of the impact of Shakespeare upon traditional drama in modern and contemporary China are evident. First, Shakespeare has replaced traditional Chinese drama to become the most important and authoritative dramatic form in Chinese cultural circles today. Second, the dramatic concept of Shakespeare now dominates Chinese theatrical circles and has affected, directly or indirectly, all theatrical activities in contemporary China. And third, the impact has brought the decline of traditional Chinese drama to the point where it could die out completely as a feeble and decaying art with unfashionable beauty or survive through reform at the risk of losing its own distinctiveness. There are indications that some actors of traditional drama try to tailor their performances to the taste of contemporary Chinese with new methods that are apparently influenced by Shakespeare's dramatic ideas. For example, they try to have a tragic ending instead of the conventional happy one (*The Inspector General Returns to His Native Place* by the Yangzhou Opera Company, 1–28 May 1992); they also speed up the tempo of the performance and sometimes use a realistic acting style to express the true feelings of the character and represent individuality. There is a hope that the wheel of fashion may turn back once more. Since traditional Chinese drama is still vital in overseas Chinese societies such as Taiwan, Hong Kong, and Singapore, one may expect that when China becomes a society with pluralistic artistic tastes, traditional Chinese drama will regain its former place in Chinese cultural life and once more please Chinese audiences and readers. As a powerful national art form of long standing, traditional Chinese drama certainly has its own artistic charm. Its unique stage techniques still display great vitality and influence other theatrical activities of modern Chinese theater. Shakespeare production in China is also significantly affected by the stagecraft of traditional Chinese drama, which will be the central topic of the next chapter.

4

Shakespeare on the Chinese Stage:
The Convergence of Shakespearean
and Traditional Chinese Drama

OVER TIME Shakespeare's plays have been performed in a wide variety of forms, particularly when they appear on the foreign stage. In most cases the actors tend, consciously or unconsciously, to interpret Shakespeare's plays from the perspective of their own culture or to use indigenous dramatic conventions to add color to the productions. Looking back on Shakespearean theater in China, one can see the same phenomenon. Besides the standard productions, which maintain the original manner of the plays by using spoken drama and Western costumes and settings, numerous Shakespeare productions have created sinicized versions of Shakespeare's plays. As I pointed out in the last chapter, Shakespeare has had a great impact on traditional Chinese drama in modern and contemporary China. Nonetheless, as a type of drama with long-standing traditions and unique aesthetic qualities, traditional Chinese drama has also greatly affected Shakespearean theater in China, particularly during the 1980s, because it is an ideal vehicle by which Chinese directors and performers can present truly sinicized Shakespeare productions.

This chapter, therefore, discusses the different attitudes of the Chinese towards the adaptation of Shakespeare's plays into traditional Chinese dramas and investigates the feasibility and advantages of performing Shakespeare's plays in this style. It also deals with the achievements of some of these Shakespearean productions as performed by traditional Chinese drama groups such as Beijing, Kunju, Shaoxing, and Huangmei operas, in addition to other metamorphoses of Shakespeare's plays on the Chinese stage, and pays special attention to the significance of these productions to both Shakespearean and traditional Chinese theater in contemporary China.

There has been some debate whether Shakespeare's plays should be adapted into traditional Chinese drama in the first place. The

The Winter's Tale, Zhejiang Shaoxing Opera Troupe, 18 April 1986. Photograph courtesy of the author.

The Revenge of the Prince (Hamlet) by Shanghai Shaoxing Opera Troupe, 24 September 1994. Photograph courtesy of the author.

The Revenge of the Prince (Hamlet) Shanghai Shaoxing Opera Troupe, 24 September 1994. Photograph courtesy of the author.

uncertainty derives first from ordinary Chinese audiences. It may not be easy for the playgoers of traditional Chinese drama to appreciate a production in which the players wear Western costumes but act and sing in the pattern of traditional Chinese drama. Likewise the Shakespearean audiences may feel it is ridiculous to see Hamlet or Macbeth using stylized movements and symbolic gestures onstage.

Some Chinese Shakespearean scholars and critics tend to be highly conservative on this issue. They worry that a production might lose its Shakespearean fascination if adapted into traditional Chinese drama; moreover, such an adaptation would distort the true nature of Shakespeare because it is very difficult to retain all the distinctions of Shakespeare's plays when they are adapted into foreign dramas. Some young radical scholars also argue that since traditional Chinese drama is a declining and "backward" type of drama, it would degrade Shakespeare's plays rather than enhance and polish them. Other Shakespeare scholars take the middle road, believing that conditions are not ripe for such an amalgamation because many ordinary Chinese people still do not know Shakespeare's works. It would be better, they say, if we first presented Shakespeare's plays in conventional productions and then, when the plays are familiar, in productions using a traditional Chinese style. For the time being Shakespeare's plays should be staged mainly in the form of spoken drama.

The adaptation of Shakespeare's plays into traditional Chinese drama also creates embarrassment for the performers. Usually when a Shakespearean play is adapted into traditional Chinese drama, the acting is undertaken not by players using spoken drama but by traditional drama actors. Their training, which can take more than ten years and is given privately by senior actors, is based on repertoire and conventional stage techniques. Thus it is very difficult to ask these performers to act in a play having a totally different content and style from what they had been taught. The obstruction sometimes comes directly from the leaders of traditional drama companies: "Our conventional theater has already lost more and more audiences. If we use our drama to perform Shakespeare's plays, the production might be 'neither fish nor fowl,' which would make the situation of our conventional theater even worse and damage the intact theatrical tradition."[1]

Yet many broad-minded Chinese Shakespeare critics, directors, and performers advocate presenting Shakespeare's plays in the form of traditional Chinese drama. They hold that such an adaptation would be not only practicable but also successful. They also believe that it could be a very beneficial theatrical activity for both types of theater in contemporary China, as the celebrated director and Shakespeare expert Huang Zuo Lin has pointed out:

> We can find a lot of common characteristics in Shakespeare's drama and traditional Chinese drama. We can also see some strong points in each which the two types of drama may learn from each other. There is no doubt that we shall make more contributions to the theatrical circles of the world if we perform Shakespeare's plays by using some stage techniques of traditional Chinese drama when we introduce the works of this great dramatic poet to Chinese audiences. And in the meantime we can make our brilliant theatrical tradition and consummate stage techniques known to countries all over the world.[2]

Other critics as well emphasize Huang's last point:

> It is indeed a new theatrical exploration to adapt Shakespeare's plays into traditional Chinese drama . . . . As is known to all, Shakespearean drama is a bright pearl of Western culture and traditional Chinese drama is a treasure of Eastern art. If we mix them together, it will not only make Shakespeare known to more Chinese audiences but also cause traditional Chinese drama to exert a widespread influence upon the theatrical circles of the world. Thus it is really a matter of great importance.[3]

The critics who favor blending the dramas do not think it would be difficult for Chinese audiences to get used to the new mingled style in view of the rapidly changing artistic taste in contemporary China. As a matter of fact, they say, China is now in transition from a single to a multiple aesthetic taste. Soon a Shakespearean play in Chinese style will be compatible to the taste of Chinese audiences, considering that the presentation of Shakespeare's plays in a foreign manner has been fashionable on the modern Western stage. As a Chinese Shakespeare scholar has pointed out,

> When seeing an actor wearing an ancient Chinese costume perform Shakespeare's plays some people feel that it looks like a square peg in a round hole. Actually, to wear different costumes is merely a matter of form. If English actors, when performing Shakespeare's plays, can wear Cossack uniforms and modern German steel helmets, if American players can wear Indian clothes and the Canadian performers Eskimo clothes, why can't Chinese performers put on ancient Chinese costumes? There can be no doubt that so long as we preserve the Shakespearean spirit, the adaptation of Shakespeare's plays into traditional Chinese drama will further prove the universal appeal of Shakespeare and add extraordinary splendor to the Shakespearean theater of the world.[4]

In reviewing the history of modern Chinese theater, one can also argue that the adaptation of Shakespeare's plays into traditional Chinese drama is feasible because numerous excellent works of modern Chinese spoken drama have also been adapted into traditional Chinese drama. For instance, Guo Mo Ruo's historical plays *Hu Fu*, *Wu Ze Tian*, and *Cai Wen Ji* were adapted into Beijing, Kunju, and Shaoxing opera. Cao Yu's *The Thunder Rain*, *The Sunrise*, and *The Open Field* were adapted into Shaoxing, Pinju, and Hainan opera respectively. Yang Han Sheng's *Spring and Autumn in Heaven* was adapted into Beijing opera and his *Greenwood Hero* was adapted into Sichuan opera. Thus, if modern Chinese spoken drama can be adapted into traditional Chinese drama, why not Shakespeare's plays? Furthermore, modern Chinese theater has already shown the practicability of adapting Western stories into traditional Chinese drama. For example, there were two Beijing operas adapted by Xia Yue Ren, *Napoleon* (1910, Shanghai) and *Mrs. Warren's Profession* (1911, Shanghai). *Robin Hood* was adapted into Beijing opera by Zhang Chun Hua (1928, Beijing). Oscar Wilde's *Lady Windermere's Fan* was adapted into Shanghai opera (1924, Shanghai) and was well received by the audience. In addition, Shakespeare's plays are easier to adapt than other Western writers' works because, as Chinese critics have often said, many similarities exist between Shakespeare's plays and traditional Chinese drama as far as theatrical concepts are concerned.

As I pointed out in chapter 2, the poetic language used in Shakespeare's plays and traditional Chinese drama is not the ordinary language of daily life employed in other types of drama. In most cases the texts of Shakespeare's plays and traditional Chinese drama are recited by the actors, and sometimes sung by them, as in traditional Chinese drama. When Shakespeare's plays are adapted into traditional Chinese drama, therefore, the performers easily appreciate the lyrical style of Shakespeare and have no difficulty in using his poetic language.

The free employment of time and space on the stage is to be found in both Shakespeare's plays and in traditional Chinese drama. Both can have very long plot time spans and frequent changes of place. Both types of drama use an "open" structure in most cases and have plots that suggest that the story might be continued. All of these similarities make it easier for Chinese writers and directors to rearrange the structure of their sinicized Shakespeare productions.

More important perhaps is another theatrical concept that Shakespeare and traditional Chinese drama have in common. Traditional Chinese drama is based on supposition rather than on verisimilitude, which has been characteristic of Western theater since 1800. Shakespeare also uses the principle of supposition to transcend the limits of the stage. Neither Shakespearean nor traditional drama intends to create an illusion of reality but instead asks the audience to visualize a scene or an event that cannot be easily presented on the stage. This is most explicitly stated in several Shakespearean chorus speeches. In *Henry V* we read:

> . . . But pardon, gentles all,
> The flat unraised spirits that hath dar'd
> On this unworthy scaffold to bring forth
> So great an object. Can this cockpit hold
> The vasty fields of France? Or may we cram
> Within this wooden O the very casques
> That did affright the air at Agincourt?
> O, pardon! since a crooked figure may
> Attest in little place a million;
> And let us, ciphers to this great accompt,
> On your imaginary forces work.
> Suppose within the girdle of these walls
> Are now confin'd two mighty monarchies,
> Whose high, upreared, and abutting fronts
> The perilous narrow ocean parts asunder.
> Piece out our imperfections with your thoughts:
> Into a thousand parts divide one man,
> And make imaginary puissance;
> Think, when we talk of horses, that you see them
> Printing their proud hoofs i' th' receiving earth;
> For 'tis your thoughts that now must deck our kings,
> Carry them here and there, jumping o'er times,
> Turning th' accomplishment of many years
> Into an hour-glass: for the which supply,
> Admit me Chorus to this history.

(Prologue, 8–32)

Serving mainly as a way to appeal to the imagination of an audience, supposition also leads to greater freedom in handling stage space and time, as we read in the speech of Gower in *Pericles:*

> Thus time we waste, and long leagues make short;
> Sail seas in cockles, have and wish but for't,
> Making, to take our imagination,
> From bourn to bourn, region to region.
> By you being pardoned, we commit no crime
> To use one language in each several clime
> Where our scenes seem to live. I do beseech you,

To learn of me, who stand i' th' gaps to teach you
The stages of our story. . . .

. . . .

while our scene must play
His daughter's woe and heavy well-a-day
In her unholy service. Patience then,
And think you now are all in Metelin.

(4.4.1–9, 48–51)

In turning to traditional Chinese drama, we find that the concept of supposition runs through every aspect of its stagecraft. Similar to the function of Shakespeare's chorus, traditional drama's chorus (called *fu mo,* a supporting male role) sets the place or time of the story or describes the surroundings of the scene, always in the prologue. For example, in *The Tower of Lei Feng* the chorus first recites a poem depicting the beautiful scenery of West Lake of Hangzhou, which is the setting of the play. Then he discusses with an actor who remains backstage the title, author, and other related information about the play. Finally he gives the gist of the story in a longer poem. The acting skills of traditional Chinese drama also appeal highly to the imagination of the audience. For instance, when the characters need to travel a long way to another place, the actors simply walk around the stage twice with very beautiful stylized movements and say "Oh, here we are," and the audience then knows that the characters have arrived at their destination. In Shakespeare's plays the same technique is employed, as in *Romeo and Juliet* 1.4. To imitate the act of climbing over a wall, the actor just jumps over a table. The concept of supposition in traditional Chinese drama clearly creates an effect of alienation that is very similar to the distancing technique of Brecht. Or rather one could say that Brecht's method was influenced by the alienation effect of traditional Chinese drama, since he attended a performance by the famous Beijing opera actor Mei Lan Fang in Moscow in 1935 and wrote an article discussing the characteristics of traditional Chinese drama the next year.[5] In many aspects traditional Chinese drama indeed tries to avoid an illusion of reality and instead lets the audience know that this clearly is a performance. For instance, stage workers often change props in the presence of the audience. During the performance an assistant goes up on the stage to operate a special device, as for example one that makes "raging flames." The actors' makeup is unique and beautiful, yet it is too exaggerated to resemble real people.

The supposition concept of traditional Chinese drama can also be seen in the symbolic acting that is also often employed by Shakespeare. When Shakespeare presented vast scenes such as a war or a gathering of citizens, he did not cram great numbers of actors onstage. Instead, he employed symbolic methods: for instance, a general with a standard-bearer represents an army (*Antony and Cleopatra* 3.8–10), and several people talking with one another on the stage take the place of a gathering of many citizens (*Julius Caesar* 1.1). Symbolic acting has also been used to a great extent in traditional Chinese drama. For instance, a few groups of *longtao* (a general and some soldiers) can stand for thousands upon thousands of horses and soldiers; likewise the fight between them symbolizes a great war. If a scene is set at night, the actor will sometimes move as if groping in the dark, even though the stage is well lit. The use of torches and lanterns in Shakespeare's plays also achieves a similar effect (*Romeo and Juliet* 5.3.120–26). The makeup in traditional Chinese drama is also highly symbolic and relates to the type of character being portrayed. For example, red makeup stands for loyalty and bravery, as does that of Guan Gong, a valiant general in the plays adapted from the famous classical Chinese novel *The Romance of the Three Kingdoms*. Black usually symbolizes uprightness, as for example the makeup of Bao Gong, a wise and just judge in *The Dream of a Butterfly*. White makeup represents treacherousness, for example Qin Hui in *The Flag of Loyalty*.

The sets and props of both Shakespeare's plays and traditional Chinese drama tend to be simple and allusive, often signifying many objects and occasions. Both types of drama rarely if ever use scenery to change space and time, which is instead very conveniently accomplished through an actor's speech. Shakespeare normally used only a few tables and chairs or perhaps a bed as props. On a traditional Chinese stage, the most conventional props are one table and two chairs, sometimes fewer or more as required. In some of the plays, the table and chairs are covered with cloth relating to the story. If an emperor appears on the stage, the table and chairs will be covered with yellow cloth depicting an embroidered dragon. If a high-ranking official or a county magistrate is to appear onstage, the table and chair will be covered with red cloth, the symbol of power. There are almost twenty special ways to arrange these tables and chairs onstage in accordance with particular scenes and settings, as for example a private house, banquet, hotel, restaurant, official hall, law court, and so on. Two tables put together with a chair on top are used to depict a tall ship with several decks or a reviewing stand for a general or a hillside. In contrast to the simple sets and props of Shakespearean and traditional drama, the costumes of both are gorgeous and carefully made, intended to produce special visual and symbolic effects, as we see in the symbolic costuming at the coronation of several kings (*2 Henry IV* 5.5 and *Richard III* 4.2). In traditional Chinese drama the costumes not only help to create beautiful images on the stage but also provide an opportunity for the actors to show special performing skills. For example, swinging long sleeves is a very complicated technique that represents the emotion and disposition of the characters. A warrior in traditional Chinese plays always wears a helmet with long pheasant tail feathers that represent his power, grandeur, and high position. Playing with the feathers is also an important technique, showing how the character copes with different situations. All these skills, which take a long time to practice and use correctly, contribute crucially to the theatrical achievement of a performer. In sum it appears that both Shakespeare and traditional Chinese drama try to make the audience concentrate on the performers rather than on supporting stage elements.

One of the most obvious theatrical conventions that Shakespeare's plays and traditional Chinese drama have in common is the device of the prologue and epilogue. A prologue is frequently used in Shakespeare's plays, among them *Romeo and Juliet, 2 Henry IV, Henry V, Henry VIII*, and *Troilus and Cressida*. Here the prologue is usually presented by a chorus, but sometimes Shakespeare uses other interesting and symbolic methods to present it. For instance, in *2 Henry IV*, the chorus has become a personified Rumour. In *The Winter's Tale*, Time goes onstage to present the prologue to act 4. The function of the prologue in Shakespeare's plays is to introduce the setting of the play and the principal characters and to briefly give the gist of the story. In some of the plays, such as *The Winter's Tale* and *Pericles*, the chorus connects two acts between which a long period of time has elapsed and provides a psychological transition for the audience to accept the unrealistic development of the plot. Often the epilogue is also assigned to the chorus, as in *2 Henry IV, Henry V*, and *Henry VIII*, while in other cases it is spoken by a character in the play. For example, at the end of *The Tempest* Prospero recites a rhymed epilogue. In *Twelfth Night* the epilogue is a song delivered by the clown. In *2 Henry IV* the epilogue is spoken by a dancer. *As You Like It* ends with a speech by Rosalind. If Shakespeare's prologues serve as a guide to bring the audience into the plays, then his epilogues take the audience out of the performance. The epilogue provides an opportunity for the actors to address the audience directly and to invite their applause in response to the performance. The epilogue also acts as a final unit summing up the theme of the play and providing further information concerning the future of the chief characters, as in 2 Henry IV, or predicting forthcoming historical events, as in Henry V.

Similarly, traditional Chinese drama also uses prologues and epilogues frequently, but in a slightly different way. In some traditional drama, particularly in Yuan plays, the prologue—called a "wedge" (xiezi)—is formed by an additional short unit before the regular acts. This type of prologue is presented by several main characters of the play and provides important background information, outlining possible developments in the plot, as we see in The Romance of the Western Chamber, The Orphan of the House of Zhao, Autumn in the Han Palace, and A Slave to Money. In later plays, especially those of the Ming and Qing dynasties, the prologue is greatly simplified and looks similar to that of Shakespeare's plays. It is presented by a fu mo, who takes the role of the Shakespearean chorus. The form of this kind of prologue also is very simple. As discussed earlier in this chapter, the fu mo first recites a poem related to the relevant background information or the setting of the story. Then he talks about the play to be performed with an actor who remains backstage. Finally he recites a longer poem recounting the plot and a very short poem summarizing the theme and gist of the play. This pattern can be found in many famous Ming and Qing plays, such as The Fan of Peach Blossom, The Hall of Longevity, The Story of the Honest Subjects, and The Tower of Lei Feng. There is also a clear pattern for the epilogue of traditional Chinese drama, which, unlike that of Shakespeare's plays, is presented only by the characters of the play and not by the chorus (fu mo). The main purpose of the epilogue is to heighten the jubilant atmosphere caused by the play's happy ending. The epilogue in most cases, therefore, is formed by the poems and songs recited and sung by the hero and heroine, together with other characters at the wedding or banquet.

Monologues, soliloquies, and asides are used quite often in both Shakespeare's plays and traditional Chinese drama, through which the two types of drama try to establish direct communication with the audience. Shakespeare's plays are noted for their long and brilliant soliloquies, which serve as an effective way to reveal the character's innermost feelings, represent the complex disposition of the characters, and discuss profound philosophical ideas. The aside in Shakespeare's plays also frequently expresses the real thoughts and feelings of the characters and their response to the action of other characters. Compared with Shakespeare's plays, traditional Chinese drama uses more monologues and fewer soliloquies because in most cases the character talks to the audience directly rather than to himself. Normally the characters of traditional drama rarely use soliloquies in a Shakespearean sense because there are no complex natures and strong inner conflicts to present. Monologues, however, are sometimes used by Chinese actors to express their thoughts and emotions. In such cases they are written in poetry, recited, or sung by the actors and are shorter than those in Shakespeare's plays. Traditional drama has a lot of explanatory monologues that provide objective information about the character and openly acquaint the audience with his background and intentions.

Generally speaking, traditional Chinese drama attempts to establish a more direct contact with the audience than do Shakespeare's plays, which can be seen by the use of another device of straightforward exposition of the character called self-introduction or self-identification (*zi bao jia men*). When a character comes onstage, he generally announces his identity and states why he conducts himself as he does, giving further background facts about himself, as in the play-within-the-play in *A Midsummer Night's Dream* (5.1.216–52). For example, in *Looking over the Wall,* after entering, the hero introduces himself to the audience: "My name is Pei Shao Jun, son of the Minister of Works. I was able to speak well at the age of three, to read at five, to write well at seven, and compose an extempore poem at ten. And I have both talent and good looks, so the people of the capital call me 'handsome boy.' I'm seventeen years old now but still single. What I like to do is read poetry and books. I've never associated with women so far." Then he explains that he has come to Luoyang city to buy exotic flowers and rare plants for the emperor. In this way the audience becomes acquainted with the hero and can predict possible plot developments.

This brief discussion of the common stage techniques of Shakespeare's plays and traditional Chinese drama points out that advantages do exist for Chinese actors to perform Shakespeare's plays in the form of traditional Chinese drama. The Chinese adapters, directors, and players should have no difficulty in finding corresponding devices to represent particular Shakespearean stage techniques.

It is important to note, however, that traditional Chinese drama also possesses its own unique stage techniques. To be sure, the content and some dramatic concepts are out of fashion, yet its distinctive techniques still demonstrate extraordinary artistic charm. There is no doubt that they will contribute to the sinicization of Shakespeare's plays.

One of the most obvious performing skills of traditional Chinese drama is the employment of an extensive set of stylized movements. These gestures derive from the actions of daily life but have gradually become graceful dance movements through a long process of refinement and beautification. They are used to present many actions on the stage: opening and shutting doors, drinking, writing, walking, running, going upstairs and downstairs, and so on. On the Western stage it is difficult for an actor to imitate the action of riding a horse, and it would be awkward to bring a real horse on the stage. But traditional Chinese theater can easily cope with this problem. With a whip in hand, an actor can represent vividly the act of riding a horse with beautiful and smooth movements that please the eye and look true to life as well. When it is necessary to paddle a boat, the player will gracefully imitate rowing motions. Other performing patterns represent feelings and emotions such as sorrow, joy, crying, laughing, excitement, and hesitation by a set of stylized movements such as swinging hair and sleeves, spreading a cloak, and pacing up and down with dance movements. An excessive employment of these patterns may slow down the tempo of the play and bore the audience, but proper use of them adds seasoning to the performance. Thus when Shakespeare's plays are presented in the form of traditional Chinese drama, these movements are ideal for displaying various passions and inner conflict.

In recent years the Chinese martial art of Kung Fu has been well known to Westerners through movies. In traditional Chinese theater, acrobatic fighting that has evolved from Kung Fu is often used to present fighting scenes. It is a consummate skill characterized by a mixture of dance and acrobatics that enables the actors to handle the fights expertly and efficiently with perfect timing and body control. Using this skill to stage combat scenes in Shakespeare's plays would be extraordinarily effective. The addition of Chinese percussion instruments to the scene would also achieve a good effect, as would the orchestra of traditional Chinese theater. Chinese instruments are useful in presenting the music associated with combat, especially fanfares, flourishes, and the use of trumpets.

In addition, numerous other unique stage techniques can meet the special needs of presenting Shakespeare's plays. For instance, to show a god descending from heaven a performer comes onstage, gently waving a horsetail whisk, which creates the illusion of crossing a cloud. Other methods depict ghosts, thunder, and flames. The symbolic makeup of traditional Chinese theater can be used for certain Shakespearean characters such as Othello, Caliban, and clowns. It should be pointed out that particular types of Chinese drama often have their own special techniques, even though they share the stagecraft I have described above. According to incomplete statistics, more than three hundred types of traditional Chinese drama now exist in various parts of China, but only about twenty of them have nationwide influence. Some of these are the Beijing, Kunju, Shaoxing, Huangmei, Guangdong, Sichuan, and Henan operas. The main difference between them lies in their use of unique musical patterns and diverse local dialects.

This brief discussion shows that the adaptation of Shakespeare's plays into traditional Chinese drama is possible and practicable. Theatrical practice so far has proved that the endeavor has been indeed fruitful, particularly in the 1980s. During that time spoken drama was the most prevalent form of presenting Shakespeare's plays, but some Chinese performers adapted his plays into various types of traditional drama right from the beginning of Shakespearean theater in China. As I pointed out in the last chapter, the first Chinese Shakespeare production, which was presented as spoken drama, appeared on the stage in 1913. The next year, in Sichuan province, the Ya An Sichuan Opera Troupe played *Hamlet* in the form of Sichuan opera. The play was adapted by Wang Guo Ren with a Chinese-style title: *Murdering His Elder Brother and Marrying His Sister-in-Law*. Performed in some areas of Sichuan province, the play was well received by the audience. It is thought that other Shakespearean productions were presented as Guangdong and Shaanxi opera at that time, but no detailed references are available. Shaoxing opera is one of the major types of traditional Chinese drama and is very popular in Shanghai and in Zhejiang province. Since Shanghai has been an important cultural center in modern China and a place where many of Shakespeare's plays have been performed, it is understandable why many Shakespeare productions have been adapted into Shaoxing opera in this district. Early in the 1940s and the beginning of the 1950s, some performers of Shaoxing opera tried to present Shakespeare's plays in this type of traditional Chinese drama. In 1942 the celebrated Shaoxing opera performer Yuan Xue Fen, who created a new performing school of Shaoxing opera, presented a production of *Romeo and Juliet* in Shaoxing opera at Shanghai's Da Lai Theater. The title was changed to *Affection and Hatred*. Three years later another Shaoxing opera troupe, led by Fu Jin Xiang, performed a production of *King Lear* adapted into Shaoxing opera at Shanghai's Long Men Grand Theater, with a title of *The Filial Piety of the Daughter*. After the liberation, in 1952, a production of *Othello* was adapted and performed by the Shanghai Shaoxing Opera Troupe in Shanghai. Beijing opera, as the most representative type of traditional Chinese drama, was also used to present Shakespeare's plays before the establishment of the People's Republic of China. In 1948 a Beijing opera production of *Everlasting Love*, adapted from *Romeo and Ju-*

liet, was performed in Beijing under the well-known director Jiao Ju Yin.

With the new push to assimilate Western culture and present Shakespeare's plays in the 1980s, more and more of Shakespeare's plays have been adapted into various types of traditional Chinese drama. Shakespearean scholars, directors, and actors of traditional Chinese drama have explored this valuable theatrical field more earnestly than ever before. Numerous Shakespeare-Chinese productions have been very successful and evoked nationwide repercussions. For instance, in 1983 the Experimental Beijing Opera Troupe performed a production of *Othello,* recreated in a convincing Shakespearean-Chinese tradition. The play caused a sensation in the capital. Later in the same year, in Guangzhou city, a production of *The Merchant of Venice* was presented by the Experimental Guangdong Opera Troupe under the famous director Zhang Qi Hong and starring the Guangdong opera performer Hong Xian Nu. The play was well received by the audience, having a run of twenty-five performances. In 1985 Shanghai's Hong Kou Shaoxing Opera Troupe presented another production of *Everlasting Love* under the direction of Xie Hong Ling and Zhou Zhi Gang. The structure of the original play was adapted into nine scenes, each with a title describing the scene's content. This play was also successful, having a very long run of three years with more than two hundred performances.

In the Inaugural Chinese Shakespeare Festival, four of the plays being performed were adaptations into different types of traditional Chinese drama.[6] They were a production of *Macbeth* called *Bloody Hands,* adapted into Kunju opera by the Shanghai Kunju Troupe; a production of *Twelfth Night* adapted into Shaoxing opera, presented by Shanghai's Shaoxing Opera Troupe; a production of *The Winter's Tale,* also adapted into Shaoxing opera and presented by the Hangzhou Shaoxing Opera Troupe; and a production of *Much Ado About Nothing,* adapted into Huangmei opera, presented by the Anhui Huangmei Opera Troupe. All four productions were highly praised by both Shakespearean scholars and the artists of traditional Chinese drama for their success in combining the two types of drama. They were regarded as genuinely sinicized Shakespearean plays, mixing the fascination of Shakespeare and the charm of traditional Chinese theater. After the festival, in 1987, the play *Bloody Hands* in Kunju opera was invited to be performed at Edinburgh. The achievement of Chinese theatrical professionals in adapting Shakespearean plays into traditional Chinese drama for the Inaugural Chinese Shakespeare Festival inspired them to explore further this fruitful field. Consequently, in 1987 the Henan Opera Troupe of Zhou Kou prefecture,

Henan province, presented a Henan opera *Romeo and Juliet*. Their success evoked a strong repercussion in overseas Chinese communities as well. In January 1989 Shanghai's Hong Kou Shaoxing Opera Troupe was invited to visit Hong Kong to perform their version of *Romeo and Juliet* in the second Kui Qing Art Festival.

The Shakespeare productions adapted into traditional Chinese drama have shown a wide range of variation, each with its own distinction, although they are all intended to follow the common principle of maintaining the fundamental Shakespearean spirit while interpreting the plays from the perspective of Chinese culture and performing them in the manner of the Chinese theatrical tradition. It would be difficult to discuss all of them in detail. The following selected examples will have to suffice to demonstrate the wide variety of approaches to adaptation.

Chinese actors have used two major methods in adapting Shakespeare's plays into traditional Chinese drama, the "Chinese manner" and the "Western manner." In the Chinese manner the adaptor changes all the characters, places, times, and customs of Shakespeare's plays into Chinese style. The original texts are sinicized and the stories are reset in ancient China. The characters have Chinese names, wear Chinese costumes, and follow Chinese customs. This method obviously produces thoroughly sinicized Shakespearean productions. The Western manner tries to keep intact most of the original texts, plots, scenes, and lines of Shakespearean plays so that the outward appearance of such a production would still resemble a Western play. The characters still have their original names, wear Western costumes, and observe Western customs, yet they speak, sing, and act in the patterns of traditional Chinese theater.

Each method has its strong points. A production in the Chinese manner is easily accepted by an audience unfamiliar with Shakespeare. This approach, however, risks offending Shakespeare scholars and devotees because it would change the production completely and obscure the glamor of Shakespeare. The key point, as adapters and directors have realized, lies in keeping a balance between the Shakespearean spirit and the sinicized methods. The Western manner has the obvious advantage of being faithful to the spirit and original manner of Shakespeare's plays, thus avoiding the loss of Shakespeare's artistic charm. The main problem of this method is how to make the audience accept the unconcealed exotic flavor through the acting, singing, movements, and other performing patterns typical of traditional Chinese drama. Such a mixture might cause a feeling of disharmony at the outset, disconcerting the audience, which needs time to get used to a combined performing mode. There is no doubt, however, that both approaches can bring about successful productions through careful adaptation and representation.

BEIJING OPERA'S PRODUCTION OF OTHELLO

Beijing opera, noted for its beautiful music and rich stage techniques, has been the most popular and representative type of traditional Chinese drama in modern China. It possesses all the performing patterns and stagecraft mentioned above. Of all the Beijing opera/Shakespearean plays presented in modern China, the production of Othello by the Experimental Beijing Opera Troupe is the most successful example. The play premiered in Beijing on 23 May 1983 and then toured Shanghai and other cities with more than twenty performances. It was performed again in the Inaugural Chinese Shakespeare Festival in Beijing. As the first Shakespeare production presented in the form of traditional Chinese drama after Deng Xiao Ping's "open-door policy," it caused a sensation throughout the country and aroused great interest among Western experts working in the capital. The troupe invited the famous dramatic critic Weng O Hong to be its literary adviser. The play was textually adapted by Shao Hong Cao, Zheng Bi Xian, and Lu Xing Cai, under the direction of Zheng Bi Xian, with Zhang Yun Xi as an invited drama coach and Huang Bo Shou as dancing instructor. The play had a strong cast that included several famous names. Ma Yong An played the part of Othello and Li Ya Lan took the role of Desdemona. The other roles were Lian Hong Xian as Iago; Wang Yong Quan as Cassio; Cheng Duan as Emilia; Xuan De Hua as Brabantio, Lu Dong Lai as the Duke.

Since this production of Othello was to be in the Western manner, the major task of the adapters, director, and performers was to retain the essence of the play while adding the style of Beijing opera. The major plots and scene divisions were kept, along with the characters' original names. Structurally, traditional Chinese drama tends to center each scene on a subtheme, presented by a title. The adapters followed this convention and rearranged the play into seven scenes plus a prologue. The prologue was called "Under the Triumph Arch," and the titles of the other scenes were "The Tender Affection," "Follow You Forever," "The Bright Pearl of the Island," "Honey-mouthed and Dagger-hearted," "The Blood-red Setting Sun," "Humiliation and Injustice," and "The Eternal Regret." These titles were designed to give clues about the development and ending of the plot. A common difficulty that all Chinese adapters encounter is how to adapt the lines of Shakespeare's plays into the textual pattern of traditional Chinese drama, even though most Chinese translations of Shakespearean plays have been carefully written in the Chinese literary mode. To solve this problem, Shao Hong Cao, the chief adaptor, used a bold method to cut down the text. Shao tried to keep most of the original lines of the spoken parts or just slightly rewrote them, for the translation had already been written in smooth Chinese prose and was basically suitable for the dialogue and monologue patterns of Beijing opera. For the singing parts, however, Shao rewrote most of the lines to suit the special verse forms of the songs, particularly the long soliloquies of the characters. In explaining his method Shao said, "Some Shakespeare scholars blame me for my bold cutting. They believe that Shakespeare's work is the Bible of the artistic world and that any small change in the texts would be wrong. But I don't agree with them. I would argue that adaptation does not mean that we must adhere to every word and sentence of the text. The crux of the adaptation lies in conveying the spirit and flavor of Shakespeare's plays, but not in retaining all the particular lines and scenes."[7] As it turned out, the reworked script of *Othello* was considered by the audience and theatrical circles to have been the best way to represent the basic features and poetic flavor of the original play while using the textual patterns and music of Beijing opera. To help the audience understand the libretto more easily, the words of the songs were shown on the front wall of the theater when the play was performed. While the playgoers were familiar with the librettos of the entire Beijing opera repertoire, they might have had difficulty in understanding the musical content of a new play.

The ingenuity of the director of the Beijing opera's presentation of *Othello* would have been unbelievably taxed if it had been necessary to present the characters in the same role types of their usual productions. Like other types of traditional Chinese drama, Beijing opera has four major character types: *sheng, dan, jing,* and *chou,* each with a different code of behavior based on sex, age, personality, and social status and each exhibiting the strong influence of Chinese social and cultural backgrounds. It would be difficult to apply these character types to Shakespearean characters for two obvious reasons: first, Shakespearean characters come to Chinese audiences with manners quite different from those of the ancient Chinese. Second, as I have mentioned in previous chapters, Shakespeare's characters are more complex and various than those of traditional Chinese drama, and it is not easy to group them into simple moral and social types. It is evident that a mechanical application of the character types of

Beijing opera to the characters of Shakespeare's plays will lead to an incompatibility. Nonetheless, the director and performers of the Experimental Beijing Opera Troupe solved this problem in their production. Othello was treated as a type of *jing* (also called *hua lian*, meaning "a colored face" because the type wore tinted makeup) and acted by an excellent *jing* actor, Ma Yong An. As luck would have it, the characteristics of the *jing* type almost exactly suit Othello's case. Generally, a *jing* character is a male with a bold, heroic, and forthright personality having a high social position such as a general, a minister, or a judge. All the stylized techniques of *jing* would work together to represent his personality and social status. A *jing* character often has makeup in a dark or red color, which is just right for Othello's racial distinction.

Desdemona was treated as a type of *dan*, which is used to present female roles in Beijing opera. There are more than ten subtypes of *dan* according to personality and social status. In this play Desdemona was acted as a *zheng dan* (the leading female role in a play and possessing many virtues, a graceful manner, and physical beauty). Here too there were no problems in treating Desdemona as a *zheng dan* type.

A more flexible employment of the character types of Beijing opera can be found in the treatment of Iago. As a sinister and treacherous character, it was supposed before the performance that Iago would be acted as a *jia zi hua jian* (a subtype of *jing*) or a *chou* type (a clown or a stupid or nasty role) because conventionally these two types are used to present corrupt ministers at court or vicious officials in local government. But when the play was performed in public, to its surprise the audience found that Iago was being acted by a *lao sheng* actor (a subtype of *sheng*). For those who were familiar with Shakespearean characterization, this arrangement was quite ingenious. The *lao sheng* type normally represents a middle-aged or older character with morally positive qualities, as a faithful official. Obviously the director felt that if she presented Iago as a *jia zi hua jian* or a *chou*, it would bring about a morally superficial and one-sided character because, due to the special makeup of the two types, the audience would recognize Iago as simply a villain the minute he appeared on the stage, contradicting Shakespeare's interpretation. The advantage of presenting Iago as a *lao sheng* was that at the outset the audience would regard him as an honest and sincere person, judging by his makeup and appearance, but gradually come to see the other side of this character, his vicious and nasty mind, through his speech and action. Although this treatment completely violated the conventional principles of character types, it suits the taste of modern Chinese audiences and conforms to the characterization of Shakespeare. It can be seen as an innovation in the theatrical practices of Beijing opera and is a typical example of the influence of Shakespeare upon traditional Chinese drama. A more conventional character treatment occurred with the sophisticated comedy revolving around the suitor Roderigo, for the director treated him as a comic character even though he ended up being murdered. Roderigo was acted by a player of the *chou* type, a clown or a bumbling, laughable character.

The performers of *Othello* successfully employed conventionally stylized movements to represent the dispositions of the characters, particularly Ma Yong An, who played the part of Othello. Wearing a black velvet cloak and carrying a bright sword, he vividly showed the audience a powerful image of a heroic warrior. He also represented effectively Othello's emotions and inner conflict with a set of stylized movements, such as laughing in a special pattern of *hua lian,* playing with his cloak, and moving his head and body rapidly in time with the rhythm of the drum and gong. Yet Ma Yong An did not limit himself to the performing patterns of Beijing opera. For example, to display the physical characteristics of Othello as a black man, Ma sometimes looked sideways or showed the whites of his eyes, which was completely against the rules of Beijing opera, particularly when the role was a positive character.[8] The play made some innovations in Ma's music as well. For instance, as a role of the *jing* type, Othello should not sing the melody of *nan bang zi,* which was designed for other types. But to express his feeling of immeasurable joy after winning the affection of Desdemona, Ma sang a duet with Desdemona to the tune of *nan bang zi,* which heightened the moment's happy atmosphere. The acting of Jiang Hong Xang, who played the role of Iago, also broke through the character type rule. As a *lao sheng* type, he was expected to act with a slightly bent shoulder. Since this would conflict with Iago's manner, Jiang abandoned the conventional rule and used a natural posture, which clearly produced an exotic style.

As in other Beijing operas, *Othello* did not use a complex set. A cyclorama simply was erected at the back of the stage and was lighted with blue and occasionally red spotlights. It can be seen as a neutral setting that symbolically represents, for example, the sea, sky, and sun.

In sum, the achievement of *Othello* has proved that a Shakespeare production in traditional Chinese theater with a "Western manner" can be appreciated by Chinese audiences. Although at the outset the audience may be surprised by its novelty, they soon become accustomed to it. The achievement has also convincingly proved that the employment of conventional performing techniques in presenting Shakespearean plays can produce an unexpectedly wonderful effect that combines the artistic qualities of both Shakespeare's plays and traditional Chinese drama. After the experience of the Beijing opera *Othello*, many Chinese adapters, directors, and performers realized that a more flexible use of the performing patterns of traditional Chinese drama would be the critical factor in achieving the desired results.

SHAOXING OPERA'S PRODUCTION OF *TWELFTH NIGHT*

Another remarkable Shakespeare production produced as traditional Chinese drama in the Western manner was the Shanghai Shaoxing opera's version of *Twelfth Night*, presented during the Inaugural Chinese Shakespeare Festival in April 1986. The play was directed by the famous director Hu Wei Min of the Shanghai Youth Spoken Drama Troupe, who had previously directed productions of *Romeo and Juliet* and *Antony and Cleopatra*, and was performed by a young and strong cast. Of all the plays performed at the festival it received the most critical attention from theatrical and academic circles. The company used a unique way to adapt this Shakespearean comedy. Similar to Beijing opera's *Othello*, *Twelfth Night* retained most of the plot details and cultural background of the original play. The characters wore Western costumes and kept their original names. The decision to use the Western manner was made by the director after careful consideration. He held that both the Western and the Chinese styles could be used to present Shakespearean plays and that the choice should be made according to each particular play. In this case he chose the Western version because he believed that it would better present the theme of *Twelfth Night*. Although *Twelfth Night* seems to be simply a love comedy like that of traditional Chinese drama, it in fact displays a rich vein of humanism and competitive individualism—exactly, as I discussed in earlier chapters, what traditional Chinese drama lacked. Thus Hu Wei Min felt that for his *Twelfth Night*, a discrepancy would arise if the players wore traditional Chinese costumes while acting in the style of Western humanism during the Renaissance.[9] The general principle underlying the adaptation of *Twelfth Night* was "Chinese-Shaoxing opera-Shakespeare," which meant that the production was intended to create a Shakespearean play with a Chinese style and Shaoxing opera flavor. It would make the Chinese audience see it as both a traditional

Chinese play and a Shaoxing opera. It would also make both Western and Chinese audiences admit that it was a Shakespearean play as well. The adaptor and director of the play tried to find a basic point on which all the work would be centered, finally setting up a trinity of Shakespearean, Shaoxing opera, and poetic flavors.

The Shakespearean quality, they believed, was to be found not only in the outwardly exotic aura of Shakespeare's plays. Rather it lay mainly in the ideological and emotional spirit of Shakespeare, as for example the celebration of individuality, the affirmation of the freedom to seek love and happiness, and the presence of a strong romantic vein. The flavor of Shaoxing opera obviously meant the artistic distinction of this type from traditional Chinese drama. In the big family of traditional Chinese drama, Shaoxing opera was an up-and-coming youngster. It appeared in an embryonic form in 1906 in the countryside of Shaoxing prefecture in Zhejiang province and flourished in 1930s in eastern China around Shanghai and Zhejiang. After the establishment of the People's Republic of China, the theatrical activity of Shaoxing opera developed rapidly and enjoyed a large audience all over the country. More than twenty provinces, including Taiwan, have set up their own professional Shaoxing opera troupes. In Zhejiang province alone there are about seventy professional Shaoxing opera troupes. The rapid popularity of Shaoxing opera was due to its unique performing style, although it shared some of its stagecraft with other types of traditional Chinese drama. Shaoxing opera is noted for its graceful acting, refined singing, and elegant dancing; the performance pleases the audience with its extraordinary lyrical atmosphere. The stage design of Shaoxing opera often appears brightly colored and soft. The charm of this opera type derives mainly from its beautiful and sweet music. In comparison, the music of Beijing opera is loud, sonorous, and a little bit noisy. During the development of Shaoxing opera several schools have evolved, each differentiated by various styles of singing. Usually all the roles in Shaoxing opera are acted by women, which helps to shape its gentle and lyrical style. Since the 1950s male players have also been used occasionally for performances. The exquisite and graceful style of Shaoxing opera is especially suited for the performance of romantic love stories. This was one of the main reasons why the troupe selected *Twelfth Night* for the festival: as the director, Hu Wei Min, said, it would be an embarrassing task to adapt the solemn and stirring *King Lear* or the serious and tragic *Coriolanus* to Shaoxing opera's style.[10] Thus the graceful and sweet qualities of Shaoxing opera were to be mingled with Shakespearean traits in the production. The third element to which the director paid special attention was the poetic nature of the play, which the production was expected to represent fully. As I pointed out in chapter 2, both Shakespeare's plays and traditional Chinese drama are poetic drama, so the director intended to represent this element through the stagecraft of Shaoxing opera, including performing skills, music, and stage design. The achievement of the Shaoxing opera's version of *Twelfth Night* derived mainly from its expert mixture of the above three qualities.

The adaptation of the text of *Twelfth Night* was undertaken by Zhou Shui He and director Hu Wei Min. Since the play aimed to achieve a Western effect, it evaded the thorny problem of cultural discrepancies and accordingly made the script closer to the original text of the comedy. As patrons saw in the festival, the two main plots of the play—the elegant love story of the young aristocratic men and women and the mischievous trick of the lowlife character Sir Toby—were retained. The five major love stories—Olivia and Orsino, Olivia and Viola, Orsino and Viola, Malvolio and Olivia, and Sir Andrew and Olivia—were also kept. To help the audience, especially lovers of Shaoxing opera, easily understand the development of the characters' passions, the adaptor and director showed originality by adding scenes to the original text. Shakespeare does not tell us clearly why Viola suddenly decides to go to the Duke's palace, disguise herself as a servant, and try to marry him. Since she has never met the Duke, it looks as if Viola has no sufficient reason to show such an interest in him. Errors in logic are not unknown in Shakespeare's plays, although in most cases they do not run counter to the logic of art. Yet the Chinese audience, particularly those who know little about Shakespeare, could have misunderstood the action of Viola and regarded her as an ambitious and snobbish woman. The adaptor, therefore, created an extra scene in which Viola meets Orsino and falls in love at first sight. After she learns what has happened between Orsino and Olivia from the captain, she decides to serve the Duke by disguising herself as a servant. This extra scene, like a musical prelude, was heightened by beautiful music performed by both Chinese and Western instruments and warm-colored lighting, paving the way for the logical development of Viola's passion in the play. Another additional scene also provided an interesting treatment. In it Olivia asks the clown to imitate her voice and sing a love song under the Duke's window. Her real intention is to show her affection for Viola. Dramatically, the Duke and Viola have very different reactions to the clown's singing. The Duke is infatuated and flattered, for he thinks that Olivia still yearns for love, while Viola feels very frustrated because she knows very well that Olivia has mistaken her for a man and has fallen deeply in love with her. Obviously the adaptor and director intended to enhance the emotional line of the play by creating more opportunities to give full play to the lyrical flavor of Shaoxing opera through these added scenes.

Like the adaptor of Beijing opera's *Othello*, the adaptor of *Twelfth Night* was also faced with the hard task of fitting the original lines into the textual pattern of Shaoxing opera, and in most cases he had to simplify the long monologues and soliloquies. He followed the principle of representing the main ideas of particular passages while putting them into the relevant verse form of Shaoxing opera. For example, in *Twelfth Night* Malvolio reads a prose passage from the letter he has found in the garden and that he believes is a love letter from his lady:

"If this fall into thy hand, revolve. In my stars I am above thee, but be not afraid of greatness. Some are born great, some achieve greatness, and some have greatness thrust upon 'em. Thy Fates open their hands. . . . Go to, thou art made if thou desir'st to be so; if not, let me see thee a steward still, the fellow of servants, and not worthy to touch Fortune's fingers. Farewell. She that would alter service with thee, the Fortunate-Unhappy."

(2.5.143–47, 155–59)

To adapt this passage into the libretto form of Shaoxing opera, the adaptor simplified and rewrote it as rhymed verse.[11] It can be roughly translated as follows:

> Humble as you are and great I am,
> But be not afraid of greatness.
> Some are born great,
> Some achieve greatness,
> Some have greatness thrust upon them,
> Don't decline your Fortune,
> Cast thy humble slough,
> Be confident to take your new position.
> Be assertive with a kinsman,
> And surly with servants.
> Let thy tongue relish arguments of state,
> And be reserved and arrogant.
> Wear your fine yellow stockings,
> And fasten crosswise your garters.
> If you desire to be great,
> Do go and touch Fortune's fingers.

A common problem that Chinese directors encounter when they adapt Shakespearean plays into certain types of traditional Chinese drama is the lack of sophistication of the performers, who are often only semieducated. Their skills might be superb, but their general cultural and artistic accomplishments are comparatively weak because of their narrow professional training. When Hu Wei Min directed Shaoxing opera's *Twelfth Night* he recognized that this was a serious barrier for the play's successful presentation. Most of the young cast from the Shaoxing Opera Troupe had finished elementary or middle school and only a few had read any Shakespearean plays, although many knew the name of the English playwright. Consequently Hu began a program to enhance the cultural background of the players and acquaint them with Shakespeare. For instance, all the performers were asked to read Shakespeare's plays, Shakespearean criticism, and Shakespeare's biography, and then to talk about what they had gained from the reading at seminars. Celebrated Shakespeare scholars were invited to give lectures about Shakespearean art and theater and make reference to material from *Twelfth Night*. A special "Shakespeare Night" party was held, attended by Shakespearean critics and translators, postgraduate students of English literature, and performers with experience in presenting Shakespeare's plays from other spoken drama troupes. At the party Shakespearean sonnets and soliloquies from his plays were recited in both English and Chinese. Scenes from *Romeo and Juliet* and *Antony and Cleopatra* were performed under the direction of Hu. The singing of Elizabethan folk songs and the performance of a rehearsed fragment from the Shaoxing's *Twelfth Night* heightened the lively atmosphere of the party. Hu also had the cast watch videos of Shakespearean productions, see photographs of Shakespeare's theater, and view films adapted from Shakespeare's plays. To better imitate the manners of the characters, the performers learned classical Western dance and court etiquette. Besides giving the actors more knowledge of Shakespeare's theater and dispelling their sense of mystery about the English playwright, these measures provided the confidence they needed to perform their roles.

The performance of *Twelfth Night* demonstrably mingled the stage techniques of traditional Chinese theater with those of Western theater because of the employment of the Western manner in the play. Compared with Beijing opera's *Othello*, more Western methods were mixed with Shaoxing's traditional opera performing patterns in this production. For example, sword fighting, which took place in two scenes, displayed a wonderful combination of orthodox French fencing and the acrobatic fighting skill of traditional Chinese theater. The fights between Sir Toby and Antonio, Antonio and the officer, and Toby and Sebastian revealed a Zorro-type swordplay and the movements of Xuanzi, Danti, Bengzi, Lunbei, Aizibu, Zuibu and other fighting patterns of traditional Chinese theater. The two styles were merged so smoothly that a layperson was unable to distinguish one from the other. It was a rare opportunity for both Chinese and Western audiences to see realistic fighting.

The movements of social etiquette were also performed in a combined mode. When the characters saluted, played with their cloaks, and twirled their hats, the audience felt that the actors were using a Western style. On careful examination, however, one could notice that they were tinged with the stylized movements of *sheng* or *dan* character-types of traditional Chinese theater such as *yunshou* and *yaozi*, which made the posture of the characters look more relaxed and beautiful.

As in the performance of Beijing opera's *Othello*, the Shaoxing opera's version of *Twelfth Night* used the performing patterns of different character-types flexibly and creatively. A typical example could be found in the performance of the well-known actor Shi Ji Hua, who played the part of Malvolio. To represent the bearing and different expressions of Malvolio in several situations, Shi employed the multiple performing patterns of various types of traditional Chinese theater such as *lao sheng, hua lian (jing), xiao sheng,* and *chou.* When Malvolio assumed great airs before other servants, Shi used the movements of *lao sheng* and *hua lian* (the same type used by Othello in Beijing opera's *Othello*). When the character was reading the love letter from "Olivia" in high spirits, the actor employed the performing pattern of *xiao sheng* to represent his manner of getting dizzy with success. The stylized movements of *chou* were used by Shi when Malvolio affectedly paid court to Olivia.

The players also adopted some Western dancing movements. For instance, in the scene of the garden trick, Malvolio came onto the stage with a ballet step. While imagining that he had become Count Malvolio and when showing his superiority to the servants and Sir Toby he moved with a waltz step as well as with the stylized movements of *wu sheng.* When he went offstage he used the steps of an English folk dance. All of these movements were mixed so smoothly that they helped to make the character of Malvolio more vivid while heightening the humorous atmosphere of the play.

One of the great distinctions of the Shaoxing's *Twelfth Night* was an innovative use of music. Traditionally there are several schools in Shaoxing opera, each differentiated by the style of its music and named after its originator; examples are the Yuan School (*yuan xue fen*), the Lu School (*lu ru ying*), the Fan School (*fan rui juan*), and the Xu School (*xu yu lan*). Normally a Shaoxing opera player follows only one school, yet the director felt that a mechanical application of the musical patterns of a certain school might be inadequate for the presentation of Shakespeare's complicated characters. The rules of the different schools of singing were broken, therefore, so that richer and multiple musical styles could be composed for particular characters. The actress who played the part of Viola usually followed the Lu School but her songs were mingled with the music of other schools to suit her disguised identity as a young man. Some Western musical elements were also used to express her emotions in particular situations. Another good example was the singing of Malvolio. Basically following the Fan School, Shi Ji Hua incorporated the singing pattern of the Xu School and even the melodies from Beijing, Sichuan, and Hebei Banzi operas. To represent the bragging laugh of Malvolio, Shi combined the method of sound production in Western singing with his falsetto, which produced a wonderful effect.

KUNJU OPERA'S PRODUCTION OF MACBETH

Of all the sinicized Shakespearean productions using the Chinese manner, the Kunju Opera Troupe's *Macbeth* (*Bloody Hands*) was one of the most successful. It premiered in Shanghai during the Inaugural Chinese Shakespeare Festival in 1986, arousing great interest among critics, artists of traditional Chinese drama, and the general audience. It was brought to London and Edinburgh in the autumn of 1987 and caused a sensation among English audiences. This much-abbreviated Kunju *Macbeth* was adapted by Zheng Shi Feng and presented by the Shanghai Kunju Opera Troupe under the direction of Li Jia Yao, Shen Bin, and Zhang Min Lai. The famous theatrical artist Huang Zuo Lin, who once studied Shakespeare in Cambridge for a master's degree in the 1930s, was invited as a special artistic instructor. The part of Macbeth (with the Chinese name of Ma Pei in the play) was given to Ji Zhen Hua; Lady Macbeth (Tie Shi) was acted by Zhang Jin Xian; King Duncan (King Zheng in the play) was played by Shen Xiao Ming, and Banquo (Du Ge) by Fang Yang.

Of the various types of traditional Chinese drama, Kunju opera is assumed to be one of the oldest and is regarded as the forerunner of major types of traditional Chinese drama such as the Beijing and Shaoxing operas. Kunju began to flourish in the sixteenth century in the area now called Jiangsu province and then spread rapidly to a large part of the country, soon becoming the chief type of traditional Chinese drama. It gradually declined at the end of the Qing dynasty, losing its dominant position. In modern China theatrical circles attached great importance to Kunju, again because of the unique stage techniques found in old-style opera. Kunju is seen by many Chinese as the culmination of Chinese theater tradition, but close to Shakespeare, like the Beijing and Shaoxing operas, in that it maintains continuity of action and abstains from lavish scenery and decoration. The fascination of Kunju opera stems mainly from its rich performing skills and beautiful music. The rules for the stylized movements of the different character types and the form of the libretto in Kunju opera are more strict than those of Beijing and Shaoxing operas. Moreover, the language of Kunju opera is often refined and elegant.

As a consummate type of traditional Chinese drama, Kunju opera was thought to be an ideal form for presenting Shakespeare's plays. Unlike the adapters and directors of the Beijing opera's *Othello* and Shaoxing opera's *Twelfth Night,* those producing the Kunju opera *Macbeth* intended to produce an out-and-out sinicized Shakespeare production. Their work began by changing the title of the play to *Bloody Hands,* which signified the theme of the play and was in a Chinese style, for the Chinese usually prefer titles to indicate a theme rather than use a name. The main plot was retained but was reset in ancient China with sinicized names for the characters. Macbeth became General Ma Pei, who served under King Zheng. Lady Macbeth now was Lady Tie Shi, who helped her husband assassinate King Zheng when he stayed at the couple's house. The plot was nearly identical to the original text, yet the Chinese audience would be more likely to accept it as a genuine Chinese historical play because there were numerous incidents similar to the assassination of members of a royal family in Chinese history. For those who knew Shakespeare the play would still be received as the Shakespearean Scottish tragedy but with an outward Chinese style. The adaptor and directors, therefore, were not reluctant to acknowledge that they had caught the spirit of this great tragedy while making it accessible to Chinese Kunju lovers. Since the story had become Chinese, the actors all wore the costumes of ancient China and observed the etiquette of the Chinese royal court. According to the convention of Chinese theater, the five acts of the original play were rearranged into nine scenes, like Beijing opera's *Othello,* and each scene was given a title. The titles read as follows: "Promotion to a Higher Rank," "Conspiracy," "Shift the Accusation onto Others," "The Assassination of Du Ge" (Banquo), "The Disturbed Banquet," "The Isolated Dictator," "Consulting the Witches," "The Madness of Lady Tie Shi" (Lady Macbeth), and "Blood Must Atone for Blood." A royal doctor was invented to function as a chorus to connect these scenes. The lines of the original play were adapted into the singing and speech patterns of Kunju opera, which emphasize exquisite diction and gave the play a strong Chinese flavor. On the whole the play can be seen as a successful adaption in the Chinese manner. Some Chinese Shakespeare scholars expressed their regret over the omission of the Porter's monologue, which they believed was indispensable to the tragedy. This viewpoint was obviously influenced by Thomas De Quincey, who had investigated the profound philosophical meaning behind the scene. Yet it would have been a knotty problem for the adaptor to tackle for at least two reasons. First, he would have had to completely rewrite the monologue for his Chinese counterpart. Second, much of the Porter's dialogue with Macduff would have had to have been cut because of its explicit sexual content. While references to sexual matters are not avoided in traditional Chinese drama and are used to "spice up" plays, direct and explicit descriptions of sex on the stage or in the movies had been taboo in China since the government began to "clean up" public entertainment in the 1950s. It was evident that the producers did not want to stir up trouble even though they well knew that in recent years the attitude of the Chinese towards sex had become more flexible and even that contemporary literary works, especially fiction, increasingly contained pornographic elements.

Differing from *Othello* and *Twelfth Night*, in which Western performing skills were also used to produce a Western style, *Macbeth* had to rely on the conventional stage techniques of Chinese theater since its goal was to be a completely sinicized Shakespeare production. During the performance the audience indeed got a panoramic view of all the performing skills used in traditional Chinese theater while being asked to appreciate the spirit and humanistic ideals of Shakespeare. Considering that Macbeth was not simply an ambitious and corrupt general like those of traditional Chinese dramas, Ji Zhen Hua used many typical Kunju performing patterns to represent the two sides of Macbeth's character. All of his stylized movements and gestures helped to delineate the inner conflict of the protagonist. For example, when Macbeth was anxious and horrified at how events were turning out, the beads and cotton balls on his helmet quivered continuously, a special skill that shows the inner conflict of a character. Zhang Jin Xian also did her best to represent the personality of Lady Tie Shi by using a variety of performing skills of a *dan* type of Kunju opera. This was particularly obvious in the scene entitled "The Madness of Lady Tie Shi," in which the actress broke through the strict rules of the character types of Kunju opera and ingeniously incorporated the performing patterns of *gui men dan, xua dan,* and *po la dan*, vividly portraying the physical beauty yet inner cruelty and madness of the character. Representing the three witches, important to the revelation of Macbeth's ambition, was difficult for the performers because no comparable character type exists in Kunju opera. In the play, therefore, the director had to use three men disguised as women who acted as a mixed type of *xiao gui* (elf), *cai dan* (female clown), and walking *ai zi bu* (dwarf-gait). This treatment effectively created a mysterious and supernatural atmosphere.

To intensify the play's horrific atmosphere and the supernatural element, a scene was added in which the ghosts of King Zheng (King Duncan), Du Ge (Banquo), Lady Mei (Lady Macduff), and a green parrot (Lady Macbeth's pet but killed by her for its divulgence of their plot) went up on the stage one by one to haunt Lady Tie Shi. To show their anger the ghosts spat streams of fire from time to time, a unique skill in traditional Chinese theater used to create a ghostly atmosphere. There are two methods of producing the effect of fire-breathing. In one way the actor keeps a special paper bag containing pine-tree rosin powder in his mouth. When he blows on a torch the powder will be blown out and become ignited. In the other method the performer keeps a small container with burning paper in his mouth. The container has a few small holes in it, and when the performer exhales, the sparks are blown out, looking like a stream of fire. This unique skill has evolved from the acrobatics used in the "Variety Plays" of the Han dynasty, a dramatic genre regarded as the embryonic form of traditional Chinese drama.

Other conventional performing skills were also employed in the play to represent the inner conflicts of the characters, such as swinging the hair, playing with artificial whiskers and beads, changing face (a special skill that changes the color of an actor's complexion), and so on. Since *Macbeth* is the "darkest" of Shakespeare's tragedies, most scenes take place in gloomy places or at night, but Kunju opera is usually presented under bright spotlights. After much consideration the director decided to retain the traditional bright-light performance so as to keep the flavor of Kunju. However, the technique of light-shifting was used at times to heighten the tense atmosphere of the play.

As in *Othello* and *Twelfth Night*, many of the monologues and soliloquies in *Macbeth* were sung, rather than recited by the performers, and were accompanied by a Kunju orchestra. To reinforce the tragic mood of the play, the composer relaxed the strict limitations of Kunju music. The slow rhythms of both Kunju and Beijing opera were especially suitable in representing the fluctuation of the characters' emotions. Western instruments such as electronic piano and bass, the percussion instruments of Sichuan opera, and the drum and gong also played an important part in representing the psychological rhythm of the characters.

It would have been interesting to know the response of English critics to this sinicized Shakespeare production because such a response often serves as an important way to know whether a Shakespeare play performed in a foreign manner has succeeded. In August 1987 the Kunju operas *Macbeth* and *The Peony Pavilion* were invited to perform in Edinburgh. It was really an extraordinary event, not only because it was the first time that a Chinese drama company had presented *Macbeth* in the country of its setting, but also because the plays of the two great dramatists and contemporaries, Shakespeare and Tan Xian Zu, were on display at the same festival. Although the company worried whether the exotic style of *Macbeth* would be comprehensible to British audiences, the play received much acclaim from the audience and was highly praised by British critics:

> Several scholarly, imaginative and highly experienced men of the theater collaborated in making the Kunju *Macbeth,* performed by the Shanghai Kunju Company, a triumphant success; fascinating, exciting, moving, and amazingly true to Shakespeare, the exotic style of the production notwithstanding.[12]

In the end the unique techniques of Kunju opera were not difficult for the audience to understand. Moreover, the audience also recognized similarities between Shakespeare and Chinese theater:

> The words are recited or sung in a stylised but expressive way, accompanied by the richly varied melodies played by the Kunju orchestra, and European spectators have no trouble in understanding the Chinese conventions. . . . Elizabethan actors made great use of stylised gestures, and it is likely that Shakespeare would have found much that was comprehensible in this production. Indeed, his play comes to life with extraordinary vitality, done in the Kunju manner with gorgeous costumes on a nearly-bare stage.[13]

The response of the audience led me to believe that they were satisfied with the artistic fusion of Kunju style and Shakespeare's spirit in the production. Another British critic agrees:

> The Kunju *Macbeth* was certainly closely related to Shakespeare's *Macbeth;* but there were as many changes as retentions, making "Adapted from Shakespeare's *Macbeth* by Zheng Shi Feng" an appropriate credit. Here were three witches whose acrobatic skill made them astonishing

creatures indeed. Here was a striking onstage murder of Duncan. Here was a spectacular sleepwalking dance drama of Lady Macbeth confronted by the ghosts of Duncan, Banquo, and Lady Macduff. . . . Here was language with image and metaphor adapted to the sensibilities of another culture and with rhythms and sonorities derived from Kunju tradition. Here were bold gestural depictions of trust, duplicity, violence, ambition, accusation, fear, grief, confusion, triumph. Here was a visual and sonoral realization of *Macbeth* performed in Scotland by a company steeped in Chinese traditions, vividly demonstrating the universality of Shakespeare and of the art of Kunju theater.[14]

The *Peony Pavilion* also impressed the audience with its stunning visual impact, as another writer comments:

> This Chinese company may have appeared at the tail-end of the Festival, but they have brought with them a rare treat for theatre-goers. While the symbolism which dominates their ritualistic drama is lost on much of the audience, Westerners cannot fail to be impressed by the stunning visual impact.[15]

The relevant background of the playwright was also mentioned and the central theme of the play was well appreciated by the critic:

> The *Peony Pavilion* is one of the classics of Kunju theater, written by a contemporary of Shakespeare when the art form was in its heyday. A resurgence of interest can largely be attributed to Hua Wen Yi, who plays the lead as well as being director of the company, having repaired the damage inflicted by the Cultural Revolution.
>
> The story is of teenage love which descends into the Underworld when the young princess dies of a broken heart, barred by her father from seeing the handsome scholar she had met in her dreams. One of the joys of the play is that of seeing the discretion with which the playwright Tang Xian Zu depicts a girl discovering her sexuality.[16]

HUANGMEI OPERA'S PRODUCTION OF *MUCH ADO ABOUT NOTHING*

As an engrossing Shakespeare production on display during the Inaugural Chinese Shakespeare Festival, the Huangmei opera *Much Ado About Nothing* was another example of how to adapt a Shakespeare play into traditional Chinese drama by using a Chinese manner. The play was presented by the Anhui Huangmei Opera Troupe under the direction of Jiang Wei Guo and Sun Huai Ren. The celebrated Shakespeare scholar professor Zhang Jun Chuan was invited to be a special literary advisor. The cast included Ma Lan (Beatrice), Wu Gong (Hero), Huang Xin De (Benedick), Jiang Jian Guo (Claudio), Wang Shao Fang (Don Pedro), Li Ji Min (Don John), Chen Xiao Cheng (Leonato), and Huang Zong Yi (Dogberry). At the festival the play drew large audiences, and then toured Beijing in September 1986, evoking strong reactions from the capital's theatrical circles.

Huangmei opera is another major type of traditional Chinese drama. It took shape at the end of the nineteenth century in the An Qing area of Anhui province and flourished in the 1950s, becoming a major local opera type. Since then Huangmei opera has gradually earned a national reputation. There are more than fifty professional Huangmei opera troupes in the country, with most of them in south China, including Taiwan, Hong Kong, and Macao. This opera type is noted for its beautiful songs and performances. The duet "The Couple Returning Home" from the opera The Fairy Couple is known to the whole country.

As a Shakespeare production adapted into traditional Chinese drama using the Chinese manner, every aspect of Much Ado About Nothing had been sinicized, as in Macbeth. The players wore ancient Chinese costumes and were given familiar Chinese names. According to the adaptor, Jin Zhi, the production adopted the Chinese manner partly because it could give full play to the unique performing skill of Huangmei opera and enable the performers to feel at ease in playing Shakespeare's characters. But another reason may have been that the use of the Chinese manner helped to attract large audiences, which knew little about Shakespeare, in small towns and villages when the play went on tour after the festival.[17] The adaptor and directors did not intend to completely sinicize the Shakespearean comedy, however. Their aim was to use the theatrical form of Huangmei opera to present Shakespeare's ideas and artistry—-the beauty, greatness, and common bond of humanity, a wide variety of characterization, and his beautiful language. The play would not be recreated as a "purely Chinese play," though it would come across to the audience in a Chinese manner. It was designed to make the audience feel clearly that it was a Shakespearean play in the form of Huangmei opera. The adaptor and director believed that the theme and story of the comedy would not be unfamiliar to a Chinese audience living in modern times. The hedonistic mood and the desire for personal happiness and freedom displayed in the twists and turns of the love plots could also be easily understood by Huangmei opera fans.

Yet the adapting work did not turn out to be plain sailing. Compared with Macbeth, Much Ado About Nothing was more difficult to adapt because the original play contains many Western customs such as the masquerade, the Christian wedding, the free social contact between men and women, and so on. A mechanical adaptation would inevitably result in cultural discrepancies, making the audience feel that such alien customs were strange in a Chinese cultural context. The question of cultural discrepancy also was raised in the treatment of character in the play. For instance, in ancient China it would have been impossible to find a bold and audacious girl like Beatrice, who displays complete freedom of action in dealing with her personal affairs and social milieu. To be sure, similar characters could be found in traditional Chinese drama, such as Li Qian Jin in *Looking over the Wall,* who has the courage to elope with her lover and argue with an intimidating minister in defending her brave behavior against a feudal ethical code. But obvious differences between Beatrice and Li Qian Jin can be seen in their personalities. The former sometimes is so bold that she engages in a battle of words with young men while the latter always treats men politely and gently, which is regarded by the ancient Chinese as one of the major virtues of a woman, unless she is complaining about the injustice done to her. Beatrice tries to oppose conventional institutions by remaining single, but to Li Qian Jin, as well as to all Chinese women from that period, such an idea is entirely inconceivable. More cultural discrepancies can be found in the behavior of the characters. For example, the marriage of Beatrice and Benedick is actually brought about by a trap designed by the elders, which could never happen in ancient China because at that time old men made all the decisions in domestic affairs and hardly needed to rack their brains devising such a plan.

Thus the adaptor, recognizing that a direct transplantation of the story into feudal China would be troublesome, found an alternative way to solve the problem. The play was reset in ancient China without mentioning any definite dynasty, in the border region of China where a minority kingdom existed in comparative freedom. In Chinese history, minorities were less influenced by feudal ideology and retained their own institutions. Their customs were similar to Western ones: they had free contact between the sexes, freedom to find their own mates, parties similar to Western masquerades, and so forth. This treatment had the advantage of retaining most details of the original plot while reducing cultural discrepancies. As an integral part of the play the masquerade scene was kept but sinicized by adding a traditional Chinese lantern-playing dance, which cleverly combined with the Chinese local flavor of the scene. To avoid another cultural discrepancy, however, the church and Friar Francis had to be removed from the wedding scene.

As in the three operatic versions of Shakespeare's plays that I discussed above, the adaptor of *Much Ado About Nothing* rearranged the play into seven scenes to suit the structural pattern of Huangmei opera. The first scene contains the basic plot of act 1 of the original text. The second scene is an adaptation of the masquerade scene in act 2. The third scene combines the content of 2.3 and 3.1 and is centered on the "love trap." The fourth scene concentrates on the plot of Don John, containing mainly the story from 3.3. The main event in the fifth scene is the unexpected turn of the wedding, as well as the "death" of Hero from 3.4 and 4.1. The sixth scene is adapted from 4.1 and concentrates on the interrogation at the jail. The last scene is basically adapted from act 5. As in other Shakespearean productions adapted into traditional Chinese drama, the adaptor of *Much Ado About Nothing* took much care in putting the original lines into the textual pattern of Huangmei opera. The work had been done in three stages: first, he kept the original lines, especially the language of Dogberry and his followers; second, he grasped the main ideas of the lines and reorganized them into the verse form of Huangmei opera without impairing the play as a whole; and third, he reinforced the emotional atmosphere by composing new lines. For example, the song sung by Hero to express her joy before the wedding in scene 5, the song revealing her great sorrow caused by the injustice done to her in scene 7, and the song sung by eight girls at the grave scene were all the creation of the adaptor. These new songs were joined smoothly with the original lines, adding a strong flavor of Huangmei opera to the poetic quality of Shakespeare.

The director and players showed much originality in performing the play. They tried hard to find a corresponding Chinese style to replace a scene that showed a noticeably Western cultural vein. For instance, as I mentioned above, a traditional Chinese lantern-playing dance was the setting of the masquerade, achieving the same humorous effect as the original scene. Since the church and Friar Francis had been removed from the play, the adaptor replaced the original Christian wedding with a conventional Chinese wedding displaying many typical rites. Yet the treatment provided an ideal setting for the original plot. In this unique scene a traditional performing pattern artfully heightened the at once joyous and sorrowful atmosphere, as when the bride's face was unveiled by taking off the scarf that covered her head. Solos, duets, and choruses expressed the different feelings of the characters. In the scene it was Beatrice who suggested that Hero should "die to live," instead of Friar Francis, as in the original play. The advantage of this change, the adaptor believed, was that it created another opportunity to display Beatrice's resolute and resourceful character.[18]

The treatment of scene 7 also demonstrated the creative spirit of the adaptor and director. Its central event was Claudio's obsequies at Hero's "grave." To reinforce the mournful mood, the entire set was designed in white. The "grave," which consisted of eight girls in white, wearing veils, suddenly split apart after Claudio's repentance, and the girls, Hero included, sang and danced around Claudio. The atmosphere had rapidly changed into a happy one. Claudio had his new choice, which turned out to be his reunion with Hero. This unique treatment gave full play to the dancing and singing skills of the Huangmei opera, which made the scene look beautiful and lyrical, brimming over with a fairy-tale atmosphere.

Another inventive transformation of the original play can be found in the performance of Constable Dogberry and the watch. To sinicize this group of characters, the adaptor changed them into their Chinese counterparts. Dogberry became a typical officer in the city guards. With a Chinese name, Du Bai Rui, he was acted as a *chou* type since its performing pattern was well suited to the manner and disposition of the constable. Wearing an eccentric costume, the officer set the audience roaring with laughter as soon as he came onstage. His odd appearance was helped by an ox horn that hung from his neck, a winged black gauze cap with only one wing intact, and a costume that was only half of an official uniform. As is customary, he introduced himself: "My name is Du Bai Rui, a city guards officer without rank. My single-wing cap always shivers with the wind, no matter what the direction is." Then he had a disorderly dialogue and a funny dancing chorus with the guards. Admonishing the guards, Du Bai Rui asked them to take off their hats together with him, which exposed his bare head to the public. Swaying his head, he recited a piece of doggerel making fun of his bare head. The scene was humorous in a very Chinese way. Behind this performance, however, one could still see clearly Dogberry the foolish and conceited constable.

As in other Shakespearean productions adapted into traditional Chinese drama, Huangmei opera's *Much Ado About Nothing* used conventional stylized movements and symbolic gestures that strongly appealed to the imagination of the audience. For example, a special technique represents the infatuated psychology of lovers who fall in love at first sight. When they look fixedly at each other's faces, they seem connected by an invisible string. If a third person plucks this invisible string, the lovers will move correspondingly. Such a performance can be seen in Sichuan opera's *The Palace of King Fan* and

The White Snake Lady (The Tower of Lei Feng) and Shaoxing opera's *A Dream of the Red Mansion.* In *Much Ado About Nothing,* this exaggerated movement was used to depict the love between Claudio and Hero when they first met. When they looked at each other, their eyes seemed to be tied together. Noticing this situation, Beatrice naughtily plucked this imaginary string and led the lovers around the stage, accompanied by beautiful music.

Other traditional techniques used in Huangmei opera were also used by the players. For instance, Huangmei opera is noted for its frequent use of duets accompanied by dances, which was well suited for the expression of the battle of words between Beatrice and Benedick. The stylized movements called "drunken gait," "turning," and "leg-sweeping" vividly showed Benedick's ecstasy at the news that Beatrice was in love with him.

When the adaptor, director, and actors were rehearsing the production, they were afraid that it would not look like a typical Huangmei opera; once it was shown in public, however, they worried that it would not be received as a Shakespearean play. However, the production turned out to be successful. The adaptor and director in the end achieved their original goal of merging the spirit of Shakespeare and the artistic charm of Huangmei opera.

This brief survey of a few of the Shakespearean productions adapted into major types of traditional Chinese drama shows how successfully Shakespearean drama and traditional Chinese drama have been merged on the contemporary Chinese stage. I have noted above that the two types of drama have also benefited from each other: Shakespeare's plays have brought new vitality to the sluggish traditional Chinese drama and aroused a sense of innovation in its performers. At the same time traditional Chinese drama, with its unique stage techniques, has added an extraordinary splendor to Shakespearean theater in modern-day China. As a form of drama with a long-standing tradition, traditional Chinese drama still greatly influences all the theatrical activities in today's China, directly and indirectly. Consequently it has been used not only as a primary vehicle for the adaptation of Shakespeare's plays but also as a supporting method for performing the plays by other approaches. Indeed, the most important dramatic form employed by Chinese directors and actors for presenting Shakespearean drama has been spoken drama, which was introduced from the West at the beginning of the twentieth century and has since become a major type of drama in China. Yet in many influential Shakespeare productions presented in spoken drama, one can still see the frequent use of the stagecraft of traditional Chinese theater.

China Youth Art Theater's Production of
The Merchant of Venice

An example of this approach is the production of *The Merchant of Venice* presented by China Youth Art Theater in the 1980s, which had a long run of two years with more than two hundred performances. It was highly praised by Shakespearean scholars, dramatic critics, and audiences as one of the best Shakespeare productions on the modern Chinese stage. Since it was performed largely in spoken drama, the production impressed the audience as being part of traditional Chinese theater. The director, Zhang Qi Hong, who trained at the Moscow Art Theater for six years, said that she did not intend to follow either English or Russian patterns of Shakespearean theater: the play would be treated in a Chinese style. By this she meant that the actors would adopt various performing skills of traditional Chinese theater while using the stage techniques of spoken drama.[19] The performance was further mixed with a few performing methods of traditional Chinese laudatory comedy. Against the symbolic setting of Venice upon water, the characters used gracefully stylized movements to depict the rowing of a boat, about which one Western Shakespeare scholar, Philip Brockbank, wrote:

> It was a specifically Chinese kinetic skill, however, that accented the graceful but precarious movement of wits upon water by evoking a gondola in the opening scene. In the manner of an episode in Beijing opera, gondolier and courtiers bobbed, swayed, and flourished on what became an almost audibly lapping canal, distantly echoing the notion of Antonio's mind "tossing on the ocean" and the "roaring waters" of Salerio's apprehensive imagination.[20]

One original touch was the appearance of an ancient Chinese moneylender on the stage, who was designed to embody the psychology of Shylock. When he lamented over his lost money and was angered by his daughter's action, a phantom moneylender, as an image in his imagination, came onstage, talking with him about their mutual business interests in both Venice and China and expressing sympathy. This interesting treatment—or Chinese theatrical joke, as the late Professor Brockbank called it—was much enjoyed by the Chinese audience. It obviously served the director's purpose to deal with the play as a comedy about money, which would avoid both the thorny problem of offending Jews and the difficulty of the Chinese audience understanding the complex historical relationship between Jews and Christians. As stagecraft, such a treatment was able to depict logically the inner suffering of Shylock and to represent his isolation in a society where most of the people around him are enemies. Another obvious advantage of this device was that it could create a common ground for Shakespearean comedy and traditional Chinese drama because the scene reminded the audience of the moneylenders in traditional Chinese drama. An example is Cai Po in *The Injustice to Dou E*, the mother-in-law of the wronged heroine Dou E and probably more greedy than her Jewish counterpart. She lends money to Dou Tian Zhang, Dou E's father, and just one year later the amount has doubled. Because he cannot repay it, Dou Tian Zhang has to give his daughter to the lender in payment, which serves as the root cause of the tragedy. When I asked Zhang Qi Hong if she had an historical reference to back such a treatment, her answer was yes. She told me that according to the historical records, Jewish and Chinese businessmen indeed had had trade contacts in past centuries. Many Jewish businessmen had once visited China during the Northern Song dynasty (960–1127 A.D.) and Chinese businessmen have also traveled to Venice. As a result she believed that the treatment was by no means without foundation and that Shylock should have some sort of common bond with his Chinese counterpart.[21] As a dramatic effect, the scene helped to reinforce the romantic atmosphere of the play. Even so, however, some people disagreed with the director about the treatment. They felt that it was the same as "drawing a snake and adding feet to it," meaning gilding the lily or ruining the effect by adding something superfluous. They were also dissatisfied that the rich Jew was simplified as a miser, similar to a character type in traditional Chinese drama.[22]

The treatment of the casket-choosing scene also displayed the ingenuity of the director. In these scenes the caskets were held by three young women in different costumes. When the wooing took place, the three were in constant motion, dancing gracefully in different styles to suit the qualities of each casket. The suitors sometimes joined them when they tried to make a decision. This arrangement created an extraordinarily lyrical atmosphere, which was manifestly influenced by the characteristic of traditional Chinese theater to frequently use dancing to enrich the power of representation.

THE CHINA COAL MINER'S DRAMA TROUPE'S PRODUCTION OF *A MIDSUMMER NIGHT'S DREAM*

One of the most engrossing productions staged during the Inaugural Chinese Shakespeare Festival in Beijing was that of *A Midsummer Night's Dream*, presented by the China Coal Miner's Drama Troupe under the direction of Xong Yuan Wei. The play was acted as spoken drama but was mixed with the stage techniques of traditional Chinese theater. The result was a lyrical and romantic atmosphere with an Asian flavor. As Xong declared in his program notes, his intention was to present "a Chinese midsummer night's dream of the nineteen-eighties" in such a way that foreigners would suppose it to be Chinese and the Chinese would take it to be new. Giving the gist of the story, Xong wrote that the young men and women leave the city for the forest for the sake of love while the workmen leave it for the sake of art. The program says, "Although the tranquillity of the fairy and natural worlds, like that of the human world, is flawed, all discord is resolved into a harmonious nocturne that may be found only in a dream." Finally the director wrote that the artistic goal he intended to achieve was "to use Eastern aesthetic taste and modern rhythms to realize Shakespeare's lyrical sentiments and make of them a flowing poem for the stage."

All the stage designs worked to embody the director's idea. Eleven thick ropes, hung over the stage in several groups, and many thin vertical ropes formed an image of a forest, accompanied by unusual lighting. This setting served the director's purpose in creating a symbolic and abstract space for the imagination to compose a "flowing poem" on the stage. The performing skills of traditional Chinese drama were used at times to enhance this symbolic and imaginative climate. The carryings on in the woods gave considerable scope for the employment of stylized movements and symbolic gestures such as the actions of groping forward in the dark and fog, fighting the wind, and sleeping while standing.

Another interesting treatment by the director was the sinicization of the workmen. In the play Bottom and his friends became their Chinese counterparts. Wearing the clothes of modern Beijing workers, they spoke a Beijing dialect (slightly different from Mandarin Chinese) to suit their status. Their movements were of the *wen chou* type (a subtype of *chou*) of traditional Chinese drama, used to depict lower-class people. They still kept their original names, however, and followed the original lines of the text. Occasionally, fashionable terms used in contemporary China reinforced the comic atmosphere of the dialogue, as for example "to have your wages raised," which got a laugh from the audience. Xong appeared keen to interject a few modern references into the play. The most noticeable example was the substitution of a digital watch for the "little changeling boy." Such a treatment looked a little incompatible in the context of the plot, yet it was enjoyed by the audience although criticized by a Shakespeare scholar as a "cheap theatrical joke."[23]

In recent years it has been popular for Chinese actors to present Shakespearean plays in the form of spoken drama. Such a play uses the performing skills of spoken drama, but the story is sinicized, as in the productions adapted into traditional Chinese drama using the Chinese manner. The play, therefore, outwardly appears to be an ancient Chinese play. The adaptor and director using this method, of course, still have to solve the same problems of cultural discrepancy as those who adapted Shakespeare's plays into traditional Chinese drama in the Chinese manner. The two most typical examples of this style of adaptation are the production of *King Lear* by the Central Drama Academy and the production of *All's Well That Ends Well* by the Xi An Spoken Drama Troupe, which were presented, respectively, in Beijing and Shanghai during the 1986 Festival.

With the Chinese title *King Li Ya*, the Central Beijing Drama Academy's production took place in the setting of a solemn and splendid ancient Chinese court decorated with symmetrical ornaments and a high central throne on a raked platform. The characters wore beautiful ancient Chinese costumes and observed the etiquette of the Chinese royal court. The play succeeded in getting the audience to believe that the plot was a stirring tragedy that happened in the long-ago history of Chinese feudal society. Those familiar with Shakespeare's works, however, knew immediately that it was the great Shakespearean tragedy that was being performed on the stage, although at the very outset they had thought it was a Chinese historical play. According to Jin Nai Qian, who took the part of King Lear, one of the advantages of using the Chinese style was that the central theme of the play could be more easily understood by the audience because it would tend to associate the story with numerous similar historical incidents. In Chinese history emperors often encountered the same problem of investing their successors with hereditary titles and territories, which frequently resulted in bloody wars. On being praised for his successful performance, Jin admitted that it was hard work to depict Shakespearean tragic protagonists because the performing style of spoken drama asks the actor to identify with his or her role.[24] The influence of traditional Chinese drama upon Shakespearean theater in China was so all-pervasive that even in *King Li Ya*, presented in the pure form of spoken drama, one could still find deployment of the techniques of traditional Chinese theater. The acting of the fool, for example, appeared to use the performing style of the character types *wen chou* and *wu chou*. The conventional movements the actor used included "dwarf-gait," "tiger-leap," "somersault-turning," and so on.

The "modernization" of Shakespeare's plays has been very popular in Western Shakespearean theater since the 1920s, yet it sounds quite new to Chinese audiences. Generally speaking Chinese Shakespearean scholars tend to be conservative and are opposed to any attempts to seek novelty. Most Chinese directors, however, seem to have a good appetite for something new and unusual. Consequently in the 1980s the modernizing style of adaptation gradually became accepted by Chinese directors, players, and audiences as a practical way to stage Shakespeare's plays. Yet up to 1993 audiences had not seen any completely modernized Shakespearean production on the Chinese stage that resembled the production of *The Comedy of Errors* by the Royal Shakespeare Company in 1990 or the production of *Twelfth Night* by the English Shakespeare Company in 1992. The only examples of this adaptation style so far are two partly modernized Shakespeare productions: *Love's Labor's Lost* by the Jiangsu Spoken Drama Troupe and *The Taming of the Shrew* by the Shanghai People's Art Theater, both presented in Shanghai during the festival. In these two productions, modernizing treatments were mingled with orthodox methods, for the directors did not want to go too far in transforming the plays.

Xong Guo Dong, the director of *Love's Labor's Lost,* maintained that the employment of the modernizing method—such as wearing modern costumes, speaking modern languages, and using modern props—could help the audience, especially its younger members, to appreciate the play and bring the story closer to their tastes. However, he tried to avoid updating the play too obviously. Instead he used this method to serve the play's central theme. The production tried to demonstrate how humanity frees itself from asceticism through the ages.[25] The play began with a glimpse of medieval life in Europe, with the costumes, props, and mannerisms all belonging to this period. The pace of the action was slow and the atmosphere depressing. Then as the plot began to develop, the costumes, props, and demeanor began to change gradually to match each succeeding historical period (about one century per act), becoming increasingly modern. Accordingly the play's pace became faster and the atmosphere brisker and livelier. When the play ended, the audience saw a vivid scene of modern life on the stage. The characters wore Western suits, jackets, and miniskirts and carried fashionable handbags and tape recorders. The scene was accompanied by pop music and the roar of an airplane's jet engines. Some modern references and language were also used to suit this up-to-date setting such as using a telephone, sending a registered letter, taking a photograph, and so forth. The play displayed an optimistic attitude towards social progress. To establish close contact with the audience, the performance took place on an extended stage. The whole theater was decorated as a royal park, which made the audience feel as if they were participants. To achieve a "distancing effect" during the performance, the players sometimes invited the audience to dance with them or help put on a magic show in the audience, which enlivened the atmosphere and entertained the audience. Some critics, however, felt that these distancing techniques weakened the actual performance. Nevertheless the production was praised, on the whole, for its profound ideas and novel style.

Chinese audiences and theatrical professionals have evidently become more open-minded about theatrical modernization because *People's Daily* reported that a production of *Hamlet* was performed on 28 December 1994 in the Capital Theater, Beijing, by the Beijing People's Art Theater. This completely modernized production with modern settings, costumes, language, and sound effects was well received by the audience.[26]

In showing the convergence of Shakespearean plays and traditional Chinese drama and other major metamorphoses of Shakespeare on the Chinese stage, I hope that the magnificence of the spectacle when the two long-standing theatrical traditions combine, like the confluence of two great rivers, is quite clear. I also hope that the above discussion convincingly demonstrates how much Chinese dramatists have enriched Shakespearean theater in China by basing their plays on Chinese theatrical tradition while flexibly adopting other modes of Western theater. Such a convergence has a profound and lasting significance: it helps to vitalize traditional Chinese drama and greatly advances contemporary Chinese theater. Moreover it contributes to the further popularity of Shakespeare in China by presenting a variety of Shakespeare's plays on the Chinese stage. In a sense, the mixing of Shakespearean plays and traditional Chinese drama can be seen as a convergence of the two cultural traditions because Shakespeare has become a major figure in every aspect of China's culture. This will be the central topic of the next chapter.

Part III

5

Looking Ahead: Shakespeare in the Cultural Landscape of China

THE chapters in Part II of this study have shown the general reception of Shakespeare by the Chinese and the relationship between Shakespearean and traditional Chinese drama. The connection between the two dramatic traditions was found to be interactive. On one hand, Shakespeare has had a great impact upon traditional Chinese drama, replacing its authoritative central position in modern China and infusing new blood into the old Chinese dramatic tradition through joint theatrical activities. On the other hand, traditional Chinese drama has also contributed to the wide variety of Shakespearean productions on the Chinese stage. The significance of the Shakespeare industry in China, however, is not confined to theatrical and literary circles. In fact, Shakespeare has entered into every domain of Chinese culture and exerted a tremendous influence upon it. From National Youth Intelligence Competition questions to wedding gifts of complete editions, from the design of the commemorative gold coins issued by the Central Bank of China to advertisements in local newspapers, Shakespeare has permeated Chinese life like no other great Western cultural figure before and since. In a sense Shakespeare has become a Chinese institution, and due to his wide popularity he has entered the consciousness of many Chinese people, some of whom may not have even read his plays.

As in Japan and other Asian countries, the existing culture in contemporary China is a double one, characterized by the mixture of traditional and Western cultures. What impresses foreign tourists most when they visit China is always the conspicuously conjoined cultural framework. Traditional Chinese architecture and modern Western buildings, Chinese and Western food and clothes, Chinese folk songs and pop music, Chinese dance and Western ballet all are accommodated simultaneously into one hybrid culture. The Chinese have emphasized the Western part of this blended culture more than their indigenous traditions because the former is often associated with prosperity and progress, while the latter represents the past and the nation's identity. So it is understandable that Shakespeare, as a "hero" of Western culture, has been a major figure in the cultural landscape of contemporary China and that every expression of interest in the English playwright is interpreted as a manifest sign of cultural advancement.

In this chapter, therefore, I attempt to investigate the widespread and profound influence of Shakespeare upon modern Chinese culture, to demonstrate how the plays and their legendary author have flourished and functioned in varied and diverse cultural forms such as theater and education, entertainment and artistic creation, academic activity and literary criticism, politics and ideology, and so on. I also discuss how Shakespeare has become a cultural phenomenon in the customs and daily life of the Chinese, who now recognize Shakespeare wherever and whenever his name crops up, whether it be in newspaper advertisements, television game shows, dinner parties, or wedding ceremonies. We shall then see how Shakespeare is used in China as a means of constructing cultural meaning and how he has contributed greatly to the construction of the "New Culture" of China (the culture of China since 1919, characterized by a combination of traditional Chinese culture and some elements of Western culture).

As one of the important areas of Chinese culture, theatrical practice of modern China has been directly and obviously influenced by Shakespeare. Besides Shakespearean productions and theatrical activities linking Shakespeare and traditional Chinese drama, the entire modern Chinese theater shows a clear connection to Shakespeare and his plays. From dramatic creation to theatrical training, from direction to performance, almost every aspect of theatrical practice bears the imprint of the great English playwright. Many of the works of modern Chinese dramatists reveal apparent Shakespearean influences. Shakespeare is often associated with the great playwrights of modern Chinese theater, and my discussion in this chapter centers on the most important of them: Tian Han, Cao Yu, and Guo Mo Ruo.

As one of the founders of modern Chinese theater, Tian Han (1898–1968) was a very influential figure in cultural circles. His works, unlike those of traditional drama, were written in the form of spoken drama and represented the turbulent reality of modern China, which strongly aroused the will of the people to examine their moribund society. There can be no doubt that his interest in drama and his ambition to become a dramatist stemmed directly from the inspiration of Shakespeare. In his youth Tian Han was fond of

Shakespeare's plays. When he studied in Japan he read many of them and developed aspirations to study drama and take up dramatic writing as his profession. As I mentioned in chapter 3, he made a great contribution to the translation of Shakespeare's works and the campaign to publicize the playwright in China. He was the first to translate a Shakespearean play (*Hamlet*) in its original dramatic form. He also published a translation of *Romeo and Juliet*.

Besides his translation work, Tian Han also introduced some useful information about the staging of Shakespeare in the West by publishing an article on the evolution of Shakespeare theater on the Western stage.[1] In 1935 he was jailed by the ruling National Party because he led the left-wing Cultural and Dramatic Movement, which advocated resistance against the invasion of Japan. Shakespeare's works accompanied him when he entered jail. He took an English edition of the complete works, and each day he sat on the floor of his cell, tirelessly reading the texts aloud for hours on end.

Since he was such an admirer of Shakespeare, Tian Han was naturally inclined to follow his artistic style, so Shakespeare's influence on Tian's drama is not hard to find. First and foremost his themes were Shakespearean: he described the miserable life of the people, revealing serious social problems in tragedies that had an unhappy ending, unlike conventional Chinese tragedy. Most of his successful and influential plays are tragedies, such as *The Night in a Cafe, The Night of Tiger Hunting, The Tragedy on the Lake, The Return to the South, The View of a Village on the Edge of a River,* and *The Death of a Famous Player.* When he worked as an editor for a publishing house, he once had a plan to translate ten Shakespearean plays. Of these, only three were either a comedy or a romance (*A Midsummer Night's Dream, The Merchant of Venice,* and *The Tempest*); the rest were tragedies. Like many Chinese intellectuals, Tian Han lamented the lack of a real tragic sense in traditional Chinese drama. The "happy ending" pattern in drama served to alleviate social contradictions and support the interest of the ruling class. By contrast, Shakespearean tragedy, he believed, exposed profoundly social problems and led people to examine their society. As I mentioned in chapter 4, in his preface to the translation of *Hamlet* Tian Han asked Chinese readers, particularly the young, to associate the play with the seamy side of modern China. Shakespearean tragedies inspired Tian Han to represent the suffering and struggle of Chinese people in a true tragic form. For instance, in *The Night in a Cafe* and *The Night of Tiger Hunting,* he illustrated how young Chinese men and women suffered from the unreasonable feudal marriage system, which resulted in numerous tragedies like that in Shake-

speare's *Romeo and Juliet*. In *The Night of Tiger Hunting*, the leading characters, Han Da Sha and Lian Gu, are an ordinary young
man and woman in the countryside who are confronted with the
powerful feudal force. It is quite clear that the situation will inevitably lead to a tragic end, owing to the great disparity of strength
between the lovers and the character of the feudal political force. Yet
the lovers dare to fight their enemies to seek the freedom to marry
each other. The author abandoned the outmoded happy-ending pattern and gave no false remedy for the problem in order to reinforce
the tragic conflict in the play, help the audience realize the gravity
of the problem, and, most important, spur them to reform society.

The early works of Tian Han are imbued with a romantic atmosphere that is obviously influenced by a Shakespearean style. In *The
Night of Tiger Hunting*, *The Return to the South*, and *The Tragedy
on the Lake*, this romantic atmosphere is represented by various
means of artistic expression. For example, in *The Night of Tiger
Hunting*, a romantic story of tiger hunting is mixed with the realistic
description of the suffering and struggle of the Chinese farmers. The
play is marked by noticeable local color of the mountain area in
Hunan province. Moreover, since Shakespeare's plays are characterized by lengthy eloquent and poetic soliloquies and monologues describing scenes and revealing inner conflict in characters, Tian Han
often adopted this technique in his own works. For example, in *The
Night of Tiger Hunting*, *The Tragedy on the Lake*, and *The Return to
the South*, many long monologues and soliloquies help the characters
reveal emotion and express resentment at their grim society as well
as show their intention to find happy new lives.

Like other modern Chinese writers, Tian Han was dissatisfied
with the simple and morality-oriented characterization of traditional
Chinese drama. By contrast, he showed great interest in the richness
and variety of Shakespearean character portrayal, so in his plays he
intentionally followed Shakespeare's method; most of his characters
are vividly portrayed with distinctive personalities, coming to the
audience and readers as individuals rather than moral types. Lian
Gu, the heroine in *The Night of Tiger Hunting*, is such a character.
In the play the author successfully depicted Lian Gu's gentleness,
honesty, courage, and insight, helping to create a new image of the
younger generation in the rural areas of modern China.

Tian Han's skill in portraying individualized characters was more
mature when he wrote his three-act play, *The Death of a Famous
Player*. Almost every role in the play is vividly delineated as an individualized character. The hero, Liu Zhen Sheng, a well-known
Beijing opera player, is an experienced and extremely skilled actor.

He devotes all his life to his career while being an honest, upright, and brave man who dares to resist the oppression of evil forces. Like the players in ancient China, the performers in modern China, especially before the 1940s, had a low social status and were treated like prostitutes. They were often bullied by the upper class and hooligans alike. As the antithesis of Liu Zhen Sheng, Lord Yang was also vividly created as a mean and cruel representative of the evil local gentry. The disposition of Liu Feng Xiang, apprentice to Liu Zhen Sheng, suggests Shakespeare's technique of creating dual-sided characters. He is a pure and innocent young man, but the other side of his character shows weakness and vanity. Finally he took to evil ways, corrupted by Lord Yang. It is evident that Tian Han had completely distanced himself from the conventional mode of characterization since his characters were not simply portrayed as moral types. Unlike Zhou Shun Chang, Yu Fei, and other heroes in traditional Chinese drama, Liu Zhen Sheng's courage to fight against evil forces does not stem from any specific conventional moral doctrine such as loyalty and filial piety. On the contrary, his action is backed by a sense of general social justice and the desire for equality and freedom. It is clear that, like Shakespeare, Tian Han paid special attention to general human nature and emphasized the multifaceted qualities of his characters.

Tian Han also employed Shakespearean techniques to help develop the plot, play up the surroundings, and heighten atmosphere. The atmospheres of his plays are often heightened to produce audience involvement, as we have seen in *The Night of Tiger Hunting*. Tian Han also used Shakespeare's device of a "play-within-the-play" to good effect in *The Death of a Famous Player*, where it not only describes the professional activity of the leading role but also enhances his temperament. In the play-within-the-play, Liu Zhen Sheng, the principal character, takes the part of the heroic innocent who fights against the decayed feudal system, while in the play itself he also portrays a hero resisting the oppression of evil forces. The plots in both the play and the play-within-the-play are skillfully interwoven to produce stirring scenes and reinforce the tragic mood.

The relationship between Shakespeare and the great modern Chinese dramatist Cao Yu can be clearly seen from the two major posts that Cao holds. When this book was published he was president of both the Dramatists Association of China and the Shakespeare Association of China. Cao Yu's dramatic achievement constitutes both the peak and the heart of modern Chinese theater. His three greatest plays, *The Thunderstorm, The Sunrise,* and *The Open Coun-*

try, are known to almost every household. He was elected president of the Shakespeare Association of China not only because he has enjoyed high prestige in Chinese theatrical circles, but also because he has made a great contribution to the country's Shakespeare industry. He taught Shakespeare at the university level in the 1930s and 1940s and actively took part in Shakespearean theater at the National Drama School during the Sino-Japanese War. His translation of *Romeo and Juliet*, accepted as one of the best translations of any Shakespeare play in China, is characterized by its smooth poetic language and suitability for stage representation.

Like Tian Han, Cao Yu admired Shakespeare's works early in life, starting when he was a student in middle school. He first read Lamb's *Tales from Shakespeare*, translated by Lin Shu, then *The Merchant of Venice* and other plays. He even bought a gramophone record of Ellen Terry's *Romeo and Juliet* with money saved from his allowance and listened to it again and again, intoxicated by the recitation of the actress and the imaginative illusions created by the lines. After entering Qing Hua University to study Western literature, Cao Yu had more opportunities to read Shakespeare's plays in English. The more he read, the more he admired the uniqueness of Shakespearean drama. He specially liked the "great tragedies" and *Julius Caesar*. He felt that the remarkable nature of Shakespeare's works derived not only from their profound philosophy but also from their artistic appeal.[2] Asked who was his favorite of all the dramatists he had known, he answered without hesitation, "Shakespeare, of course." Then he added, "Like Leonardo da Vinci, Shakespeare is a great genius and a miracle of mankind."[3] Thus it is understandable why he praised the great English writer so highly in his speech at the opening ceremony of the Inaugural Chinese Shakespeare Festival in 1986.

Shakespeare's works inspired Cao Yu to take up dramatic writing and influenced many aspects of his work. Cao himself admitted that he had learned a lot from Shakespeare. He writes,

> Shakespeare's plays are so great and profound that they are as miraculous as the universe. I once learned some techniques from Ibsen, yet I learned more from Shakespeare. His works exhibit the richness and variation of humanity, exquisite structure, beautiful poetic flavor, humanistic enthusiasm, and a fertile imagination. No genius can bear comparison with him.[4]

In Cao Yu's works, characterization, plot design, structure, and language all show Shakespeare's influence.

What attracted Cao Yu most to Shakespeare's plays was the complexity and colorfulness of Shakespeare's characterization. This was also the main quality that he intended to emulate in his dramatic writings, as he told young Chinese dramatists: "The most important technique of Shakespeare that we should learn is his brilliant characterization."[5] As I pointed out earlier, modern Chinese writers were dissatisfied with the simple characterization found in traditional Chinese drama because it was based on moral values and unable to portray the real people of modern China. In using the Shakespearean style of characterization, Cao Yu achieved his goal perfectly: most of his characters, particularly in his masterpiece, *The Thunderstorm*, are highly individualized with colorful and complex qualities.

If *The Thunderstorm* can be seen as the monument of a remarkable genius, it can also be considered the highlight of a remarkable age. The play reflects the social life of the Chinese, who are in transition from a collapsed feudal system to an industrialized country and who are undergoing great changes in every aspect of life. Through the sad story of a family, Cao Yu mirrors the crises of the dying Chinese feudal system. One way that his tragedy is "Shakespearean" is that it lacks the artificial happy ending of conventional Chinese drama. Another way is in the eight roles he created for *The Thunderstorm*, each having a distinctive character composed of complicated qualities and shaped by humanity at large, conventional institutions, and the changing times, as well as by their social status, age, sex, personality, and so on. Although the play clearly reveals a political and moral program, the characters are not simply good or bad. As in Shakespearean tragedy, they act in accordance with the logic of their passions but not by a particular moral doctrine. Zhou Pu Yuan, the leading character, represents the Chinese patriarchal system. In traditional Chinese drama, as the head of a family he would be a highly praised character with many virtues since the entire Confucian ideological system is based on a patriarchal feudal society. But in this play his role is as complex as those of Shakespearean tragedies because his vices and weaknesses are emphasized. Selfishly and callously he forsakes Lu Ma, the woman who lives with him, leaving her in a dreadful plight. Driven to despair, she intends to commit suicide but is rescued by another man. Zhou Pu Yuan is also an imperious and despotic husband and father, requiring his wife and children to submit absolutely to his will. Yet in reflective moments he has a clear awareness of what he has done, like Macbeth and Claudius. To show repentance for his cruelty to Lu Ma, whom he believes has killed herself, he keeps the room in which he lived with her untouched for many years. This may be regarded as a hypocritical action, yet it is true to human nature. Although he always treats his children sternly to maintain his authority, he also displays affection for them and finally commits suicide when he is informed that his errors caused their deaths.

His wife, Fan Yi, is also vividly portrayed as a typical character produced by the changing society in which the feudal family relationship is breaking up. She comes across to the audience as representing the modern Chinese women who rebel against the harsh rule of Chinese patriarchy. She suggests both Ibsen's Nora in *A Doll's House* and the Shakespearean women who interrogate or challenge the dominant position of men, such as Adriana, Beatrice, and Katherina. She does not resign herself to the control of Zhou Pu Yuan and claims equality between the sexes. Her boldest action is to seek true love by falling in love with her stepson Zhou Ping, which would be regarded by the apologists for feudal ethics as the worst offense one can commit.

From the above examples it is clear that in his character portrayal, Cao Yu follows the Shakespearean mode, creating characters whose passion and will are universally shared. Like Shakespeare, the playwright also closely associates the passions of his characters with the historical context and political system. The characters cannot be completely blamed for the dying moral order and the self-destructive contradictions of the divided society; obviously, *The Thunderstorm* can be seen as an individual tragedy in the Bradleian mold, but it can also be regarded as a social tragedy. Indeed, almost all the techniques of Shakespearean characterization are deployed in this Chinese masterpiece: the revelation of the inner world of the character, the complexity of the role, dual personalities, the changeability of the nature of a role, the contrast between characters, and so on.

Cao Yu also painstakingly bases his plot designs on Shakespearean models. *The Thunderstorm* has a familiar double-plot structure that is manifestly different from the structural patterns of traditional Chinese drama. It consists of two parallel plots, one centered on Zhou Pu Yuan's family and the other on Lu Gui's family, and both are carefully interrelated. This structure reminds us right away of the plots of *Hamlet* and *King Lear,* although the social status of the two families in Cao Yu's play is much lower than that of the protagonists in Shakespearean tragedies.

As I discussed in the second chapter, the mixture of tragedy and comedy has been used in both Shakespearean plays and traditional Chinese drama, although in different ways. In Cao Yu's works, this mingled mode frequently produces a specific stage effect. And in most cases, we find a striking similarity between his style and that of Shakespeare. In *The Thunderstorm* Cao Yu skillfully mixes comic elements with the basic tragic mood. For instance, Lu Gui, the head of the second family in the play, is a humorous character, similar to Polonius in *Hamlet*. Although he is just an ordinary person with a lower social status, he always puffs himself up before lower-class people while currying favor with the powerful and acting servilely. Another comic character in this tragedy is Zhou Chong, the youngest son of Zhou Pu Yuan. He is an innocent, simple, and rather childish young man. Whenever he comes onstage, the atmosphere is enlivened. Some happy scenes in which the lovers show their affection for each other are also designed to form a sharp contrast with the serious and depressing mood of the play. The mingled mode of Cao Yu's plays does not derive from traditional Chinese drama, for it is not used in conventional patterns. For example, Cao Yu does not use a happy ending to relieve the gloomy mood of his tragedies. In addition, the comic characters in his tragedies are not used merely to lighten the ambiance by making impromptu gestures and remarks. Rather, Cao Yu's style is similar to Shakespeare's because his comic scenes in his tragedies are closely related to the development of the plot and serve the central theme. Being representatives of different social classes, the comic characters also have their own importance. Furthermore, as in Shakespeare, the main function of the mingled mode in these plays is to represent life as a whole, in which joy and sorrow can both be found.

Many other of Shakespeare's dramatic skills were used to enhance Cao Yu's plays. For example, he admired Shakespeare's technique for beginning and ending a play and even asked other Chinese dramatists to imitate it. He thought that *Romeo and Juliet* had a very good beginning that was full of action. The fight between the two families attracts the attention of the audience and asks them to get involved in the story at once. Cao Yu also admired the first scene of *Hamlet*. It was, he believed, a very exciting and thrilling beginning, characterized by a wonderful mixture of plot development and recapitulation.[6] Cao Yu successfully used this technique in his works. For example, in the first scene of *The Thunderstorm* Lu Gui tells his daughter a story about a ghost. Similar to Shakespeare's method, it is a very dramatic scene that also gives the audience the previous story of the plot. Cao Yu also paid special attention to the endings of Shakespeare's plays. He particularly liked the ingenious treatment of Othello's suicide because it was logical, conforming to moral law and to the character of the hero. Inspired by the skill of Shakespeare, Cao Yu declared that he would not start writing a play until he had fully worked out its ending.[7] Another Shakespearean dramatic skill emulated by Cao Yu was the style of the language. When reading

Cao Yu's plays, one is often enchanted by the wide variations in his lively, eloquent, and individualized language. He used both graceful and vulgar styles according to the status of the characters. Pun, metaphor, slang, simile, and proverb can all be found in his texts. He is rightly regarded as a master of language.

From the above discussion we can conclude that although Cao Yu's dramatic creations were also influenced by other foreign dramatists such as Ibsen, Chekhov, O'Neill, Galsworthy, and Wilde, there is no doubt that his reputation as a great modern Chinese dramatist can be largely attributed to Shakespeare.

Shakespeare's impact on the modern Chinese theater can also be found in the creation of historical plays. Generally speaking, modern Chinese drama can be classified into two categories according to subject matter. Real incidents and events are taken by the dramatists to reflect realistic social life while historical figures, stories, and events are used to reproduce life in ancient China. But unlike traditional Chinese drama, which can be regarded by modern Chinese people as historical drama in a broad sense, modern Chinese historical plays are not intended simply to resent the past of the Chinese. With their clear political bias, they use the past to disparage the present.

The dramatic works of Guo Mo Ruo represent modern Chinese historical drama at its height. As a giant of modern Chinese culture, Guo Mo Ruo was a versatile writer and scholar. His six historical plays caused a sensation throughout the country in the 1940s during the Sino-Japanese War with their brilliant artistic charm and immense patriotic zeal. Shakespeare has influenced Guo Mo Ruo's historical plays; this was not only discovered by later scholars through careful studies but was also pointed out by his contemporaries. It seemed no accident that, like the works of Tian Han and Cao Yu, Guo Mo Ruo's dramatic creations were also largely affected by Shakespeare's plays, for the Chinese dramatist was an ardent admirer of Shakespeare when he was very young. In his autobiography, "My Childhood," Guo Mo Ruo recollected that Lin Shu's translation of *Tales from Shakespeare* was one of his most loved books.[8] When he studied at the Imperial University in Tokyo, he read many of Shakespeare's plays, including *Hamlet, King Lear, The Tempest,* and *Romeo and Juliet,* which greatly influenced his own later plays. It is quite clear that he used Shakespearean tragic concepts in his historical plays because most of the plays are historical tragedies displaying the vigorous and solemn style of Shakespearean tragedy. In his discussion about the spirit of tragedy, Guo held that tragedy was more instructive than comedy. The essence of tragedy, he argued, was the conflict between the new social force and the old one. The value of tragedy was to turn grief into strength, not simply to appeal to one's sympathy and pity.[9] Obviously his understanding of this tragic concept was based on Shakespearean tragedy rather than on traditional Chinese drama, though there is also a touch of Hegelianism and Marxism in his approach.

The Chinese Cherry Bush (Tang Li Zhi Hua) is one of the most influential historical plays of Guo Mo Ruo, drawing its material from a tragic and heroic story in Chinese history during pre-Qin period (see the Appendix). In the play the hero, Nie Zheng, assassinates a tyrant, King Xia Lei. But before the hero commits suicide, he mutilates his face in order not to get his twin sister, Nie Ying, into trouble. After he dies, the court displays his body in public to let people identify him. A thrilling scene occurs near daybreak, as a rooster crows occasionally. Two soldiers are guarding a platform with Nie Zheng's body on it. They talk about the body and his ghost, frightened by the terrifying atmosphere. Suddenly they see, in the dark, a figure approaching, looking just like the dead man. The soldiers run away in great fear, for they think it is the ghost of the hero. This scene resembles the first scene in *Hamlet:* both have a chilling atmosphere, sensational effect, and immediate audience involvement. In *Hamlet* the scene's function is to unfold the story while in *The Chinese Cherry Bush* the scene paves the way for the play's climax. The character of Nie Zheng has much in common with that of Brutus in *Julius Caesar.* Both fight heroically against dictators and die a heroic death. In his later articles Guo Mo Ruo frankly admitted that Shakespeare's works had inspired him to write this and other historical plays.[10]

The most typical example of Shakespeare's influence upon Guo Mo Ruo's historical plays can be found in his other very famous tragedy, *Qu Yuan,* which attracted much attention when it was performed in public during the Sino-Japanese War. The play was characterized by tremendous momentum, a stirring and solemn atmosphere, and intense emotion. It is a political tragedy, quite different from traditional Chinese drama. Qu Yuan, the hero, was a great classical Chinese poet and politician whose tragic story is known to every household in China. He was a faithful and upright minister and a great patriot, serving King Chu during the pre-Qin period, yet he was framed by treacherous subjects and wronged by the king. Sent into exile, he lived a miserable life. When his country was subjugated by another powerful state, he threw himself into a river and drowned. A special occasion—the Dragon Boat Festival—now commemorates this great poet and patriot. Based on this historical story, the plot of the play was greatly enhanced by the playwright to represent the spirit and ideology of the new age. Unlike the heroes of traditional Chinese political tragedies, Qu Yuan was not portrayed as an honest subject eager to defend the feudal system. Instead the audience sees him as a champion fighting for justice against evil forces and as a great patriot defending state sovereignty. Obviously the hero was an embodiment of the "anger of the age" (as the emotions of the Chinese during the war were described), strongly voicing the desire of the Chinese to fight against the invasion of Japan.

Although the play deals with a genuine Chinese story, its artistic style, characterization, and tragic atmosphere are so similar to that of Shakespearean tragedies that many Chinese scholars and critics immediately felt that the play exhibited an evident Shakespearean style. Some of them even directly pointed out that Qu Yuan bore a strong resemblance to Hamlet.[11] The events in which Qu Yuan gets involved are different from those in which Hamlet participates, but both characters are rebels who challenge the seamy side of society and misanthropes who detest the world and its ways. The lengthy soliloquies and monologues that are frequently used in the play also reveal a Shakespearean style.

In act 5 of *Qu Yuan,* a scene entitled "Ode to Thunder and Lightning" evoked a particularly strong reaction from the audience. In the scene, the hero, filled with grief and indignation, shouts with great agitation to the wind, thunder, and lightning to express his anger. Many Chinese critics immediately perceived the influence of *King Lear.* The famous poet Xu Chi even wrote a letter to the playwright pointing out the similarity between *Qu Yuan* and *King Lear* while praising the achievement of the play at the same time.[12] This scene indeed has something in common with the scene on the heath in *King Lear* in which the King, facing the storm, angrily curses his daughters' ingratitude and the evil world. Admittedly the contents of the two scenes are different, yet the central theme and expressive mode of both are similar, particularly when Qu Yuan shouts to the thunder and lightning, asking them to destroy this evil world with their great power. This stirring scene, which made *Qu Yuan* famous, served as a vehicle for spreading political ideas and expressing society's anger. In fact, some years later Guo Mo Ruo himself also admitted that he drew great inspiration from *King Lear* when he wrote the scene,[13] though he seemed reluctant to admit it at that time.

In 1937 the president of the National Drama School, Yu Shang Yuan, who was a famous dramatic artist and educator, wrote an article explaining why the first graduating class of his school would perform a public Shakespearean production. He held that it was of great significance to use Shakespeare's plays for drama training because they had been universally accepted as one of the most important theatrical activities in the world and even as the highest standard of stage representation.[14] Just as Yu Shang Yuan recognized, Shakespearean drama has indeed played an important role in training actors and has greatly influenced the creative work of the modern Chinese theater. Throughout the drama schools and institutes in modern China Shakespeare's works have been used extensively as teaching material and as the subject for staging practice, helping to develop a new team of theatrical workers and artists.

The National Drama School in Nanjing was set up in 1935 as the first spoken drama school in modern China. As I previously mentioned, its president, Yu Shang Yuan, had a clear goal of using Shakespeare as both a means and a standard for the training in his school. Consequently the school made a rule that every graduating class must perform a Shakespearean play in public. During the Sino-Japanese War, the graduating students of the school successively presented *The Merchant of Venice, Othello,* and *Hamlet,* all of them receiving much acclaim from their audiences. The performances served not only to demonstrate the acting skill of the students, but also as tests of their ability to undertake other stage work. The students realized that it was not an easy matter to play a role in Shakespeare's plays, so they went all out to fulfill the task, using the knowledge they learned from the training and giving full play to their performing skills. For instance, Yie Zi, who played Portia in the inaugural graduation performance of *The Merchant of Venice,* fully represented the character of the heroine in different situations, displaying her remarkable acting talent. Her performance was highly praised by the audience and critics, and she was immediately employed as a professional actress by two well-known drama companies, the Shanghai Experimental Drama Troupe and the Wu Han Angry Tide Drama Troupe. The second graduation performance of the school, a production of *Othello,* repeated the same story, enjoying a highly successful season at Guo Tai Theater in Chongqing city. Ling Guan Ru, who played Desdemona, and other students were invited to work in the Shanghai Drama Company. The graduation performance also provided a good opportunity for the students to undertake other stage work. For example, for the inaugural graduation performance the graduates did all the stage work including set design, costumes, makeup, and lighting, fully displaying their originality. The students also took an active part in the publicity for the performance, publishing many articles in national and local newspapers to introduce Shakespeare's works to the readers.

After the establishment of the People's Republic of China, Shakespeare and his plays were emphasized by the drama schools and institutes more than ever. In state drama institutes and most provincial drama schools, Shakespeare has been a required course in the curriculum. In the Analysis of Play Texts course, many of Shakespeare's plays were on the syllabus, particularly popular plays such as *Hamlet, Othello, Romeo and Juliet,* and *The Merchant of Venice.* Other courses using Shakespeare are the Study of Writers and Their Works and the History of Foreign Drama. The students are taught (and they themselves also recognize) that as tomorrow's theater professionals, they must have sufficient knowledge of Shakespeare no matter what job they take up, whether as writer, director, actor, or stage designer. Since Shakespearean works have been universally regarded as the greatest achievement of world theater, knowledge of his plays should be a basic accomplishment in their training.

Shakespeare has been the most frequently selected dissertation topic of graduate students, especially those of dramatic literature departments in major drama institutes. For example, just after the collapse of the Gang of Four and the end of the Cultural Revolution, the students of the Department of Dramatic Literature at Shanghai Drama Institute set off an upsurge in the study of Shakespeare, writing many dissertations on the playwright. One of the titles was "On the Relationship between Renaissance and Enlightenment Drama." In it the student highly admired Shakespeare's achievement and criticized the attitude of the Gang of Four towards Shakespeare and Western culture. Another student chose *Othello* as his topic. By analyzing of the social and historical context of the play, he came to the conclusion that Shakespeare's plays are indeed a mirror of social life, profoundly instructing and pleasing us at the same time.[15]

By using Shakespeare's plays in the teaching of directing, acting, and stage design, instructors contribute to the improvement of their students' ability to analyze and appreciate dramatic works. At the Shanghai Drama Institute, for example, one-third of its graduation performances in the last three decades have been Shakespeare's plays. Many more excerpts from Shakespeare's plays are used in teaching demonstrations. The Central Drama Academy also heavily uses Shakespeare's plays for practice and graduation performances. Many of them draw large audiences, such as *Macbeth* in 1981 and *The Tempest* in 1982. A directing class for advanced studies at the Shanghai Drama Institute used *King Lear* for its teaching practice in 1980, and at the Shanghai Drama Institute a teacher asked every student in his class to make his or her own set design for *King Lear*. Then they discussed and commented on each design model, finally choosing the best one. In 1984 the class of stage design of the Central Drama Academy jointly created a set design for *Hamlet* with extraordinary results. Both teacher and students felt that using Shakespeare's work was the best way to teach the practice of stage design because his plays allowed a wide scope for imagination and creativity.[16]

Many film stars and celebrated actors owe their achievements to their training in Shakespeare as students. Zhu Yang Ping, a television star, is noted for his successful performance in a film series entitled *Wu Song*. According to Zhu, his performing skill comes mainly from his training at the Shanghai Drama Institute, particularly from acting practice in Shakespeare plays. In a program of optional acting practice, he chose the fifth act of *Othello* because of its difficulty. Through much effort, in the end he portrayed the heroic Moor's complex character on the stage, greatly enhancing his acting skill.[17]

Similar to this story is the experience of the well-known actor Zhu Yi, who took the role of Othello in a successful production by the Guangdong Drama Company at the Guangdong Art Festival in 1984. Early in the 1960s, when Zhu Yi studied at the Shanghai Drama Institute, he became an admirer of Shakespeare after attending a course, showing a special interest in *Othello,* and fostering an aspiration to portray the title role someday on the stage. To achieve his goal he grasped every opportunity to gain more background. When a Russian film version of *Othello* was shown, he saw it again and again, more than ten performances altogether. One day, taking some food with him, he even stayed in the cinema all day to see four performances back to back. His ambition was disrupted by the Cultural Revolution, but twenty years later his goal at last came true with the Guangdong Drama Company production.

It is hard to calculate the widespread and profound influence of Shakespeare on modern Chinese theater. Every expression of interest in Shakespeare in theatrical activity is interpreted as an unambiguous sign of theatrical advancement. Moreover, Shakespearean dramatic ideas have been prevalent in contemporary Chinese theatrical circles, affecting both stage representation and dramatic criticism. In theatrical circles the highest measure of a director's artistic level is whether or not he can direct a Shakespearean play. Consequently almost all of the famous directors in contemporary China have experience in this type of directing. For instance, the country's most authoritative director and theatrical artist, Huang Zuo Lin, who started his profession soon after finishing his Shakespeare studies at Cambridge, has directed numerous Shakespearean plays in his long stage career. Ying

Ruo Cheng, the famous director and actor of the Beijing People's Art Theater, is noted for his production of *Measure for Measure* and his translations of several of Shakespeare's plays. Many other celebrated names are also associated with Shakespeare. Zhang Qi Hong of the China Youth Drama Theater has directed many of Shakespeare's plays, including a very influential production of *The Merchant of Venice*. Shanghai Youth Spoken Drama Troupe's Hu Wei Min directed *Romeo and Juliet, Antony and Cleopatra,* and the beautiful Shaoxing opera version of *Twelfth Night*. Nearly all of the directors working in state-level drama companies have had some experience in presenting Shakespeare's plays. For instance, Yang Zong Jing of the Central Experimental Drama Theater once directed a production of *The Merry Wives of Windsor* and the director of the China Railways Drama Troupe, Cheng Ping, guided a stirring *Othello*. Chinese actors and actresses consider it a great honor to act in Shakespeare's plays, so most of the best-known performers have acted in Shakespearean productions.

In today's China Shakespeare's art has been commonly accepted as a fundamental principle of dramatic criticism, particularly since the end of the Cultural Revolution. In the 1960s and during the Cultural Revolution, so-called class-struggle theory was the only safe principle in literary and dramatic criticism, which made all literary and dramatic works material for political propaganda. When this period ended, Shakespeare became especially valued by the theatrical profession and was used as the authoritative critical standard in every aspect of dramatic criticism. In the middle of the 1980s a lively discussion ensued in theatrical circles about the crucial problem of dramatic creation at that time. Some critics thought that most of the dramatic works created in that period failed to express the true feelings and emotions of human nature and still exhibited an inclination to portray the characters as political types. Yet other critics held that the major problem was the lack of a philosophy of life in the plays. It is obvious that both approaches viewed the problem from the standpoint of Shakespeare's art.[18]

It is quite understandable why Shakespeare has permeated the education of contemporary China since knowledge of his works is interpreted as evidence of cultural maturity and advancement by the Chinese, even though China has its own splendid civilization. A section on European Renaissance in the world history textbook used in junior middle schools introduces Shakespeare as one of the greatest figures of the Renaissance. An account of his life and theatrical achievement is given and the titles of his popular plays mentioned. Generally speaking, traditional Chinese literature, particularly poetry, and the works of modern Chinese writers have remained at the center of the language and literature program in the curriculum of elementary and secondary schools because Chinese is a difficult language and it takes a long time to learn it. Yet a few outstanding Western writers have been carefully selected to give impressionable Chinese pupils of middle school age a taste of Western culture. The names on such a list change according to the political climate, but Shakespeare has occupied a stable place on it. His plays in translation are required reading in senior middle school classes: *The Merchant of Venice* is included in the syllabus of the second grade of senior middle schools. This means that each year more than five million Chinese teenagers study the popular Shakespearean comedy. As a rule the teacher provides the student with additional knowledge about Shakespeare's life and major achievements and the student then shows a greater enthusiasm for reading more of Shakespeare's plays. A teacher at the Fourth Middle School in Beijing who was my student when I taught at the Beijing Open University told me that her students sometimes even asked her to recommend particular Shakespearean tragedies, for they were already familiar with the titles of the great tragedies through newspapers and television. While doubting whether the students could understand them, she nevertheless recommended *Hamlet, King Lear,* and *Macbeth.* She said that her students seemed able to grasp the major themes of the tragedies, although it was a little difficult for them to analyze deeply the characters and historical context.[19] To ensure the quality of the teaching of Shakespeare in middle school, the State Education Commission makes the knowledge of his life and works an item in the qualification examination for those teaching language and literature. The examination is designed for those who have not obtained a bachelor of arts degree in higher education, for all the language and literature degree holders have already taken a Shakespeare course in order to graduate.

In Chinese universities and colleges Shakespeare has been taught more seriously. In the Chinese, English, foreign language, and language and literature departments of most national and provincial universities Shakespeare is a required course. The students of a Chinese department or a language and literature department will be trained as writers, editors, critics, or scholars undertaking research on language and literature (mainly Chinese language and literature). Nevertheless higher-education authorities clearly recognize that graduates cannot be competent in their jobs in the near future without an adequate knowledge of Western literature, particularly that of Shakespeare. Students must not isolate themselves from the outside world and the cultural reality of contemporary China, for Western culture is so prevalent in China that nobody can ignore its existence and influence. Thus a one-year Western literature course in which Shakespeare occupies the longest section is arranged for the students. During their last year students are offered an optional course on Shakespeare in which they learn more of the English dramatist and his works. In most cases this elective becomes a required course because the students always show immense enthusiasm for Shakespeare and none want to miss it. In 1988 Professor Meng Xian Qiang, the general secretary of the Shakespeare Society of Jilin province, told me that when he offered an optional Shakespeare course in the Chinese Department at Northeast Teachers' University, all of the students of the fourth year enrolled in it. By contrast, only one-third of the students chose the department's optional course on traditional Chinese drama. Professor Meng even felt a little guilty when the professor who taught the traditional drama course half-jokingly said to him, "Please tell Shakespeare not to try to lure the students away from my course. I don't understand these young people. They should pay special attention to our own cultural tradition because they'll teach and research Chinese literature rather than Western literature. Why do they show such an interest in Western literature and culture?" Both Professor Meng and I understood that although the professor's complaint was a fact that no one could deny, it was also a trend that no one could reverse. So Professor Meng gave a sophisticated answer: "I think Shakespeare can probably provide one more way for the students to approach traditional Chinese drama."[20]

My own teaching experience repeats this story. When I offered an optional Shakespeare program (an important section of my course on comparative literature) for fourth-year students in the Department of Language and Literature at Beijing Language Institute, all the students enrolled in my program and showed an extraordinary enthusiasm for the subject matter. During the program I organized a seminar to discuss the character of Hamlet. I expected poor results because I knew that Chinese students had been trained as stereotyped thinkers, influenced by both conventional culture and Marxism-Maoism, even though there had been a strong call for reform in the education system since the 1980s. Yet the discussion turned out to be successful, full of the original views and independent thoughts of my students. Almost every participant described his or her own Hamlet. Their understanding of the hero was so often associated with the social reality of contemporary China that I had to guide the discussion carefully through the delicate political issues because it turned out to be impossible to confine the seminar to a purely literary discussion.

Compared to the language and literature departments the English or foreign language departments of Chinese universities emphasize Shakespeare even more because such knowledge will directly concern the future of the students. Even if the graduates do not undertake literary teaching or research work, they still should possess some basic knowledge of the great writer to avoid embarrassment when in social contact with Westerners. Some departments offer a course on Western literature in translation that features Shakespeare. It aims to give students some general knowledge of Western literature, especially English, French, and German literature. In most departments, however, Shakespeare is taught directly in English by either Chinese professors or foreign experts from Britain, America, or other English-speaking countries. Courses in the departments of key national and provincial universities are normally undertaken by foreign instructors simply because the universities can afford it. At the beginning of their work these teachers may not appreciate the instructional style of their Chinese colleagues or the learning method of their students, although they have absolute freedom to offer their courses in any way they like. The Canadian professor Edward Berry published an account of his interesting experience in teaching Shakespeare in a provincial university in China in 1987. He described both his achievements and problems in his teaching and expressed his concern about the possible political influence upon Shakespeare studies in China.[21]

Generally, if the course is taught by a foreign teacher, it will center on individual plays. If a Chinese scholar offers the course, he will tend to concentrate on wider topics such as Shakespeare's life, the social and historical background of Shakespearean plays, the ideology in Shakespeare, the aesthetics of Shakespeare, Shakespearean criticism, and so forth. Many Chinese critics and scholars turned away from textual research in the 1980s for two reasons: they grew weary of traditional pedantic textual criticism and they came to they believe that it would be more profitable to encompass large issues within the whole corpus of literary criticism and research.

This trend has inevitably affected both Shakespeare teaching and Shakespearean studies in contemporary China. In art institutes and colleges, for example, Shakespeare has been an indispensable part of the curriculum because knowledge of Shakespeare's art is seen to be not only an important intellectual accomplishment for a modern artist but also a productive inspiration for many sorts of artistic creations. Thus in all the national music institutions, fine arts institutes, dancing colleges, film institutes, broadcasting institutes, and in most provincial art colleges, Shakespeare is taught as either a required or an optional course. Shakespeare's reputation even attracts students who study science and technology. Most national universities offer numerous elective courses to all students, no matter what their area of study, because the higher-education authorities encourage them to have a wide range of knowledge. Among these courses Shakespeare has been one of the most popular, drawing many students from the faculties of science and technology who recognize that Shakespeare is an essential part of the intellectual baggage of an educated person in modern society.

After the academic degree system was resumed by the Chinese government in 1978, Shakespeare was the first Western literature speciality that the State Education Commission approved for masters' and doctoral degrees. At first only a few respected Shakespearean scholars were entitled to enroll postgraduate students, owing to the high academic standards set up by the commission. Doctoral students in Shakespeare Studies were recruited by Professor Cheng Jia at Nanjing University, Professor Sun Jia Xiu at the Central Drama Academy, and Professor Wang Zuo Liang at Beijing Foreign Studies University. Masters of art students were found by Professors Zhang Jun Chuan at Hangzhou University, Zhang Si Yang at Jilin University, and Shui Tian Tong at Lan Zhou University, among others.[22] Since the middle of the 1980s increasing numbers of Chinese scholars have been entitled to offer upper-level programs in Shakespearean studies. In recent years almost all of the national universities and most provincial universities enroll postgraduate students in Shakespeare for a three-year research course.

Shakespeare has also become part of the curriculum of Chinese adult education. Each year about six hundred thousand people study in evening colleges and television universities (similar to the Open University in Britain). Shakespeare is an important course on the syllabus for the language and literature major in all these adult education institutions. One of the examination questions for the students of the National Television University was "How do you interpret the character of Hamlet?" According to Professor Tao De Zhen at Beijing Teacher's University, who was in charge of the university's program, the students' understanding of this question was even deeper than that of the undergraduates in universities because most of them were in their thirties or forties and had seen more of the world.[23] A student who has no time to enroll in an adult education course can still obtain a degree by taking the State's self-education examination. Each year several million people take this examination. Those who intend to get a degree in Chinese language and literature must learn, on their own, some knowledge of Shakespeare, who forms an important part of the examination.

The impact of Shakespeare upon Chinese education can also be seen in the number of Shakespeare productions staged by students at universities and institutions. In the 1980s many of these plays were presented in English by the students of English departments. These performances served a double purpose: they enhanced the students' mastery of the English language and gave all of them a taste of English culture. In November 1980, for example, the students of the English Department at Shanghai Foreign Language Institute presented *A Midsummer Night's Dream* in English, under the direction of an American scholar, giving five performances altogether. On 22 April 1985, to commemorate the 421st anniversary of Shakespeare's birth, the drama group of the English Department at Fudan University performed acts 4 and 5 of *The Merchant of Venice* at the celebration organized by the Shakespeare Association of China. The same group also presented *Much Ado About Nothing* in English at the University Hall during the Inaugural Chinese Shakespeare Festival in April 1986 (not included in the program of the festival). The student performances of Shakespeare's plays in Chinese have been even better received by audiences. In April 1986 the Student Drama Society of the Chinese Department at Nanjing University presented *The Taming of the Shrew*, which received much acclaim from both students and community. Generally speaking, as amateur theatrical activities, the campus Shakespeare productions by Chinese students are not good enough for commercial performances, compared with those of British students. Some British campus Shakespeare productions have impressed me with their skillful performances, bright styles, and original interpretations, much like a production of *Henry V* presented by Southampton University Players at the Nuffield Theater on 17 January 1989 and a production of *A Midsummer Night's Dream* by the Southampton University Theater Group on 7 March 1992. To me these performances were by no means inferior to some professional performances. Admittedly only a few Chinese student drama companies manage to demonstrate their potential when they present a Shakespearean play on a formal occasion. For instance, a very good student drama group, the North China Drama Society of Beijing Teacher's University, presented, at the same time, an all-women version of *Twelfth Night* and *Timon of Athens* at the Inaugural Chinese Shakespeare Festival in April 1986. The performances were satisfying and commonly praised by the audience and theatrical circles. The players, like those of other student drama groups, used a refined classical style, whereas their British counterparts tend to combine high classical standards with a challenging contemporary approach to Shakespeare.

In China Shakespeare's works are enjoyed not only as theater but also as many other forms of entertainment. Ballet has been regarded as a "highbrow" artform in China and serves as one of the main forms of entertainment in big cities. In the 1980s a version of *Romeo and Juliet* was frequently performed as a ballet in China. For example, in October 1984, to celebrate the thirty-fifth anniversary of the founding of the People's Republic of China, the Shanghai Ballet Company presented *Romeo and Juliet* in Shanghai, with Romeo acted by the famous ballet dancer Shi Hui and Juliet by the famous dancer Wang Qi Feng. In September 1990, at the festival of the Eleventh Asian Games in Beijing, the opening program was a ballet of *Romeo and Juliet* performed by the Central Ballet Company. About five hundred million Chinese people saw it on television.[24]

In recent years some Chinese opera troupes have tried to adapt Shakespeare plays into opera. Opera troupes are those performing companies presenting musical plays in a Western style that is mixed with Chinese folk songs or modern compositions. Early in April 1986, when I gave a talk at a conference in Beijing, a director of the Central Opera Theater who showed an interest in my topic, which was about the relationship between changing artistic taste and the staging of Shakespeare in contemporary China, told me that someday he hoped to adapt Shakespeare's plays into opera. His wish apparently came true, for I read in a major Chinese daily newspaper in early January 1992 that the Central Opera Theater had just presented *The Taming of the Shrew* in Beijing and had received much acclaim from the audience and the cultural circles of the capital. The paper quoted the Minister of Culture as saying that the performance was fascinating. He believed that Shakespeare's humanism was still of great importance to today's China and was glad that Chinese theatrical artists had tried to interpret Shakespeare from their own perspectives but had not rigidly adhered to the text.[25] One of Shakespeare's plays was even presented as a puppet show by Chinese puppeteers. On 23 April 1986 the Shanghai Puppet Play Company presented a performance of *The Twin Brother and Sister* (*Twelfth Night*) that was appreciated by the audience, particularly the children.

As modern means of communication and forms of entertainment, films and television have played an increasingly important role in Chinese cultural life. Both are very effective channels through which Shakespeare exerts his influence on Chinese culture. The earliest Shakespeare film that was screened throughout the country was Laurence Olivier's *Hamlet*, which electrified thousands of Chinese audiences. I can still clearly recall how shocked I was by the ghost scene and how much the solemn atmosphere of the film moved me when I first saw it thirty years ago. The film was excellently dubbed with two attractive titles: *The Ghost Travels West* (part 1) and *The Revenge of the Prince* (part 2). In the 1960s more Shakespearean films were shown in China, including several Russian productions of *Othello, Twelfth Night,* and *Romeo and Juliet.* In the 1980s Shakespeare's plays began to appear on the Chinese television screen, when most families owned a set. At first, in April 1986, the Central Television Station dubbed and broadcast a BBC version of *Romeo and Juliet* under the supervision of the country's most respected Shakespeare scholar, Professor Sun Jia Xiu of the Central Drama Academy. The BBC's *The Tempest* and *Henry IV* (both parts) followed in the latter half of the year. Their *Julius Caesar* was broadcast in 1987, with more plays in preparation. Performances of Shakespeare's plays in theaters and at special occasions were also frequently telecast live. Of all the media, television has made the greatest contribution to the popularity of Shakespeare in China because there are probably more than six hundred million viewers in the country, according to official statistics.[26]

As one of the major social media, radio broadcasting in China still has a great many listeners. In April 1986 the Shanghai People's Broadcasting Station broadcast a four-part radio production of *Macbeth,* characterized by vivid monologues and dialogues, realistic sound effects, and rich music. The station received many letters from listeners showing their great interest in the play.[27] Later that year, on 3 December 1986, the Shanghai People's Broadcasting Station produced *A Midsummer Night's Dream* in four parts, under the direction of the famous stage artist Huang Zuo Lin.

An especially ambitious project to adapt all thirty-seven of Shakespeare's plays into a series of radio programs was undertaken by the directors and producers of Jilin People's Broadcasting Station in 1988. The Shakespeare Society of Jilin province, as well as many well-known dubbing actors and actresses from the state-run Changchun Film Studio, helped to produce the plays. The general title of the program was "Stories and Scenes from Shakespeare's Plays," and it comprised forty-two episodes (thirty-seven plays plus a several-part general introduction to Shakespeare). Each episode included a short summary of the plot and some of the best scenes or passages from the play. The program was broadcast once a week and lasted almost an entire year. According to a local newspaper, the program has been rebroadcast three times since 1988.[28] Highly praised by both Chinese scholars and radio listeners, the series was an easy and convenient way to introduce Shakespeare's dramatic treasures to the public.

Another response to the increasing demand of the Chinese for Shakespeare was the Chinese Phonograph and Tape Company's 1986 production of "The Highlights of Shakespeare's Best-known Plays" in two tapes, which selected passages, dialogues, and monologues from some of Shakespeare's most famous plays. Several respected Chinese actors such as Sun Dao Lin, Qiao Zhen, Qiao Qi, and Zhu Yi participated in the recording.

Shakespeare also has found his place in the musical world of the Chinese. In 1960 the Chinese Music Publishing House published *A Collection of the Best-known Foreign Songs,* which included two songs from Shakespeare: "Cuckoo" (the song of "Spring" at the end of *Love's Labor's Lost*) by British composer Thomas Arne and "Hark, Hark! the Lark" (*Cymbeline* 2.2) by Schubert. During the dark years of the Cultural Revolution the songs of this collection secretly spread far and wide among middle school graduates who were forced to leave cities and work in the countryside.

It is hard for Westerners to realize the high degree of prestige that Shakespeare enjoys in China's literary and artistic circles. References to Shakespeare by Chinese writers and artists are common anywhere and at any time. For example, in a conference on poetic creation in China, the famous Chinese poet Ai Qing said, "As for Shakespeare, he is such a writer that he cannot write without thinking in terms of images. His works radiate with the eternal light of imagination."[29] And on the evening of 5 May 1990 a program on the Central Television Station featured a popular singer, Cheng Fang Yuan. Miss Cheng was asked many questions about her career, private life, and hobbies. Asked who her favorite writer was, she named Shakespeare. Then she told the interviewer that she was particularly interested in Shakespeare's representation of the psychology of women.[30]

Shakespeare is also admired by Chinese painters. To show his great esteem for Shakespeare, the famous painter Cao Wen Han created, in 1983, an engraved portrait of Shakespeare against a setting of the fencing scene in *Hamlet* that was printed on the front covers of many Shakespeare journals in China and Japan. In his article discussing the creation of the portrait, Cao said:

> As a Chinese painter I have admired Shakespeare for a long time. Shakespeare provides precious nourishment for my mind. I have obtained great inspiration and artistic pleasure from his works. It is not important whether the portrait is successful or not. What really matters is that it demonstrates the active participation of Chinese painters in the Shake-

speare industry of China although the participation is not as noticeable as that of literary critics. It also shows clearly how widespread and popular Shakespeare's influence upon Chinese culture is.[31]

The high prestige that Shakespeare enjoys among Chinese intellectuals can also be observed by the number of organized events. For example, on the evening of 31 December 1987, a New Year celebration sponsored by Beijing literary and artistic circles was televised live by the Central Television Station to viewers throughout the country. Watching the program with my family, I saw many well-known writers, directors, actors, film producers, and pop stars appear on the screen, talking about their work in the past year or presenting impromptu performances. The most interesting item in the celebration was a special "program" arranged at the end of the party. The host told all the participants that he felt greatly honored to introduce a distinguished guest to them. The guest would be familiar to all of them, he said, although they had never met him before. No sooner had the guest come on when I recognized that he was "Shakespeare," impersonated by a Chinese actor. After he was greeted with warm applause, "Shakespeare" addressed his Chinese counterparts, as well as the television audience. He said that there was no national boundary to literature and art: both Western and Eastern cultures were the common treasure of humanity. He expressed his admiration for the long-standing Chinese culture. He told the Chinese writers and artists that he was very pleased to know that they were creating their new literature and art while showing their interest in Western literature and art. It looked as if "Shakespeare" knew contemporary Chinese literature and art very well because he congratulated his Chinese counterparts on their achievements during the past year, which, he believed, demonstrated the vigorous spirit of the times. While this novel device apparently was used to enliven the atmosphere of the celebration, something unusual was behind it. If the organizers of the celebration had followed the usual routine, they would have invited a high-ranking party or government official in charge of cultural establishments to attend the occasion and comment on the year's artistic achievement. At the very least an actor impersonating a famous classical writer should have been invited to address his successors. It sounded as though the organizers considered Shakespeare the most authoritative person to evaluate the annual achievement of writers and artists, which provides strong evidence that Shakespeare has been regarded as the god of art by Chinese writers and artists.

The widespread and profound influence of Shakespeare, direct or indirect, affects many genres of creativity, among them fiction, poetry, film, and television. A few examples will suffice to show this phenomenon. The creation of the novel in contemporary China has been considered by Chinese critics as the top achievement of what they call the "Literature of the New Period" (1978–88). Compared to the classical and modern Chinese novel, the novel of this period shows quite a different tendency. As some critics have pointed out, most novelists writing in this period, obviously dissatisfied with the moralistic tone of classical Chinese literature and the social class orientation of the socialist literature period (1949–78), tried to portray complex characters with multiple qualities. They paid special attention to psychological description in their works and tended to discuss philosophical issues through their characters.[32] These characteristics show the clear influence of Shakespeare because his literary techniques have been so highly regarded and followed by Chinese novelists. Many Chinese novelists have discussed how they have benefited from Shakespeare's techniques, especially his characterization and psychological description.[33] Shakespeare's most important impact on the novel, however, is the representation of the central theme. Almost all the novels written during this time concentrate on delineating general human nature and the celebration of individuality instead of reflecting class struggle and proletarian revolution, which were the central themes of Chinese literature from 1949 to 1978. A typical novel representing the new theme is Zhang Xin Xin's *Man Oh Man* (*Ren A Ren*).

The poets of contemporary China have also benefited from Shakespeare, who see him as one of the greatest poets in the world and who have been eagerly following his unique poetic style and techniques. The poetry created in the New Literature period differs from that of both classical Chinese poetry and the socialist literature period. The new poems represent the anxiety, enthusiasm, and voice of the times, exhibiting an apparent influence of Shakespearean poetic style. It is evident that many poets tend to adopt the explicit, straightforward, and bold poetic representation associated with Shakespeare. The traditional restrained and refined poetic style seems to be out of favor, thus the new poetry lacks its gentleness, delicacy, and gracefulness. The famous young poet and critic Xu Jing has said that to Chinese poetic circles Shakespeare was like a breath of fresh air. In his case Shakespeare's poems, full of vitality, enthusiasm, and imagination, had been the model for his poetic creativity.[34] As for imagery, contemporary Chinese poets again seem to prefer the Shakespearean style to that of traditional Chinese drama and poetry. In the poems of famous young poets such as Bei Dao, Mang Ke, Xu

Jin Ya, and Wang Xiao Ni, the poetic images range widely and are no longer limited to a narrow number of traditional images. The images in their works are often gigantic, vigorous, disruptive, and even odd, but sometimes they are very wonderful and witty. And following another Shakespearean technique, the poets began to use symbolism to illustrate abstract concepts such as political power, democracy, ambition, faith, love, and youthfulness, which are rarely found in traditional drama and poetry.

Sensitive to the changes in both politics, literature, and art, movies and television are important media in China's cultural life. Here too Shakespeare's influence has been felt in the last decade. Many films reflecting social life during the Cultural Revolution lacked the happy endings of traditional Chinese drama or "bright endings" of socialist literature, a tendency no doubt affected by Shakespeare's tragic concept. In *A Narrow Lane* (1985) by Shanghai Film Studio, a young man and a girl suffer from the turbulence of the Cultural Revolution. The girl disguises herself as a boy to avoid being bullied because her parents are thought to be counterrevolutionaries. The two help and care for each other like real brothers, and the young man becomes aware of the identity of the girl only very late in the story. Nevertheless the film ends without a love scene and the subsequent marriage of the hero and heroine. Assuming that the audience must expect a happy ending, the director makes an apology at the end of the film for his unusual treatment. He says that events in real life do not always result in happy endings and it would be better if the audience could invent different endings on its own.

The influence of Shakespeare on the characterization of contemporary films is more evident than the presence of happy endings, however. The characters cannot be simply classified by any fixed moral or political standards and possess the varied personalities one would find in real life. Other techniques such as the use of the dual nature and psychological description make many of the characters seem Shakespearean. An example can be found in *The Demon and the Angel*, made by the Zhu Jiang Film Studio in 1988. The chief character in the film is a burglar who one day meets a young woman studying at a fine arts college and immediately falls in love with her. She is also attracted to him by his sophisticated manner. From that point on the man cannot decide if he should leave his criminal life and live with her or continue his evil ways to get more money; inevitably he suffers from a deep inner conflict. At the end of the film the man is sent to prison and the woman is forced to work on a remote island. The delineation of the chief character's inner world strongly suggests the influence of Macbeth, although the two heroes are driven by different passions. The portrayal of a character's dual nature is rarely found in earlier Chinese literature, including traditional Chinese drama, because it might arouse an ambiguous moral response that would run counter to the principles of both traditional and socialist Chinese literature.

Since the 1980s it has been fashionable for Chinese films to discuss philosophical questions, but one can often detect a Shakespearean style in the dialogues. For example, at the beginning of *The Demon and the Angel,* when the young man first meets the girl at an underground railway station, he talks on and on about the meaning of life in a flow of eloquence that sounds as though a Shakespearean character is reciting a lengthy monologue. In other cases the screen writers sometimes simply use direct quotations from Shakespeare's plays. In *The Unbridled Passions,* produced by the Zhu Jiang Film Studio in 1989, when the heroine tries to commit suicide on the seashore after being raped by her boyfriend's father, she hears a deep voice from behind the rocks reciting,

> To be, or not to be—that is the question;
> Whether 'tis nobler in the mind to suffer
> The slings and arrows of outrageous fortune,
> Or to take arms against a sea of troubles,
> And by opposing, end them. To die, to sleep—
> No more . . .
>
> (*Hamlet* 3.1.55–60)

Then the speaker, a handsome young man who is the hero of the film, comes up to comfort her. He has been wronged, too. They decide to seek their interest and happiness together, but like Edmund and other bastards in Shakespeare's plays, they try to fight fire with fire, which at last brings about their tragic end. Generally speaking, this tendency to raise philosophic issues in the films is welcomed by Chinese audiences, but sometimes the screenwriters do not use this technique as naturally and properly as Shakespeare does, and the philosophical dialogue seems a little dull and farfetched.

Shakespeare's growing reputation in Chinese academic circles stems partly from the expansion of Shakespeare studies as an academic specialization. As I mentioned in chapter 3, numerous articles and books dealing with Shakespeare have been published since the 1980s, and, as I stated earlier in this chapter, there is also a massive and well-qualified team of Shakespearean scholars throughout the country. In addition, a nationwide Shakespeare organization—the Shakespeare Association of China—was founded in 1984 by well-known Shakespeare scholars, translators, and directors, with the distinguished Chinese dramatist Cao Yu as president and the Shanghai Drama Institute as its headquarters. Since then other provincial Shakespeare associations have been established. The Shakespeare Society of Jilin Province was formed in 1985, with Professor Zhang Si Yang of Jilin University as president; among its many activities were an exhibition of Shakespeare's life and works, the translation of a documentary film, *Shakespeare's Hometown*, and other Shakespeare television films, and the production of Shakespeare radio plays. In 1989 the Shakespeare scholars in Tianjing, the third biggest city in China, founded the Shakespeare Association of Tianjing city. A famous scholar in foreign literary studies, Professor Zhu Wei Zhi, was elected president. In the same year Wuhan Shakespeare Center was founded by Shakespeare scholars in Wuhan city, with Professor Yuan Kun as president. With a long tradition of Shakespeare studies, Zhejiang province also created its own Shakespeare association in 1993. Specific Shakespeare research institutions have also been set up. In 1985 the Central Drama Academy created a Shakespeare Center to improve the quality of Shakespeare studies and collect reference material relating to Shakespearean theater and research. In the same year Fudan University founded a Shakespeare library that would serve Shakespearean research by collecting reference material in both English and Chinese. Shakespeare Research Center of Beijing University appeared in 1993, and Professor Gu Zheng Kun was appointed as its director. More recently founded is the Shakespeare Research Center at Northeast Normal University in Jilin province, with Professor Meng Xian Qiang as director.

Shakespeare journals are also published in China, including *Shakespeare Studies* by the Shakespeare Association of China, *Journal of the Jilin Shakespeare Society* by the Shakespeare Society of Jilin Province and *Shakespeare Studies* (in English), a journal compiled by members of the English Department at Fudan University.

Along with the recent expansion of Shakespearean studies, Shakespeare's art has been increasingly accepted by Chinese critics as a fundamental standard for literary criticism and theory. In fact, today Shakespeare's artistic method has become the primary source of inspiration for both traditional and socialist literature. In general, Shakespeare's artistic ideas have been employed by Chinese critics and scholars in every aspect of literary theory, literature criticism, and academic argument. For instance, in the early 1980s, there was an academic discussion in the field of literary theory about the standard of characterization in literature. The individualized style of character portrayal was considered the most mature characterization technique, and Shakespeare was taken as the ideal representative of this mode.[35] Professor Liu Zai Fu, the director of the Literature Institution of the Chinese Academy of Social Science and a radical and leading figure in Chinese literary circles, was often attacked by the conservative literary school, which adheres to the orthodox literary theory of Marxism-Maoism. In his influential book *The Constitution of the Nature of Literary Characters* (1986), Professor Liu deals with a variety of styles of characterization, showing an evident tendency to favor the Shakespearean mode of character portrayal. In the 1980s modern Western literary theories were introduced into China such as structuralism, poststructuralism, deconstruction, semiotics, psychological criticism, aesthetics of reception, and feminism. Yet most of them were considered only as useful knowledge and not as working theories of literary criticism. Evidently Chinese critics show more interest in the Shakespearean references related to these new literary theories than in the theories themselves. For example, Shakespeare's concern with the subconsciousness and abnormal psychology, now associated with Freudian theory, is quite often taken by Chinese critics as evidence of the need for writers to improve their representation of psychology in various forms and the standard for such representations. Ernest Jones's book on Hamlet's "Oedipus complex" particularly was discussed by Chinese critics, though they generally did not agree with the author, whose opinion was opposed to the psychological habits of the Chinese.[36] In China, Northrop Frye's anthropological criticism has always been associated with Shakespeare's works and was often used to enhance the artistic merit of Shakespeare and strengthen the authoritative position of his works as a major standard for literary criticism, rather than spur Chinese critics on to practice Frye's theory of literary criticism.[37]

Shakespeare has not only made a notable impact on Chinese education and cultural life but also been taken up in the politics of modern China. During the period of the Democratic Revolution (1911–49), Shakespeare's works were sometimes used as a powerful weapon to fight against feudal dictatorship. One example is a political event that occurred in 1915. In that year the chief warlord Yuan Shi Kai attempted to restore autocratic monarchy, which had been overthrown by the Xin Hai Revolution led by Sun Zhong Shan in 1911. After that China was ruled by the warlords. As the most powerful warlord, Yuan Shi Kai tried to usurp the state power and become a new emperor but his plot incurred the wrath of the people throughout the country. Chinese intellectuals used every practical means of propaganda to expose Yuan Shi Kai's plot. Shakespeare's plays were used by Chinese dramatists to satirize and attack the warlords' ambi-

tion. In 1916 the Yao Feng New Drama Company adapted and performed *Macbeth* in Shanghai, with the title *The Arch Usurper,* which
attacked Yuan Shi Kai by innuendo. In the same year, in Shanghai's
Qian Kun Theater, the Dao Drama Troupe presented a production
of *Hamlet,* using the title of *The Treacherous Lord Who Disturbs the
Country.* The play was also intended to expose Yuan Shi Kai's plan
to restore autocratic monarchy. But the most sensational political
event at that time was caused by the performance of *Macbeth* by the
Min Meng Drama Company in Shanghai. In the play the famous
actor Gu Wu Wei fiercely condemned monarchy, attacking Yuan Shi
Kai with both freezing irony and burning satire and bringing the
house down. Yuan Shi Kai flew into a rage when he was informed
of the performance, giving an order to have the actor arrested. Gu
Wu Wei was soon taken to the Shanghai Garrison Headquarters,
accused of disturbing the peace and agitating people under the pretext
of a performance. The Garrison Headquarters sentenced Gu to death
without trial. Fortunately the sudden downfall and death of Yuan
Shi Kai saved the actor from execution.[38] This political incident,
however, left an indelible impression on the Chinese democracy
movement, as well as demonstrating how Shakespeare once got involved in the politics and social progress of China.

Shakespeare's influence has even been felt in modern China's politics. The significance of many cultural activities featuring Shakespeare often goes beyond the scope of culture and takes on political
overtones. For instance, the influential Inaugural Chinese Shakespeare Festival became a political activity because it declared that
China would more strenuously put into effect its policy to absorb
Western culture and once again be part of the world's cultural life.
The attendance of both Chinese and British high-ranking officials
at the festival, together with a congratulatory letter from Margaret
Thatcher, bestowed a diplomatic significance on the festival, contributing to the improvement and reinforcement of Sino-British relationships. Another event important to international relationships and
politics was the visit of Hu Yao Bang, the general secretary of the
Chinese Communist party, to Stratford-Upon-Avon during his state
visit to the United Kingdom in June 1986. It was quite unusual for
Hu Yao Bang to visit Shakespeare's birthplace because never before
had a Chinese leader traveled to the home of a foreign writer, in
effect paying tribute to him. This trip, together with the pictures in
which he talked with local residents and tourists on the riverbank,
made front-page news with bold headlines in all the official newspapers in China. According to the reports, Hu told his English hosts
that Shakespeare belonged not only to Britain but also to the world.[39]

Obviously Hu's visit to Stratford was of political importance. His visit as leader of the Chinese Communist party and the leading figure of the reform group helped to achieve a better international image for China by declaring in effect that China would firmly carry out its "open door" policy in adopting not only the West's technology but also its cultural heritage. Personally, I do not think Hu had an extensive knowledge of Shakespeare, but his attitude towards Western culture and ideology was uniformly praised by Chinese intellectuals and strongly opposed by the powerful conservative group in the leadership—which was one of the major reasons why he was ousted from his post in 1987. His sudden death in 1989 functioned as an incident that touched off the political events on Tiananmen Square that shook the world.

In recent years Shakespeare has again become involved in political affairs in China. A nationwide political campaign to promote moral standards against the prevailing degeneration and money worship has been launched by the government since 1992. In a high-ranking meeting held at the end of 1992, Jiang Ze Min, the top leader of the government and party, used a passage from *Timon of Athens* ("Gold? Yellow, glittering, precious gold?" 4.3.26–41) to point out the harm in money worship and the importance of combating it.[40] Articles promoting the campaign, published by official newspapers, also quoted this passage.[41] Jiang Ze Min's use of Shakespeare's quotation seems not to be accidental. In fact he is a Shakespearean enthusiast and even performed in a Shakespeare production when he was young. In 1986, when he was mayor of Shanghai, he actively supported the Inaugural Chinese Shakespeare Festival, attending it with great interest.[42]

The fact that Shakespeare exists in China as a complex institutional reality can be shown by his influence on varied cultural practices and on many areas of Chinese social life. The existence of Shakespeare in Chinese life is especially noticeable in the frequent quotation of sayings, epigrams, and maxims from Shakespearean texts in publications, lectures, television and radio programs, and on many public and private occasions. It is popular to use Shakespearean quotations to enhance one's article or speech, to express an opinion or emotion, and to show erudition, which ironically brings back to the Chinese mind the compulsory use of Mao's quotations during the Cultural Revolution. Even in articles dealing with serious matters carried by official magazines or newspapers one can often find Shakespearean quotations. In 1989 an article in *People's Daily*, the most widely read newspaper in China, criticizes the new Chinese businessmen in Shakespearean terms:

Lacking the temperament to be rich, the private businessmen in contemporary China have now found themselves in a predicament as to how to deal with their wealth and social status, which can be associated with what Shakespeare describes:

He shall but bear them as the ass bears gold,
To groan and sweat under the business . . .

(*Julius Caesar* 4.1.21–22)

The incompatibility of their wealth with their personalities has resulted in an abnormal psychology for them.[43]

Shakespeare has also contributed to China's campaign against corruption in the 1980s. In 1985 a special report was carried by the local official newspaper, *Liaoyang Daily*, in which readers were told of a corrupt official who not only used his power to make money illegally but also raped several women who entreated him for help. The subtitle of the article used a quotation from Shakespeare, printed with eye-catching boldface type: "'hence shall I see / If power change purpose: what our seemers be' (*Measure for Measure* 1.3.53–54)— William Shakespeare."[44] The author had indeed used the quotation very properly because the offense of the official was similar to but more serious than that of Angelo.

Many magazines and newspapers in China have a special column that publishes well-known sayings of famous people. Shakespeare's quotations usually fill up the columns. For instance, in 1986 seven of the twelve issues of *The Youth Digest*, a very influential magazine in China with several million readers, carried Shakespearean quotations about love, life, ethics, reason, emotion, human nature, and so forth in their column entitled "The Well-Known Sayings of Eminent Persons." Due to this trend, one can see why so many books collecting "golden sayings" from Shakespeare works have been published in China in recent years, including the best-selling *Witty Remarks of Shakespeare* by Gansu People's Press in 1986 and *One Hundred Brilliant Passages from Shakespearean Works* by the Chinese External Translation Publishing Ltd in 1988.

The 1980s saw the popularity of various types of contests on television in China. One well-known national contest was the May Fourth Youth Intelligence Contest held annually by the Central Television Station in which the participants must have extensive general knowledge to win. The final usually took place in the evening of the fourth of May. In 1987 there were four contestants, ranging in age from seventeen to thirty and having different educational backgrounds. After drawing a question, Zhao Zhong Xiang, the well-known host, asked a young man, "What are the great tragedies of Shakespeare?" The young man responded to the question without

hesitation: "They are *Hamlet, King Lear, Othello,* and *Macbeth.*"
The audience congratulated him with applause and the scoreboard
recorded points for his correct answer. Watching this scene I naturally felt excited, as would any Shakespeare scholar. But what really
mattered was that a knowledge of Shakespeare was needed for the
final because the questions concerning literature and art formed only
a very small part of the whole. To me it convincingly proved the
high position of the dramatist in Chinese cultural life.

The best example of Shakespeare's combined financial and cultural
value in China might be the Bank of China's 1990 gold coin, minted
to celebrate the achievement of world culture. Five famous international figures were commemorated: Xuan Yuan Shi (the legendary
Chinese forefather who invented crop-growing and silkworm-
raising), Homer, Shakespeare, Goethe, and Edison. Obviously the
nominations came from the perspective of the Chinese, although the
influence of Homer and Goethe on Chinese culture are much less
than that of Shakespeare. As for Edison, the Chinese would benefit
from him materially rather than culturally.

Probably the most interesting example of the influence of Shakespeare on Chinese culture and social life is the use of the dramatist
in advertisements. In 1990 a local Chinese magazine (*Jilin Radio and
TV Times,* 7 February 1990, p. 4) ran an advertisement selling wedding dresses, here quoted in part:

A Wedding Dress—-the Best Choice for a Modern Bride

> Shakespeare said, Neither borrow a wedding dress from others, nor
> lend your wedding dress to others; only by wearing your own wedding
> dress can you have a happy life.
> It is really a pity that a modern bride goes to her wedding without a
> wedding dress. Changchun Fashionable Dress Factory is a state-level
> factory that specifically makes wedding dresses.

Instantly recognizable as a transformation of Polonius's famous lines
in *Hamlet,* the advertising copy took advantage of the great interest
of the Chinese for many of Shakespeare's precepts. Shakespeare
might blame the copy writer for distorting his lines, but at the same
time he might admire his resourcefulness. Here Shakespeare's cultural and commercial worth are joined to produce a cultural product
that will help to make Shakespeare an institutional reality in China.

In China Shakespeare even contributes to the formation of new
social customs. Along with rapid changes in every respect of society,
many traditional customs have become quickly outmoded. For instance, the old wedding ceremony is both overelaborate and too

costly, causing many young people to choose a simple wedding ceremony in good taste. The "tea party" wedding vogue, which began in Beijing, features a poetry reading or performance presented by the bride and groom. The love poetry from Shakespearean works is often heard at these new-style weddings, particularly sonnet 116. And in 1990 *The Youth* magazine reported that in Guangzhou city it was a fashion for guests to present the *Complete Works of Shakespeare* (in translation, eleven volumes, published by the People's Literature Press) to the bride and groom as a wedding gift instead of giving them money.[45] This information must have heartened Chinese scholars and cultural workers because Guangzhou has long been regarded as an area with a strong climate of commercialism and materialism.

From this brief survey of the widespread and profound influence of Shakespeare on Chinese culture and the existence of a culturally produced "Shakespeare phenomenon" in Chinese life, we can see that Shakespeare has been wholeheartedly accepted by the Chinese and that he functions as a major and indispensable figure in the cultural landscape of China. Considering that the Chinese cultural tradition differs completely from that of the West, Shakespeare's reception in China has furnished fresh evidence indicating his universal appeal and importance as a writer "not of an age but for all time," as Ben Jonson wrote. Yet because the worldwide appreciation of Shakespeare by no means implies that every nation approaches Shakespeare in the same way and enjoys his works for the same reason, I shall, in the next chapter, deal with the general perspective of the Chinese on Shakespeare and try to describe a Chinese vision of the dramatist.

6

The Chinese Vision of Shakespeare: Confucianism, Marxism, and Humanism

FOREIGN countries have different visions of Shakespeare, and every nation has its own cultural and social perspectives by which it views the dramatist. The reception of Shakespeare in China can be seen as proof of such an assumption because of the striking discrepancy between Chinese and Western cultures. Whenever a play is transferred to a foreign culture, the cultural discrepancy often is double-sided in that it could be a barrier to an understanding of the play or reveal elements that other societies have never seen before. In China Shakespeare is considered fortunate because his acceptance by and large has not presented difficulties. We should bear in mind too that Shakespeare's introduction into China coincided with the assimilation of Western culture into Chinese culture. Modern Chinese culture (called "new culture" in China) is actually a mixture of Western and traditional Chinese cultures, with the former often considered more prestigious than the latter, as I discussed at the beginning of chapter 5. We should also remember that China's modern education system was established with the help of Western missionaries and intellectuals, which resulted in a Western orientation. Accordingly, most educated Chinese are well acquainted with Western civilization, and even the poorly educated and illiterate Chinese acquire a sense of Western culture through today's media. Thus we can assume that Shakespeare's plays should not be alien to most people since they will have no trouble understanding their cultural context and references.

This view suggests that the Chinese approach Shakespeare in a way similar to that of Westerners. Some Shakespeare scholars indeed maintain that the Chinese, affected by the progressive Westernization of their society, interpret Shakespeare's works in the light of Western values, conceptions, and beliefs instead of Chinese ideology and institutions.[1] Such an opinion can be supported by the superficial tendency of the Chinese Shakespeare industry in China to pay attention only to what their Western counterparts have emphasized.

Yet I would argue that the actual perspective of the Chinese on Shakespeare is far from a unified West-oriented vision. On the contrary, it is, from a materialist position, a multiple, complex, and variable perspective, mingled with varied and diverse ideologies and tastes shaped by the cultural, social, and historical contexts of modern and contemporary China. First, traditional Chinese culture, which is centered on Confucianism, is still a large presence in the social and cultural practices of the Chinese today, even though it has lost its dominant position of past centuries. It has undoubtedly greatly affected the interpretation of Shakespeare by the Chinese. Second, the political power struggles that have run through the history of modern China have also affected Chinese cultural life. Marxism, which has been the dominant ideology in China for more than forty years, has impacted directly and explicitly upon the response of the Chinese to Shakespeare's plays and will continue to exert its influence on the study and production of Shakespeare's plays, even if popular interest in it has subsided. Finally, humanism, a typical Western ideology, has been regarded by Chinese scholars as the core value of Shakespeare, and many Chinese people tend to view Shakespeare from its perspective. But in fact, the understanding and use of the term often exhibit a strong Chinese flavor that is affected by the changing social and political context. In this chapter, therefore, I intend first to analyze how these three important perspectives operate culturally, socially, and historically in the process of Shakespeare's assimilation into Chinese culture; second, I will present an account of the multiple perspectives of the Chinese on the dramatist in the light of cultural materialism, determining how greatly they affect the people's interpretation of Shakespeare. Third, I shall consider the different functions of these perspectives in the formation of the general Chinese vision of Shakespeare.

The first major factor that directly affects Shakespeare's reception in China is the country's long-standing cultural tradition. It is easy to find, through careful examination, that the appreciation of Shakespeare by the Chinese often shows the obvious influence of conventional Chinese ideology, especially Confucianism, aesthetic theory, and literary bias.

Founded by Confucius in the fifth century B.C. and supplemented with Taoism in the Han dynasty and Buddhism in the Song and Ming dynasties, Confucianism had been the ruling ideology in China for two thousand years until the New Cultural Movement in 1919. Since then it has been seriously criticized by Chinese revolutionaries and radical intellectuals as a spiritual shackle and an obstacle to the progress of society. When China became a socialist country in 1949,

Confucianism was claimed to be feudalistic poison and its major classics discarded from school syllabi. The increasing Westernization of modern China served as another important factor in bringing about the decline of Confucianism. Thus to many Chinese, especially young people, and some Westerners, Confucianism appeared to have been abandoned as a backward and decadent ideology. The previous discussion in chapters 3 and 5 also demonstrates the country's declining interest in Confucianism: one of the major reasons why many Chinese people do not like traditional Chinese drama is because it often comes across as a vehicle for spreading Confucian moral doctrine. Yet all these complaints are only superficial. In today's China, Confucianism still affects deeply and comprehensively the thought and behavior of the people. What the Chinese dislike and try to eliminate is just the dross of Confucianism, particularly the ethical code that was emphasized and dogmatized by politicians and scholars in the Song and Ming dynasties. Nevertheless the essence of Confucianism has been retained deep in the structure of Chinese culture and continues to function in all phases of social practice and govern the actions of the people. Even those who think they have completely extricated themselves from the influence of Confucianism sometimes still unconsciously act by its principles. For example, many radical young people eager to follow the idea of Western democracy believe that they have broken completely with conventional Chinese ideology, but the truth is that their spirit of dedication is an essential principle of Confucianism. In a sense Confucianism has become a fundamental part of the national identity of the Chinese. In recent years more and more Chinese intellectuals have recognized that the main doctrines of Confucianism, such as a strong sense of responsibility for one's family, active participation in political affairs, dedication to the country and people, and an emphasis on virtues such as altruism, modesty, and thoughtfulness could contribute to a prosperous and democratic society, especially in view of the success of Japan, which also is a country with a past history of Confucianism as its dominant ideology.

The influence of Confucianism on the Chinese reception of Shakespeare can be easily found in the reading, translation, criticism, and production of his plays in China. Chinese people quite often tend to interpret the characters and themes of Shakespeare's plays in terms of Confucian ideology. As I discussed in Part I, the doctrine of Confucianism tells us that we should first cultivate our moral character and manage our households well, then take an active part in political affairs to build a peaceful and harmonious society. In any case, one must value public and collective interests above private concerns. Accordingly, Confucian politicians are asked to have the keen political insight to perceive social problems and the courage to expose and criticize these problems. In the meantime they must not seek to profit themselves; on the contrary, they should bravely and uncompromisingly struggle with evil forces, upholding justice and reversing the downward trend of society. If necessary they should even lay down their lives to eliminate corruption and to achieve order in the country. As time has gone by these qualities have gradually become a conventional yardstick by which the Chinese judge and evaluate historical figures, particularly heroic figures. These qualities have also largely affected the creative work of Chinese writers, particularly when they express their thoughts and emotions or portray heroic and progressive characters in their works. Thus one of the main themes of Chinese poetry is the expression of the political faith and aspiration of Confucian scholars and politicians, as in the poems of Qu Yuan, Chen Zi Ang, Wang Bo, Li Bai, Du Pu, Bai Ju Yi, Liu Zong Yuan, Su Shi, and others. In Chinese fiction and drama the protagonists commonly admired and praised by the Chinese are also incarnations of the political spirit of Confucianism, such as Zhou Shun Chang in *The Story of the Honest Subject* and Yue Fei in *The Flag of Loyalty*, whom I discussed in previous chapters. I admit that some qualities found in these heroes could be difficult for today's Chinese to understand, as for example the absolute loyalty to the monarchy that was required by the later Chinese emperors to strengthen their rule. Yet the main principles of Confucian politics shown in the heroes, such as having the courage to expose and criticize social problems, actively participating in political affairs, and being dedicated to the progress and prosperity of the country remain important values to the Chinese and still deeply affect literary creation and its appreciation in modern China. It is, therefore, understandable that Chinese audiences and readers tend to interpret Shakespeare's characters from the political perspective of Confucianism.

For example, consider the character of Hamlet, which during the long history of Shakespeare criticism has been interpreted in varied and diverse ways. We can now say that the Chinese have added a "Confucian Hamlet" to these interpretations, for the Prince of Denmark, regarded by the Chinese as a Confucian hero, is often associated with the country's greatest political figures. Of all Shakespeare's heroes, Hamlet is probably the most suitable one to be qualified as a Confucian exemplar. To the Chinese, unlike Lear or Macbeth, he is, after all, morally perfect, with a noble mind. He is not limited by personal misfortune and never drifts with the tide of corruption or drags out an ignoble existence. He sees clearly and fiercely criticizes corruption in the court and the seamy side of society. In the Chinese view Hamlet also has a strong sense of political responsibility, seeing the need to fight against evil forces. As he says, "The time is out of joint, . . . I was born to set it right!" (1.5.189–90). These lines strongly echo the belief of Chinese Confucian heroes that "everybody has a share of responsibility for the fate of his country." Chinese audiences and readers often concentrate so much on the positive qualities in Hamlet's character that they ignore or forgive those weaknesses of hesitation and vacillation that are not in line with the character of a Confucian politician. What is more interesting, the Chinese tend to explain Hamlet's melancholy in the light of *youfen* (worry and anxiety), a common quality shared by all Confucian heroes and stemming from the difficult and frustrating situations they encounter. It may be that they find no way to dedicate themselves to the service of their country or to complain about the hardships of their careers, especially when they are wronged by emperors or framed by treacherous officials. They may also worry about the plight of their country. All these fears cause them to feel worried, anxious, melancholy, and even indignant. To the Chinese Hamlet's melancholy obviously derives from the tension between his moral and political ideals and the corrupt reality, and from the fact that many evil people secretly scheme against him. So to the Chinese mind, Hamlet's psychological state nearly duplicates that of a Confucian politician.

The interpretation of *Hamlet* outlined above can be easily seen in the reading, criticism, and production of the play in China. For example, early in the 1920s, when the famous dramatist Tian Han published his translation of *Hamlet,* he directly associated the play with the great Confucian politician and poet Qu Yuan in his postscript to the translation:

> As a solemn and stirring tragedy, *Hamlet* is the best of Shakespeare's great tragedies. When I read the soliloquies of Hamlet, I feel that it looks as if I are reading Qu Yuan's *Lisao*.[2]

Lisao, the masterpiece of Qu Yuan, is a long poem in which the author describes his misfortunes in the political arena and castigates the corrupt court. Expressing his great concern and anxiety about the future of his country, Qu Yuan conveys lofty social and political ideals. In Chinese history Qu Yuan has been regarded as the earliest and one of the most influential Confucian politicians and poets of all time. His *Lisao* has greatly influenced the writing of the later

Confucian writers. In identifying the Prince of Denmark with Qu Yuan, Tian Han obviously associates Hamlet with the same political ideals and principles espoused by Confucius.

This "Confucian Hamlet" interpretation has long been accepted in Shakespeare criticism in China. In the 1950s a famous Shakespeare scholar and translator, Bian Zhi Lin, published two articles dealing with the central theme of the play and the character of Hamlet. Almost all of the points he emphasizes are Confucian in principle and spirit, although some are discussed under the label of Marxism. For instance, Bian points out that one of Hamlet's finer qualities is his keen insight into serious social issues, as when he properly compares Denmark to a prison.[3] Bian highly praises Hamlet's great concern about the future and destiny of his country and his endeavor to "Shangxia er qousuo" (which roughly means to seek truth or to find a way to achieve political goals),[4] a quotation from Qu Yuan's Lisao. In his other article Bian argues that Hamlet is not a coward in evading struggle; on the contrary, he is a hero having great courage to fight with his enemy. His hesitation is not a character flaw; rather, it stems from the process of seeking truth because it takes a long time to seek the truth that will save one's country. Bian also argues that Hamlet's melancholy derives mainly from his great concern and anxiety about the future of his country (or youfen), and not from his personal passion.[5]

The discussion of Hamlet's character by Professor Zhang Si Yang, one of China's leading Shakespeare scholars, is another good way to show the influence of Confucian political ideas on the interpretation of Hamlet. Like Bian, Professor Zhang emphasizes the positive qualities in Hamlet's character, which are identical with the principles of Confucianism. For instance, he believes that Hamlet has a keen sense of the injustice and evil in life and shows great courage in combatting these evil forces; therefore the leading qualities in his character are active, positive, and dynamic, rather than passive, negative, and weak.[6] In his writings Professor Zhang pays special attention to the analysis of Hamlet's melancholy. He disagrees with the opinion that Hamlet's melancholy stems from his pessimism and nihilism, maintaining that although personal misfortune contributes to his melancholy, the real cause comes from his strong sense of political responsibility and anxiety about the time being "out of joint." Otherwise he would be temporarily at ease, waiting for the succession to the throne that his uncle had promised.[7] It is clear that Professor Zhang has also approached this issue in terms of the psychological complexes conventionally associated with Confucian politicians. He even uses special phrases that have been employed by the Chinese to describe the character of Confucian politicians, one of which is *youguoyoumin* (to be concerned about one's country and people).[8]

The Confucian interpretation of *Hamlet* has also affected the stage representations of the play. In almost all productions the main character has been treated as a hero having the usual political spirit and enthusiasm of Confucianism. For example, during the Sino-Japanese War, the State Drama School presented a production of *Hamlet* in Jiangan and Chongqing city, Sichuan province (2–7 June 1942; 9–19 December 1942), under the direction of the famous stage artist Jiao Ju Yin, with Hamlet played by Wen Xi Ying and Ophelia by Lu Shui. The production was actually an open-air performance because the players had to use a temple as their temporary theater. As it turned out, the great hall of the temple was an ideal setting for a chamber in a king's palace and gave a strong Chinese flavor to the production. The actor who played Hamlet displayed the manner and spirit of Confucian heroes and politicians, and tried to highlight Hamlet's strong sense of political duty and his heroic struggle against the gloomy and depressing atmosphere of the setting. This Confucian treatment served to encourage the Chinese people to be concerned about the future of their country and to fight against Japanese invaders.[9] Later productions of *Hamlet* in China exhibited the same tendency, stressing the "Confucian spirit" in Hamlet's character. Two of these were by the Henan Drama Company in June 1984, under Tong Shou Ze, and the Shanghai Drama Institute in July 1984, under Cheng Ming Zheng and An Zhen Ji.[10]

It is interesting to note that on the Chinese stage there is not only a "Confucian Hamlet" but also a "Hamlet's Confucius." In chapter 5, when I discussed the influence of Shakespeare on the modern Chinese theater, I pointed out the similarity between Guo Mo Ruo's *Qu Yuan* and Shakespearean tragedies. Besides the influence of *King Lear* on a particular scene of *Qu Yuan*, the treatment of Qu Yuan, the hero and great Confucian politician, bore a strong resemblance to Hamlet, which was pointed out by many of the playwright's contemporaries.[11] One can understand why Guo Mo Ruo modeled Qu Yuan on Hamlet: both of them represent political ideals favored by Confucianism. The only available literary forms that Guo could use for *Qu Yuan* were historical biography and Qu Yuan's poetry, so when he decided to stage Qu Yuan's story, it was natural for him to gravitate towards the dramatic technique of *Hamlet*, due to the similarity between the two characters.

The Chinese understanding of the central themes of Shakespeare's plays has also been deeply affected by Confucian political and moral doctrines. This is especially true for *King Lear*. Since by any Confucian standard Lear is far from a perfect Confucian hero, Chinese audiences usually focus their attention on the social significance of the play rather than on the character of the protagonist. The gloomy picture of great disorder shown by the play, which is just what Confucianism strongly opposes and tries to avoid, in a sense mirrors the social upheaval in Chinese history. In fact, all of the Confucian moral and political doctrines, to maintain order and harmony in a hierarchical and patriarchal society, ask people to observe those principles, an idea very similar to that described by Ulysses in *Troilus and Cressida* (1.3.83–124). As I discussed in chapter 1, Confucianism requires people to honor their political and family duties: an emperor must be enlightened and benevolent, a subject must be faithful and virtuous, a father must show kindness and affection to his children, a child must show obedience to his father, a wife must be chaste, and a friend must be devoted. Family duties are particularly emphasized, and any dereliction would be seriously condemned by Confucianism. In modern China, although many people now view the relationship between an emperor and his subjects differently, a strong sense of family duty and family values still greatly affects the thought and action of the people. Thus for the Chinese, *King Lear* is a depressing and shocking tragedy in which Confucian political and moral principles are thoroughly violated. However, it can be seen as a great tragedy of Confucian social ideals, serving as a negative example from which the Chinese would draw a useful lesson. Lear neglects his duties as both a king and a father. Goneril and Regan neglect their triple duties as subjects, daughters, and wives. Edmund frames his brother and informs against his father. Only Cordelia, Edgar, and Kent are qualified to be representative figures to fight for justice and duty and to defend the order and degree of society. Chinese audiences, therefore, tend to associate the central theme of *King Lear* with fundamental Confucian ideas.

One of the reasons why the play shocks the Chinese is that there are very few classical Chinese literary works describing the action of a son against his father or the hatred and plotting among brothers, although many literary works recount the high treason of vicious subjects against their emperors, as in the traditional Chinese tragedies *The Flag of Loyalty* and *The Story of the Honest Subject*. Yet the dereliction of family duties can now be understood by the Chinese people, for since China became dominated by the rigid political policies of Mao Tse-tung and money worship spread throughout society, similar phenomena have ceased to be rare.

This Confucian approach to *King Lear* is easily seen in the translations of the play in China. For instance, Zhu Sheng Hao's translation, considered the best one in China, uses numerous terms and phrases of Confucian politics and ethics in the translation of particular lines. A typical example is Gloucester's speech describing the disorder overtaking the country:

> Love cools, friendship falls off, brothers divide: in cities, mutinies; in countries, discord; in palaces, treason; and the bond crack'd 'twixt son and father. This villain of mine comes under the prediction; there's son against father: the King falls from bias of nature; there's father against child. I have seen the best of our time. Machinations, hollowness, treachery, and all ruinous disorders follow us disquietly to our graves.
>
> (1.2.106–14)

In his translation Zhu uses many conventional sentences and phrases that are employed frequently in Confucian classics such as "fu bu fu, zi bu zi" (a father does not behave like a father and a son does not behave like a son), "gangchang lunji wanquan pohuai" (degree and virtues are abandoned and moral principles are violated), "niqin fanshang" (acting against one's father and rebelling against the monarch), and "bu ci bu ai" (a father does not show kindness and affection to his children).[12] It is quite clear from these and other phrases that Zhu translated *King Lear* from the perspective of Confucianism, which of course has affected the interpretation of the thousands of people who have read his translation.

Chinese Shakespeare criticism also reflects a Confucian approach to *King Lear*. In discussing the central theme of *King Lear*, for example, Xu Bin writes:

> *King Lear* shows us a miserable world in which truth and falsehood are confused, right and wrong are misjudged. At court, the King neglects his duty and subjects commit treason against the King. In families, the father does not behave like a father, the son does not behave like a son; wife and husband fall out; brothers act against each other. Degree and virtue are abandoned; moral principles are violated. People are obsessed with the desire for power and gain. Peace and order are disrupted. . . . It is a great social tragedy.[13]

Xu Bin's remarks again use specific Confucian political terms and phrases.

The staging of *King Lear* in China demonstrates the same tendency to add Confucian color to the play. For instance, 1986 saw three productions of *King Lear*, all presented at the Inaugural Chinese Shakespeare Festival. One was performed by the Liaonin People's Art Theater in Shanghai and the other two were by the Central

Drama Academy and Tianjing People's Art Theater in Beijing. All showed in varying degrees a Confucian treatment of the theme, particularly the sinicized version by the Central Drama Academy. When I saw the production I felt as though I were watching a tragic event that had happened in Chinese history, from which Confucius and his followers had conceived of their basic philosophic ideas as a way to avoid future chaos and to strengthen the stability of society. Shakespeare's emphasis on disorder and abnormal relationships in both the political arena and family life and the Chinese historical context created by the production's setting, costume, and other cultural references all helped to form a Confucian vision of this great tragedy. Many of my colleagues and students shared this perception with me, and my assumption was soon confirmed by Professor Sun Jia Xiu, the adaptor and literary advisor of the production. She said that the production tried to expose the seamy side of feudal Chinese society by superimposing the great Shakespearean tragedy onto Chinese culture. Although this would inevitably tinge the production with Confucianism, the director and adaptor hoped that the audience could view the play from a contemporary perspective as well.[14]

The production of *Titus Andronicus* presented by the Shanghai Drama Institute provides another good example of the influence of Confucian political ideas on the treatment of Shakespearean themes. It was performed at the opening ceremony of the Inaugural Chinese Shakespeare Festival, electrifying the audience with its power and grandeur, and was highly praised by critics and scholars. As one of the more unusual Shakespearean plays, *Titus Andronicus* is rarely presented on the Western stage. Xu Qi Pin, the director, chose this play because he believed he could enliven the bloody, jumbled, Roman tragedy and give it new social and historical meaning through an original treatment. His approach turned out to be Confucian in essence, although Xu did not point this out directly. Thus the production, which presented a shocking and horrible picture of human violence, asked the audience to condemn its brutality and to recognize that we must end humanity's history of killing each other and strive for a lasting peace. Behind this thematic treatment is the strong influence of Confucian politics. As I discussed in chapter 1, the ultimate political and moral principle is *ren* (friendly and harmonious relationships between people), which should be applied to all aspects of social life. Family members must love, care for, and help each other. In state affairs the monarch or leader must be benevolent and show good will to other countries.

Every technique and device employed by the director served his original treatment of the central theme. To convey his interpretation with a strong stage image, Xu added a prologue that showed the audience a shocking scene of a bloody battlefield. The field was cluttered with dead bodies and spattered with blood. Kneeling down before his dead son, Titus stared at the body. After he stood up, his four surviving sons and a few soldiers came slowly onstage with heavy steps, carrying three bodies. Titus then followed them off. At the same time the audience heard an offstage conversation chosen deliberately by the director from the text:

> *Tit.* . . . What dost thou strike at, Marcus, with thy knife?
> *Marc.* At that I have kill'd, my lord—a fly.
> *Tit.* Out on thee, murderer! thou kill'st my heart!
> Mine eyes are cloy'd with view of tyranny.
> A deed of death done on the innocent
> Becomes not Titus' brother. Get thee gone,
> I see thou art not for my company.
> *Marc.* Alas, my lord, I have but kill'd a fly.
> *Tit.* "But"? How if that fly had a father and mother?
> How would he hang his slender gilded wings
> And buzz lamenting doings in the air!
> Poor harmless fly,
> That with his pretty buzzing melody,
> Came here to make us merry! and thou hast kill'd him.
>
> (3.2.52–65)

The conversation was then followed by a knell. As an unusual device, these offstage voices, which strongly condemned violence and killing, explicitly served the Confucian approach of the director, directly bringing out the central theme of the production. The end of the play had the same stress on a Confucian interpretation of the theme: after the Romans had cheered him, young Lucius came up to the bloody bodies. Kneeling down before his grandfather, he stared at Titus. Facing the audience, he slowly raised his head, obviously thinking painfully. The stage lights began to dim. Meanwhile an offstage voice was heard:

> How if that fly had a father and mother?
> How would he hang his slender gilded wings
> And buzz lamenting doings in the air!
> Poor harmless fly,
> That with his pretty buzzing melody,
> Came here to make us merry! and thou hast kill'd him.

Then the words "kill'd him" were repeated continuously, the voice becoming weaker and weaker, until at last it completely disappeared.

The idea behind this device was that if the younger generation thought deeply about this bloody story, perhaps the history of human violence would not continue.[15] Both the prologue and the ending of the play were intended to arouse the enthusiasm of the audience for eternal peace and harmony in the world.

Also worth mentioning in regard to this production is the treatment of Titus Andronicus. Judging by his moral character, the Roman warrior is more like a Confucian hero than is the Prince of Denmark. To a modern Chinese audience, certain qualities of Titus Andronicus could be considered weaknesses, as for example his stubborn loyalty to the emperor. Yet this weakness makes him more similar to Confucian heroes because most of them show an evident stubborn loyalty to their emperors, even when they are wronged by them (remember Yue Fei in *The Flag of Loyalty* and Zhou Shun Chang in *The Story of the Honest Subject*). In Xu's production, all the qualities of the protagonist that would be favored by Confucianism—tenacity, courage, strong moral fiber, loyalty, sense of duty, great dedication—were strongly emphasized.

Today the Chinese tend to appreciate literary works in terms of ethics and politics because of the former influence of traditional literature and changing social circumstances. Although some outmoded moral doctrines of Confucianism such as fanatical loyalty to one's ruler and parents and an overly rigid moral code for women have been abandoned, the main moral principles of Confucianism still deeply affect the thought and behavior of the Chinese. The principle of *ren*, for instance, remains their ultimate moral ideal. It applies not only to family relations but also to all social relations. *Yi* (loyalty to one's friend) is one of the major Confucian moral principles needed to achieve *ren*. It tries to establish honest and trustful relationships between men and women and is emphasized mainly by society. The Confucian ethical code stresses *yi*, underestimates *li* (personal profit or gain), and strongly condemns actions betraying a friend or harming others to benefit oneself. Moreover, China traditionally is a nation despising commercial activity and commercialism, although this view has changed since economic reform began in 1980. There is even an old Chinese saying: "All merchants are unscrupulous." These moral principles often influence the Chinese appreciation of literary works, including Shakespeare's plays.

The interpretation of *The Merchant of Venice* especially illustrates such an influence. The play has been the most popular Shakespearean comedy in China, mainly due to its interesting and romantic plot and extraordinary artistic charm. However, another prime reason is undoubtedly because the moral of the play is compatible with the conventional moral principles of the Chinese, particularly the notion of the relation between *yi* and *li*. This may help to explain why the scene of the Court of Justice (4.1) was included in the language and literature textbook for the pupils of Chinese middle schools. In the scene the confrontation between the Jew and the Christians forms a striking moral contrast. Antonio, Bassanio, Portia, and their friends represent benevolence, mercy, loyalty, faithfulness, and kindness; by contrast, Shylock stands for greed, cruelty, and selfishness. In the eyes of Chinese teachers and pupils, Antonio is the embodiment of *yi*, someone who not only finds it a pleasure to help others, but who also has the courage to sacrifice himself for his friend's interest, a trait highly praised by the Chinese. In a sense, the essence of this Confucian moral concept is altruism. Antonio, in fact, has indeed been regarded as an altruistic hero by Chinese students. By contrast, Shylock—who is intent on nothing but profit—is seen in Chinese classrooms as the incarnation of *li*. For his own gain he is willing to harm or even destroy others. As an out-and-out egoist, he represents the spirit of extreme commercialism, detested by the Chinese. Chinese teachers usually summarize the theme of the play in this way, emphasizing the moral contrast between *yi* and *li* and ignoring the complex historical context of the relationship between the Jews and Christians.[16] There are two reasons for this: first, the relevant religious background is not easily understood by Chinese students, and second, the Chinese tend to see Shylock as a literary figure and rarely associate him with the prejudice and discrimination inflicted on the Jews. Although ordinary Chinese people have a very limited knowledge of Jewish history, most of them respect and sympathize with Jews because they are known to be very intelligent people (at least everybody knows Karl Marx was a Jew) and because Hitler killed six million of their people during the Second World War.

This Confucian moral approach to *The Merchant of Venice* can also be found in the production of the play given by the Chinese Youth Art Theater in 1980, which I mentioned in chapter 4. The director obviously tried to represent a confrontation between *yi* and *li*. Shylock was presented as a genuinely unscrupulous merchant and a greedy money lender. To reinforce this impression on the audience, the director added an ancient Chinese money lender to the plot as Shylock's Chinese counterpart. As the embodiment of *li*, Chinese money lenders used to be largely despised and hated by the people because their business philosophy ran completely counter to the moral doctrine of Confucianism. Like Antonio, the Chinese lend money to help others, particularly their friends, but not to make interest or a profit. There is even a Chinese custom that discourages someone lending money to a friend from directly asking or hinting for its return, otherwise he or she will be seen as a person who overestimates *li* and underestimates *yi*. Thus Shylock would be surely accepted by the audience as a negative moral type condemned by Confucian moral concepts, while Antonio would be admired as the model of *yi*.

The influence of *yi* and *li* on the Chinese interpretation of Shakespeare's plays can also be found in the country's enthusiasm for *Timon of Athens*. In Western countries the play is rarely presented on the stage, but in China it has been popular for both readers and audiences. Two productions of *Timon of Athens* were staged at the Inaugural Chinese Shakespeare Festival, one presented by the North China Drama Society of Beijing Teacher's University and the other by the Second Foreign Language Institute of Beijing (in English). Both tried to present a striking contrast between *yi* and *li*, with Timon portrayed as a noble-minded hero who enjoyed helping others generously and the obsequious Athenian lords and citizens presented as base and ungrateful people, bent solely on profit. Like many readers, the audiences were especially interested in Timon's curse of gold (4.3.26–43) because it vividly represented the conventional Chinese attitude towards money and profit and no doubt reminded them of the Chinese saying "You can hire even a ghost to serve you if you have plenty of money." In fact, this famous soliloquy, together with that of the Bastard commenting on the function of "commodity" (2.1.561–98) in *King John*, are quoted frequently by the popular press.[17] Yet even though the Chinese might admire Timon's condemnation of money, they would still disagree with his curse of the whole human race and his pessimistic attitude about the future. The tenets of Confucianism tell us that humanity's basic tendency is oriented towards the good and can be augmented by an emphasis on morality.

Other similar Shakespearean ideas make his works accessible to the Chinese. For example, it is not difficult to find that social idealism in Shakespeare's plays has something in common with conventional Chinese ideology, particularly Confucianism and Taoism. In *The Tempest* Gonzalo describes a utopian community—his commonwealth of the island, which he supposes to "excel the golden age" (2.1.148–69). It is interesting to note that Gonzalo's ideal society looks very similar to that of Confucius, who once talked with his followers about an ideal community that he believed was the golden age of ancient China.[18] The communities of Gonzalo and Confucius are more natural than a modern sophisticated society that emphasizes public interest and welfare and enjoys equality, peace, and harmony.

Even more interesting, the Chinese have noticed that Gonzalo's utopia compares to the social ideals of Taoism. As the second most important traditional Chinese ideology, Taoism advocates conforming to nature and letting things take their own course. Thus it favors a more natural and primitive society without artificiality, just like Gonzalo's description:

> I' th' commonwealth I would, by contraries,
> Execute all things; for no kind of traffic
> Would I admit; . . .
>
> . . . .
>
> And use of service, none; contract, succession,
> Bourn, bound of land, tilth, vineyard, none;
> No use of metal, corn, or wine, or oil;
>
> . . . .
>
> All things in common nature should produce
> Without sweat or endeavor: . . .
>
> . . . .
>
> . . . but nature should bring forth,
> Of it own kind, all foison, all abundance,
> To feed my innocent people.
>
> (2.1.148–65)

Zhuang Zi, one of the major founders of Taoism, even advocates that the most ideal society is one without a ruler, which is also in accordance with Gonzalo's idea: "No name of magistrate" (2.1.150) and "No sovereignty" (2.1.157), he says.

The "green world" in Shakespearean comedies, particularly the forest in *As You Like It,* is often associated by the Chinese with the social ideals of Confucianism. In the forest world of *As You Like It,* the human relationships almost duplicate those in Confucius's ideal society. Confucius favors harmonious relations between rulers and subjects, family members, and friends and people of different social status, emphasizing that they should respect others' parents and children as they respect their own.[19] In Arden the Duke treats his subjects as friends and Orlando looks after Adam as if the old servant were his father. To show her love for Rosalind Celia willingly gives up her wealth and rank. The pastoral atmosphere of the play strengthens the connection between the green world and the Confucian social ideal because many well-known Confucian politicians wrote pastoral poetry after being ousted from their posts and retiring to their native homes. For instance, Tao Yuan Ming, a great classical Chinese poet, composed many beautiful pastoral poems and prose after he resigned office and lived in the countryside as a farmer. In his very influential prose, together with a poem entitled "Taohua Yuan Ji" ("The Land of Peach Blossoms"), he describes a fictitious land of peace, away from the turmoil of the world, where people live a happy and peaceful pastoral life. This haven can be seen as the Chinese counterpart of the forest world in *As You Like It*. In a sense, the Confucian social ideal is better represented in the green world of *As You Like It* than in the garden world of traditional Chinese drama. As I discussed in chapter 1, the garden scene, as one of the major patterns of traditional Chinese comedies, principally serves as a paradise for the lovers. It does not reflect the relations between human beings as widely as does the forest world in *As You Like It*.

The traditional perspective of the Chinese on Shakespeare, particularly the histories, is also affected by the historical context of China and the Confucian historical concept. The Chinese usually have no difficulty in understanding the incidents and events in the plays because of the similarity between English feudal society and the vast Chinese feudal society, which lasted for more than two thousand years. For instance, the cruel and bloody power struggles for the throne in Shakespeare's royal families can also be found in Chinese history. In the Tang dynasty, in order to succeed to the throne, Prince Li Shi Min killed his two brothers and forced his father to abdicate, then becoming Emperor Tang Tai Zong. During the Wudai period, Prince Zhu You Gui even killed his father to inherit the throne. Yet he himself later was killed by his brother, Zhu You Zhen. The belief "When treacherous officials are in power, faithful subjects suffer" was one of the main reasons why an emperor's reign might fall and has been a major subject of Chinese literature. Similar events occur in Shakespearean histories, such as the plot in *King Henry VI* where Queen Margaret colludes with the Duke of Suffolk, Cardinal Beaufort, and the Duke of Buckingham to frame the loyal and virtuous protector, Gloucester. This is, as I analyzed in chapter 1, the central theme of many Chinese political tragedies. After being arrested, Gloucester warns:

> Ah, gracious lord, these days are dangerous:
> Virtue is chok'd with foul ambition,
> And charity chas'd hence by rancor's hand;
> Foul subornation is predominant,
> And equity exil'd your Highness' land.
>
> (Pt. 2, 3.1.142–46)

This passage immediately suggests Zhou Shun Chang's condemnation of the conspiracy and savagery of the corrupt officials in *The

Story of the Honest Subject (*Classical Chinese Tragedies*, scene 1, p. 510).

Peculiarities of the Chinese historical context might also encourage the Chinese to focus on certain descriptions in Shakespearean historical plays. For example, they might show special interest in the peasant uprising in *King Henry VI* but wonder why the playwright depicts the event satirically and why the rebels reconcile with the monarchy so easily, because in China the rebellious peasant has been a force not to be ignored.[20] In Chinese history numerous peasant uprisings overthrew old dynasties and established new reigns. Again, the patriotic enthusiasm displayed in Shakespeare's histories would find an echo in the hearts of Chinese people, for even though the people built the Great Wall to defend themselves, China often suffered invasion by foreign countries or other nationalities. The country was conquered and ruled by uncivilized tribes for more than four hundred years (the Yuan dynasty, 1271–1368, and the Qing dynasty, 1644–1911). So patriotism has been a major theme in traditional Chinese literature and drama, as in *Autumn in the Han Palace, The Flag of Loyalty*, and *The Fan of Peach Blossom*. We should remember too that many other plays, including comedies, have foreign invasion as a subplot or setting. Thus all the exciting and stirring patriotic passages in Shakespeare's histories, such as the praise of England by Gaunt in *King Richard II* (2.1.40–58), the Bastard's pledge to defend England in *King John* (5.7.112–18), and the King's speech before the battle at Agincourt in *King Henry V* (4.3.19–67), are enjoyed by the Chinese and quoted frequently in newspapers, magazines, and books.[21]

For Chinese audiences and readers, the fascination of Shakespearean histories stems mainly from the vivid portrayal of different types of kings. Although there are simple descriptions of the achievement of Chinese kings and emperors in historical records and annals, Chinese people rarely see excellent characterizations of the monarchy in conventional literary works, due to the reasons I described in chapter 1. So Shakespeare's histories provide a rare chance for the Chinese to appreciate the literary character of a feudal ruler by giving them insight into the ruler's inner world. Chinese people normally tend to apply the character patterns of their rulers, which were formed by both historical facts and Confucian philosophy, to those in Shakespeare. For example, Henry the Sixth is regarded by the Chinese as a weak and incompetent king, much like Emperor Li Hou Zhu in the post-Tang period, who had no ability to be an emperor but had great talent as a poet. He can also be associated with Emperor Guang Xu of the Qing dynasty who, totally controlled by his aunt, Queen

Ci Xi, was only a political puppet. Richard the Second would make the Chinese people recall fatuous and self-indulgent emperors in their own history such as Emperor Sui Yang, the last emperor of the Sui dynasty. For Richard the Third the audience would select King Shang Zhou, who was a very cruel tyrant in the Shang dynasty.

Ambiguity can be found in the attitude of the Chinese people towards a certain type of monarchs—for example, Henry the Fourth and Henry the Eighth—who are very similar to those Chinese rulers called *jianxong*. A ruler with this quality normally has a double nature. Politically, they are strong, competent, and sometimes iron-handed, but morally they are unscrupulous and treacherous. The Chinese needed such strong rulers to maintain order in the vast kingdom, but they did not like their immorality, for Confucianism held that an ideal ruler must be perfect both politically and morally. Since political trickery is completely incompatible with the political doctrine of Confucianism, the character of Henry the Eighth obviously has something in common with those of Chinese rulers labeled *jianxong*. One day in the fall of 1987, after class, one of my students at the Television University told me that he felt that Henry the Eighth was an English Cao Cao. I of course agreed with him because Cao Cao was a typical *jianxong* Chinese king in the Three Kingdom period (A.D. 220–280) and one of the protagonists in the famous historical novel *The Romance of Three Kingdoms*, known to every household in the country.

Western Shakespeare scholars have argued that Henry the Fifth is Shakespeare's ideal monarch. This theory is, to a great extent, very appealing to the Chinese as well since he is the epitome of the enlightened ruler. His character is in harmony with Confucian qualities of a competent monarch, especially the combination of political competence and virtue. This view is evident in Shakespearean criticism in China. For example, Professor Zhang Si Yang has analyzed the nature of Henry the Fifth in terms of a Confucian political idea, using specific phrases that have been employed to describe a Chinese ruler.[22]

One reason why Henry the Fifth is popular with ordinary Chinese people is because having a good emperor used to be the ultimate political aspiration of Chinese farmers, since it assured them of a peaceful life. Although autocratic monarchy was overturned at the beginning of the twentieth century in China, many citizens are still accustomed to power politics or authoritative rule, which helps to explain why Mao Tse-tung was fanatically worshiped by the people during the Cultural Revolution and why most Chinese people today still place their hopes on Deng Xiao Ping.

Another important reason for the assimilation of Shakespeare into Chinese culture probably lies in the Chinese perception of a hidden combination of Confucianism and Taoism in the plays. While Confucianism is the leading ideology in traditional Chinese culture, a joint influence of Confucianism and Taoism can be seen in many aspects of the culture such as philosophy, politics, ethics, literature, and arts. In that respect Confucianism and Taoism are considered complementary in traditional Chinese culture. Generally speaking, however, the two philosophies take different attitudes towards life. Confucianism asks people to participate actively in world affairs, to strive for both personal happiness and the public interest, and particularly to build a better political system and a harmonious moral order, whereas Taoism asks people to stand aloof from the world, to follow nature, and to do nothing for either social or personal gain. Both outlooks can be seen in Shakespeare's plays. Many characters display an active and positive attitude toward life, with some exerting themselves in the struggle for love, wealth, and status and others devoting themselves to the public interest. But negativity can also be found in Shakespeare's plays, which suggests a Taoistic philosophy. Tired of the sufferings of life, some characters—Timon and Jaques, for example—are disillusioned with the mortal world and try to renounce it, just as Hou Fang Yu and Li Xian Jun do at the end of *The Fan of Peach Blossom*. Passages concerning the illusory quality of life and the idea of resignation from the world are not uncommon in Shakespeare's works, and most of them sound quite Taoistic to the Chinese mind. For instance, consider this passage from *Timon of Athens:*

> Hoy-day,
> What a sweep of vanity comes this way!
> They dance? they are madwomen.
> Like madness is the glory of this life,
> As this pomp shows to a little oil and root.
> We make ourselves fools to disport ourselves . . .
>
> (1.2.131–36)

Macbeth's "to-morrow, and to-morrow, and to-morrow" soliloquy (5.5.19–28) also echoes the Taoistic frame of mind.

Numerous cultural figures and politicians in Chinese history exhibit both philosophies, as do some characters of Shakespeare. In a sense, Hamlet is such a person. In the early pages of this chapter I discussed the Confucian quality of Hamlet, but in fact he also shows a Taoistic outlook on life in his disillusionment with the mortal world. The political careers of Confucian politicians often displayed a double track. That is, when they achieved their political ambitions, they followed the principles of Confucianism, taking an active part in social activities and state affairs. But when they suffered setbacks or were framed by treacherous citizens or wronged by emperors, they comforted themselves with Taoism and withdrew from society to live in solitude. Some returned to society if the political situation became favorable. Such a pattern is familiar to Chinese audiences, who recognize them in Shakespeare's plays. The "court-forest-court" plot in *As You Like It* is a typical example. Belarius's case in *Cymbeline* also shows this pattern.

The differing approaches of Confucianism and Taoism toward human civilization is also noticeable in Shakespeare's plays. Confucianism believes that humanity can benefit from civilization whereas Taoism rejects all traditional values and institutions. The praise of humankind and its creative achievement is often taken as evidence of humanism in Shakespeare's works, but the condemnation of human values and institutions by the misanthropes in Shakespeare's plays— Timon and Jaques—also stirs up our feelings. For Chinese audiences, this Shakespearean contrast is even more striking than that found in traditional Chinese literature.

When transferred into Chinese culture, Shakespeare's plays are not only interpreted in terms of the country's prevailing ideologies, but are also appreciated from the perspective of their conventional aesthetic taste, particularly the literary and theatrical bias. Contemporary China's usual literature and art tastes, as I mentioned in chapters 3 and 5, have lost their exclusive position since Western literature and art were introduced into the country. But they still deeply affect the literary and artistic output and appreciation of the people, particularly in rural areas. Literary and theatrical conventions sometimes make Chinese audiences see Shakespeare's plays through a filter or focus their attention on points that Westerners usually ignore. For instance, the Chinese perception of Shakespearean tragedy often shows some influence of the traditional tragic concept and the sentimentalism of Chinese literature. Earlier I analyzed how Shakespeare had influenced traditional Chinese drama and brought about a great change in conventional dramatic concepts. While some aspects of traditional Chinese drama were seriously criticized by Chinese dramatists and scholars, many elements are still popular to the modern Chinese audience. In chapter 1 I pointed out that the protagonists in most beloved Chinese tragedies are women, which demonstrates a feminist tendency in the country's literary tradition, and that the "destruction of beauty" was the fundamental tragic concept of traditional Chinese drama, shaped by the social context of ancient China and the prevalent sentimentalism of Chinese literature. This tragic concept remains an important part of the literary and theatrical tastes of the Chinese today. In contemporary China tragic literary works with women as protagonists always attract public attention. It is hard to forget the sad story of Zhang Zhi Xin, an ordinary Chinese woman who was brutally tortured and executed by the Gang of Four merely for disagreeing with the policies of the Cultural Revolution, an incident that caused a sensation in China and aroused the righteous indignation of the people in 1980. The enthusiasm of the Chinese for Thomas Hardy's works, especially *Tess of the D'Urbervilles* and *The Return of the Native*, also illustrates the influence of the notion of the "destruction of beauty" in contemporary Chinese taste.

This conventional aesthetic concept inevitably affects the interpretation of Shakespeare's tragedy. Chinese audiences sympathize more with tragic heroines than heroes, especially when the heroine is "perfect" and the hero flawed. The idea that a tragic protagonist must be a perfect person is another traditional influence. Although today's audiences have a deeper understanding of the complexity of human nature than did the ancient Chinese, they still tend to regard characters whose leading qualities are virtuous as positive heroes. These concepts therefore encourage Chinese audiences to feel less pity for Lear than for Cordelia, due to his willfulness and folly, which are at the root of the play's great disorder and the destruction of both Cordelia and himself. *Othello* is a better example of this view. To Chinese audiences, Desdemona is really the principal character in the tragedy. As a perfect woman she possesses all the virtues that are praised by Chinese aesthetic and moral standards: beauty, chastity, courage, dedication to love. Accordingly, her suffering and death greatly appeal to their sympathy and pity. By contrast, it is very difficult for Othello to win the affection of a Chinese audience because he is the murderer of Desdemona. The Chinese cannot tolerate the fact that he is so credulous and jealous that he brutally kills his innocent wife, who has given herself totally to him, without verification of her infidelity. Although Iago is an important factor behind the tragedy, Othello is the author of his and Desdemona's misfortune. The only reason for the enthusiasm of some Chinese actors and scholars for the Moor is because the complexity of Othello's character is worth representing and discussing. This does not mean that Othello is commonly perceived as a positive tragic hero by Chinese people, however. Both classical and modern Chinese playwrights would have made Desdemona the principal character if they had had the opportunity to write the play.

These observations can be illustrated by the actual theatrical and academic practices of contemporary China. The production of

Othello by the China Railway Drama Troupe, performed in April 1986 at the Inaugural Chinese Shakespeare Festival, received much critical acclaim. When I saw the play, my feeling, as well as that of my colleagues, was that the holiness and purity of Desdemona were greatly emphasized by the gloomy atmosphere of the play, like sunshine against shadows. By contrast, the initial heroic image of Othello was maintained only a very short time; his behavior then became crude, brutal, and unbearable, like a devil against the image of hell, which formed the lower part of the set. My view was confirmed by the subsequent talk of Cheng Ping, the director, who argued that the production intended to give prominence to the holy and perfect image of Desdemona, highlighting her virtues and dedication to love. Mrs. Cheng told the participants at the conference that the directing plan came in part from the company. When she asked the performers to give their own opinions on the treatment of Othello, all agreed that he could not be treated as a positive tragic hero because his crime was unforgivable. He himself was the main source of the tragedy, not Iago, who served only as a trigger to bring about the sad ending. Asked to explain the symbolic meaning of the set, Mrs. Cheng said that its principal frame, which was a huge globe, stood for heaven and earth, while the lower part, including stage itself and its apron, represented hell. The main idea behind the design was to show the process of Othello's degeneration, demonstrating how the evil element in Othello's nature was brought out by Iago, which made the Moor a devil who destroyed the beautiful, good, and ideal.[23]

The response of the audience to the play was undoubtedly in line with the director's interpretation. The production was taken mainly as a tragedy of Desdemona and the "destruction of beauty" and its aesthetic ideal. Accordingly the audience felt much sympathy for Desdemona and very little for the Moor. Besides discussions and remarks about the production, an additional event also confirmed the response: Liang Dan Ni, the actress who played Desdemona, was selected to make a speech at the closing ceremony. The production was also the only one invited to be performed in Shanghai after the festival.

The rich vein of feminism in traditional Chinese literature often influences the interpretation of Shakespeare in Chinese culture. In traditional Chinese drama women are always depicted as the embodiment of beauty and virtue or the victims of social injustice. Chinese writers rarely portray sinister and vicious women in their works. Goneril and Regan, and particularly Lady Macbeth, would certainly make a Chinese audience feel uncomfortable. One can also assume that the Chinese reception of *The Taming of the Shrew* would be problematic because the account of subduing a woman through torment and humiliation runs counter to the conventional feelings of the Chinese. I suspect that the director of any production of this play would have to make some drastic alterations to accommodate the taste of Chinese audiences. The production by the Shanghai People's Art Theater, presented in April 1986 in Shanghai under an English visiting director (Bernard Goss), supports my assumption. Although we were not sure whether Mr. Goss intended to satisfy Chinese audiences, his interpretation indeed suited their taste. Katherina was not played as a shrew, but as a rebel against a restrictive society. The relationship between Petruchio and Katherina was not depicted as that of conqueror and conquered, but as two cooperators. Both wanting a happy marriage and a good life together, they needed each other. This unusual treatment was a considerable accomplishment, and the play was well received by both theatrical circles and the audience. As some critics pointed out, however, the achieved effect relied mainly on its compatibility with conventional Chinese taste.[24]

The aesthetic philosophy of Taoism, which rejects utilitarianism and moralizing and emphasizes intuition and imagination in literary and artistic creations, has greatly influenced traditional Chinese literature and art, especially painting and poetry. *A Midsummer Night's Dream*, performed by the China Coal Miners' Drama Troupe in April 1986 under Xong Yuan Wei, is a good example of how this view makes its way into the Chinese interpretation of Shakespeare's works. In chapter 4 I analyzed briefly how this particular production employed the stage technique of traditional Chinese drama in creating an Asian style. In fact, this "Eastern aesthetic taste" (a phrase from the program notes of the production), was basically the aesthetic concept of Taoism. Such a treatment obviously depends on elements in the play that can be linked with Taoistic literary and artistic works. The most important element that the director used is the play's magical and imaginary atmosphere, which relates to the Taoistic notion that "life is a dream." The 1986 production used a set of hanging ropes to suggest a forest and to create a floating space. The changeable lighting further added a dreamlike and illusory color to the stage. The stylized movements of the players, lyrical music, and graceful dancing helped to produce the beauty and feeling of a fairyland, creating a symbolic and illusory world full of imagination and mystery whose beauty can be perceived by intuition rather than words. Such an effect was precisely the ultimate aesthetic standard of Taoism.

Traditional Chinese theatrical concepts provide another reason for the enthusiasm of the Chinese for Shakespeare's plays. As I have discussed earlier, traditional drama mixes many kinds of art: music, dance, acrobatics, the fine arts, poetry. For this reason many people like a drama encompassing more than the spoken word, although they understand its moral and political importance. Shakespeare's plays use both mixed media and spoken lines, which is one more reason why enthusiasm for the dramatist constantly runs high in China while the interest in Ibsen and Chekhov has subsided since the 1950s. However, for some rural people such as farmers and other uneducated people whose tastes are very conventional, certain characteristics of Shakespeare might be hard to appreciate. For example, the complex and morally ambiguous characters of Lear, Macbeth, Richard the Second, and others may be difficult for them to understand because they are used to enjoying characters having a simple and fixed morality and a single passion, as is found in traditional Chinese drama. The lines revealing the inner world of Shakespeare's characters may seem tedious to these people, for the psychological description in traditional Chinese drama is quite different. They may also feel uncomfortable with the endings of Shakespearean tragedy, being used to the happy conclusions of traditional tragedy. Moreover, a few Western cultural references may prove hard to understand. For instance, bastards in Shakespeare are portrayed as important characters, normally conspirators and careerists. But very few bastards are represented in Chinese literature at all, owing to the differing literary conventions and the marriage system of ancient China. Curiously the Chinese often associate Shakespeare's bastards with the eunuchs of traditional drama (such as Wei Zhong Xian in *The Story of the Honest Subject*) because there is a striking similarity in their characters. There are also many characteristics of Shakespeare's art that are completely accessible to the convention-dominated Chinese people, however. For example, Shakespearean comedies can be very easily understood because their comic concept is quite similar to that of traditional Chinese drama. Besides, his mingled mode, complicated and interesting plots, free employment of space and time, and other techniques can be fully appreciated by anyone.

I should also point out that the enthusiasm of the Chinese for Shakespeare has clear links with the long-standing Chinese poetic tradition. In ancient China, the function and significance of poetry went far beyond being simply a genre of literature. It was concerned with many social aspects such as education, politics, and institutions, serving as an important part of Confucian culture. The founders of Confucianism, including Confucius himself, saw poetry as an effective instructional medium. (One of the major Confucian classics, *The Book of Songs,* is a collection of poems.) Confucian scholars and politicians also use poetry to express their political aspirations and misfortunes.

Ancient China was a kingdom of poetry, having numerous brilliant poetic works and famous poets, including many great names such as Li Po, Du Pu, and Bai Ju Yi. Traditional Chinese poetry is rightly taken as the crown of Chinese literary achievement, and the country's poets rank among the greatest in the world. Poetic training was very popular in ancient China and was one of the essential features of traditional Chinese humanistic education. For the ancient Chinese, writing and understanding poetry were not only necessary accomplishments for an educated man but were also important ways to seek a higher social status by passing the imperial examination, where skill at poetic composition was a major requirement. In the Tang dynasty this skill served was the decisive standard by which one passed or failed the imperial examination.[25] This poetic tradition has been carried forward by the modern Chinese. In China today children start their poetic training very early at elementary schools, and it is quite common to see a three- to five-year-old child reciting from memory twenty or thirty, and sometimes even fifty classical Chinese poems. Even poorly educated people show a great interest in poetry and have some basic knowledge of classical poetry. It is customary for the Chinese to compose a poem at the end of a speech or a letter. Numerous Chinese leaders of the Communist party and government can write poems. Mao Tse-tung was an outstanding poet even though many Chinese people have a different attitude toward his political career. His reputation as a poet derived mainly from his brilliant representation in classical poetry of the thought and emotion of modern Chinese revolutionaries.

The poetic orientation of the Chinese has so greatly influenced other forms of the culture that people are highly sensitive to poetry and are able to appreciate it. This sophistication obviously helps in the country's respect for the poetic quality of Shakespearean works. At first the Chinese tended to approach the English dramatist through his poetry and to greatly admire his beautiful and lyrical language. As I mentioned in chapter 3, the early Chinese Shakespeare scholars often paid attention primarily to the poetic quality of Shakespeare's works. The famous Chinese scholar Zhu Dong Run, professor of Fudan University, has compared Shakespeare with the greatest classical Chinese poet, Li Po, and analyzed the similarities and differences between them.[26] Thus the Chinese, particularly those who adhere to literary tradition, admire Shakespeare mainly for his poetic characteristics. This is why the famous director and actor Yin Ruo Cheng always reminded his players to pay special attention to acting when they rehearsed a Shakespearean play. He knew clearly that Chinese performers are easily intoxicated with the poetic flavor and lyrical atmosphere of Shakespeare's plays and tend to neglect the acting.[27] In contemporary China, therefore, most people are still inclined to appreciate Shakespeare's plays for their poetic and literary qualities rather than their stagings. The reason is partly because performances of the plays are often limited by financial constraints and theatrical facilities. But the reason seems also to be that many people would agree with Charles Lamb's opinion that the stage performances may spoil or reduce one's appreciation of Shakespeare because an audience's attention is often distracted by elements such as sets, props, movements, and gestures.[28] This, however, by no means implies that the Chinese do not like the stage representations of Shakespeare—it merely means that they derive greater enjoyment in reading the plays.

A few minor factors in traditional Chinese culture also affect Shakespeare's reception in China. For instance, the Chinese admire a practical philosophy of life but not an abstract and profound one like that of nineteenth-century Germany. Their taste can be seen in the short philosophical poems of ancient China and the "citizen" short stories in the Ming and Qing dynasties. The precepts in these works mainly contain the principles of Taoism and Buddhism and the practical—although now dated—maxims of townspeople. This may explain why the Chinese are spellbound by Shakespearean "golden sayings." Another factor is religion. Confucian-based Chinese culture is characterized by strong secularism. The Chinese have never taken any religion seriously, including Buddhism, and generally speaking they do not like literary works with a strong religious flavor. But Shakespeare is completely acceptable to them even though some of his plays have a Christian background. By contrast, the works of Dante, Milton, and Goethe are too difficult to be understood by ordinary Chinese people because of their complex religious context.

As China's dominating ideology since 1949, Marxism has greatly influenced the social and cultural practices of the Chinese. It is probably no accident that the socialist revolution took place under the guidance of Marxism-Leninism because Chinese culture has elements in common with the principles of Marxism such as advocating active participation in state and local government and sharing similar moral and social values. The 1950s and 1960s saw the deep imprint of Marxism on Shakespeare's reception in China. The function of Marxism in molding China's appreciation of Shakespeare is dual in nature. On one hand Marx asks his followers to embrace all of the world's cultures, including bourgeois culture, while building up a new proletarian society. But on the other hand it confines the people to a single and fixed angle from which to view the dramatist. While Marx himself tended to approach Shakespeare from a literary and artistic standpoint, his successors, especially in Russia, often interpret the playwright historically and politically to illustrate the Marxist theory of dialectical and historical materialism. The Chinese appreciation of Shakespeare from 1949 to 1978 was mainly influenced by Russian Shakespearean studies, as can be easily discovered by perusing Shakespeare criticism in China from this period. Like their Russian counterparts, Chinese Shakespearean critics maintained that since, in their opinion, Shakespeare's works show the process of social development from feudalism to capitalism, the dramatist represents progressive social forces and humanism. Consequently they concentrate their research on the social and political significance of Shakespeare's works, dealing with his realism, optimism, affinity with the people, descriptions of class struggle, and so on.

Many Chinese critics consider Shakespeare's works a good metaphorical demonstration of Marxist historical materialism. Thus there has been a prevailing tendency in Chinese Shakespeare studies to link the plays with their Elizabethan and Jacobean historical contexts. For example, Professor Chen Jia holds that in his plays Shakespeare represented a panorama of class and political struggle in English history, mainly by depicting bloody power struggles in royal families and between the monarchy and aristocracy, the most typical political conflicts of a feudal society. Marxist theory, however, states that people are the real motivating force of history. So Professor Chen, like other Shakespearean scholars, paid special attention in his article to the role of the working class in political struggles. He maintains that although the farmers and citizens in Shakespeare's histories in most cases did not operate as an independent force, their participation was often an important factor in the struggle. Sometimes they even had encouragement to fight directly with the ruling class, as Shakespeare described in 2 Henry VI.

Influenced by Marxism, Chinese critics during this period believed that all writers wrote for a particular social class, most likely their own. In his article Professor Chen also tries to determine the class status of Shakespeare. He thought that Shakespeare basically was a bourgeois writer. Because the bourgeoisie was a progressive class when capitalism was in the ascendant, Shakespeare should be regarded as a progressive playwright. In his historical plays, Shakespeare saw and described political events from a bourgeois standpoint as well as that of the working class because the interests of bourgeoisie basically coincided with those of the working class during that time.[29]

Using the Marxist method of class analysis, some Chinese critics believed that in his works Shakespeare described the conflict between the declining feudal system and the ascendant bourgeois force. Zhu Wei Zhi summarized the theme of *The Merchant of Venice* as a clash between the rising bourgeois and old feudal ideologies that was shown in different cultural aspects depicted in the play. For example, Shakespeare embodied the confrontation between old usury in Shylock and the new commercialism in Antonio, who obviously represented a progressive social and economic force. The friction between the old and new ideologies was also evident in the play's marriages. Portia and Jessica tried to marry partners of their own choice, which was contrary to the arranged marriages of feudalism. Zhu believed that the defeat of Shylock was, in a sense, the defeat of the outmoded feudal law. The victory of Portia over Shylock was actually won with the help of the new bourgeois law.[30]

Other Chinese scholars have maintained that Shakespeare was not limited by his class status as a bourgeois writer because he often exposed and criticized the negative side of capitalism. Li Fu Ning, for example, held that *As You Like It* deliberately uses the device of the forest world to form a striking contrast between the harmonious golden age of mankind and a malicious capitalist society. The moral principles and values followed by the characters admitted to the forest world, especially Orlando, Adam, and Celia, completely contradict those of the bourgeoisie, which are based on gain and money. The play's negative characters (Duke Frederick and Oliver, for example) show, to some extent, the aspirations and ambition of the bourgeoisie, ignoring the interests of others.[31]

The special interest of Marx in *Timon of Athens* has particularly affected the interpretation of Shakespeare's plays by Chinese critics. In his economic and political works Marx frequently used quotations from *Timon of Athens*, especially Timon's condemnation of gold (4.3.26–45), to discuss the essence of money and its function in a capitalist society.[32] This has almost become a formula in China for interpreting *Timon of Athens* and other plays relating to money worship. For example, Dai Xing Dong has argued that Shakespeare revealed the basic drive of capitalism through Timon's soliloquies. The play demonstrated that in a capitalist society the people's enslavement to money was the root of all evil. So through his play, Dai argues, Shakespeare in fact represented the essence of capitalism while Marx expounded it through philosophical theory.[33]

The studies of Shakespeare's philosophical ideas in China, ranging from his concept of nature to his views of history, are also greatly affected by Marxist philosophy, especially its materialism and dialectics. In 1986, Zhang Yang wrote three articles that systematically discussed the philosophical ideas in Shakespeare's plays and linked them to Marx. For instance, by examining the "golden sayings" in Shakespeare's texts Zhang discovered that almost all the laws of Marxist dialectics can be found in Shakespeare's works. The law of the unity of opposites is represented in Shakespeare's works, Zhang says, for his frequent use of polarities is one of the more obvious characteristics of Shakespearean art. The transformation of a contradiction is vividly expressed by many Shakespearean sayings, such as in this passage from *Romeo and Juliet:*

> Nor aught so good but, strain'd from that far use,
> Revolts from true birth, stumbling on abuse.
> Virtue itself turns vice, being misapplied,
> And vice sometime by action dignified.

> (2.3.19–22)

The law of the negation of negation also appears in Shakespeare's works, as in sonnet 64:

> When I have seen the hungry ocean gain
> Advantage on the kingdom of the shore,
> And the firm soil win of the wat'ry main,
> Increasing store with loss, and loss with store;

According to Zhang, other laws of Marxist dialects such as the law of quantitative and qualitative change, the law of appearance and essence, and the law of cause and effect are also represented in Shakespeare's works.[34]

Marxism has also exerted an artistic influence on the Chinese perception of the dramatist. In chapter 3, I mentioned the Russian orientation of Shakespeare production in China during the 1950s and 1960s, which was actually a Marxist approach to Shakespeare's plays. Marxist literary assessment is based on the criterion of verisimilitude. The Shakespeare productions in China during this period obviously abided by this principle because all of them tried to achieve visual and psychological reality through naturalistic performances.

Engels' theory of literary typification has often been used by Chinese Shakespeare scholars to analyze Shakespeare's characters. Following this theory they tried to find how Shakespeare reproduced "typical characters under typical circumstances," which was actually an endeavor to relate the qualities of Shakespeare's characters to the relevant social contexts shaping such qualities.[35] Both Marx and Engels highly praised Shakespeare's artistic talents but were dissatisfied with those of Schiller because they held that moral and political themes should not be explicitly explained by the author; on the contrary, they had to be naturally evident from the situation and action.[36] Since this contrast of the Shakespearean and Schillerian styles reconciled great art with revolutionary commitment, it has had a great impact not only on Shakespearean criticism and Western literary studies in China, but also on all of the country's literary and artistic practices. Obviously this notion is by no means an original literary concept, yet it reminds Communist writers not to achieve political significance at the expense of artistic merit and urges revolutionary critics to pay attention to literary values while emphasizing ideological values. And it has provided yet another angle by which Chinese Shakespeare scholars can consider the literary merits of Shakespeare's works. According to the bibliography attached to *Shakespearean Criticism in China* (Meng, ed., Beijing, 1991), twenty-five articles were published from 1980 to 1984 on the implication and significance of the Shakespearean and Schillerian modes. The attention focused on this notion in fact reflects the larger debate in China over the priority between political propaganda and artistic value. Whenever the political situation becomes tense, the former is greatly emphasized, and when the political climate is more secure, the latter is cheerfully followed. This helps to explain why so many articles were written on this topic at the beginning of the 1980s, when China was more politically tolerant under Deng Xiao Ping's "open-door" policy.

The universal appeal of Shakespeare helped him to easily adapt to the taste of the proletarian revolutionaries, even if he wrote mainly for the aristocracy and bourgeoisie. In a broader sense one could say that Marxism has contributed to the positive reception of Shakespeare by the Chinese. Marx's comments on both the ideological and aesthetic value of Shakespeare in fact provided a political umbrella for the dramatist in a closed socialist state that was antagonistic to the West during the 1950s and 1960s. The political climate, however, became increasingly unfavorable to the presence of Shakespeare in China after the country broke away from the Soviet Union in the late 1950s and the ideas and principles of Mao Tse-tung (called "Mao Tse-tung Thought" in China) came to be taken as political and cultural guidelines for all of the Chinese. Mao's literary theory stated that all literary and artistic activities should first serve the revolution and comply with the political principles of the party. This seriously fettered the practice of literary criticism, including Shakespeare studies, and in the end negated all Western culture during the Cultural Revolution.

In the 1980s, after the disaster of the Cultural Revolution, China saw the decline of Marxism and Mao Tse-tung Thought and the rise of a new enthusiasm for Western culture. Although the new leaders claimed Marxism and Mao Tse-tung Thought to be the dominant ideology in the country, the Chinese basically were able to approach Shakespeare in any way they liked, gaining their freedom from the previous dogmatic interpretation of Shakespeare's works. Yet the philosophical method of Marxism continued to have a strong influence on the Chinese appreciation of Shakespeare and was still used by critics and scholars, although their conclusions were quite different from those reached in the 1950s and 1960s. For instance, a fair number of the books and articles on Shakespeare written in the last decade have associated his works with the present state of China, comparing corruption and money worship to similar situations in the plays.[37] In all these researches Marx's historically and socially analytical method was commonly employed. This continued Marxist influence on Shakespeare studies in China is partly due to the fact that the impact of Marxism on the Chinese is so deep that some of his principles, particularly dialectic and historic materialism, have become ingrained in the thinking of the people. But another reason could be that the Marxist analytical method is well suited for contemporary Chinese literary works and criticism, which have a strong political orientation stemming mainly from the continuous social turbulence and political unrest in modern China. This same orientation also helps to explain the pronounced political color of Chinese interpretations of Shakespeare's works.

The third and last concept by which the Chinese view Shakespeare is humanism, which is closely linked with the great changes occurring in China after the Cultural Revolution, particularly the upheaval of the country's existing ideology. One cannot understand the immense enthusiasm that the Chinese have shown for Shakespeare since the 1980s without being aware of the monumental changes in contemporary China that have brought about new ideologies, values, and aesthetic tastes. Shakespeare satisfies once again all these new needs of the people. At the end of the 1970s, frustrated by the disaster of the Cultural Revolution, many Chinese people were extremely disappointed in the previous political and economic policies of the ultra-left members of the party and doubted the practicality of the political utopias of both Marx and Mao Tse-tung. Recognizing the seriousness of the situation, Deng Xiao Ping, whom the Chinese regarded as a savior at that time, decided to implement an "open-door" policy and initiate economic reform. The 1980s, therefore, witnessed a series of radical social transformations in China—the increasing demand for democracy, the boom in the market economy, the rise of a cultural "Renaissance"—at the same time that a continuous struggle in the leadership between the reform group and the hard-line conservative group was occurring. Comparatively speaking, the decades of the 1980s and 1990s so far appear to be an era of political and religious tolerance, social contentment associated with economic prosperity and an improvement in living standards, and intellectual liberty characterized by a great increase in cultural undertakings. While these years have also been an age of dreams, enthusiasm, adventure, competition, and patriotism, great potential crisis looms because of the contradiction between the economic basis and the social superstructure.

Of importance to this study is the fact that a striking similarity can be found in many aspects of both contemporary China and the Elizabethan age.[38] China today bears comparison with the Elizabethan period because it is in fact a country in transition from a feudal system (although it is called a socialist system) to a modern industrialized society. Many Chinese scholars share this view. For instance, the famous writer and political dissenter Liu Bin Yan wrote in an article, "In some aspects of social life we are experiencing a radical change similar to that of the transition period in Europe from the Middle Ages to the Renaissance."[39]

For this reason one can understand why the Chinese show such enthusiasm for Shakespeare. They see his works as a mirror reflecting almost all the features of their own society: the struggle between old and new social forces, the corruption of political power, the temptation of money, the conflict and compromise between personal passions and moral order, the emergence of new ideologies and values. It is a short step to identify with the characters of Shakespeare's plays, understand their thoughts, and share their joys and sorrows.

Since the old ideologies and values are no longer suited to China's changing society, the institution of new ones is desperately needed. As Europe did during the Renaissance, China has adopted humanism as the core of its new world view. The Chinese interpretation of humanism seems to be mingled with the European definition as it has evolved over several centuries. The Chinese understand humanism as an ideological principle that concentrates on individual rights, needs, demands, desires, and creative potentialities. It implies human rights and competitive individualism that, they believe, can be found in neither traditional Chinese culture nor Marxism because both philosophies emphasize collectivism. Marxism sees private ownership, which is based on individual desire, as the root of all evil. Confucius also asks the Chinese to restrain personal desires and adapt to a moral order. The Chinese understanding of humanism is affected not only by Western values but also by the modern social and political contexts of China. During the notorious Cultural Revolution, human rights were wantonly trampled, millions died of persecution, and all rational individual demands were claimed to be "bourgeois ideology," which made China an autocratic and poor country. So it is quite clear why the Chinese have strongly called for humanism after the nightmare years of dictatorship and asceticism. For them humanism is no longer a remote trend of thought in Western history or a bourgeois ideology. It is the very philosophy that they desperately need to develop their country and enliven their culture.

The Chinese become extremely excited when they find in Shakespeare's works the very spirit of the times that they need. Shakespeare serves as an important vehicle for spreading humanism. From Shakespeare's plays the Chinese see the celebration of individuality, the awakening of self-consciousness and competitive individualism, a moral principle against obscurantism, and the concepts of freedom, equality, and universal love. As has been proved historically, all of these qualities function as the basic ideology and values for a prosperous bourgeois society or a democratic industrialized country.

Shakespeare's humanism also seems to cater particularly to Chinese young people, who have a widespread "anti-tradition" attitude, fostered by China's serious social problems and their disappointment with Marxism-Maoism and other outmoded tenets. Thus young people often are interested in the skepticism depicted in Shakespeare's plays, especially in the tragedies. Hamlet has been their hero, both in representing such uncertainty and in examining a dislocated and dying society. The philosophical changes in China also help to explain, from another angle, why the Chinese favor the "golden sayings" of Shakespeare: they find in them many useful and practical principles that are suitable for the new era.

The changing ideology, institutions, and life styles have brought about a distinctively new aesthetic taste in contemporary China, which helps the Chinese to enjoy Shakespeare's art even more. Influenced by the spirit of the times and the faster rhythm of life, contemporary Chinese tend to appreciate literary and artistic works having a strong, vigorous, and impassioned style, and characterized by vitality, enthusiasm, variation, and rapid movement. The traditional aesthetic ideal of the "beauty of balance" is out of favor, and many Chinese people, especially the young and intellectuals, have grown weary of the endless sentimentalism of traditional Chinese literature and the political propaganda and formularizing of socialist Chinese literature. The new taste is also characterized by an immediate and direct interest in human nature itself that is affected by the central position of humanism in the ideological framework. The theory of human nature was seriously criticized in the 1960s and during the Cultural Revolution as a bourgeois literary theory and was replaced with the proletarian theory of class analysis and class struggle. This new interest in human nature results in an enthusiasm for the beauty, complexity, and inner world of humanity and helps to explain why Chinese Shakespearean scholars show great interest in the analysis of Shakespeare's characters, even though it is not presently a fashionable topic among their Western counterparts. The new taste also prefers the presentation of unflinching tragic ideas to glossing over reality, asking for a full and unrestrained representation of emotion and a true reflection of life without tedious moralizing. It is evident that Shakespeare can satisfy all these new needs in contemporary China. Shakespeare gives the Chinese not only spiritual strength but also much-needed pleasure.

The influence of the new humanist philosophy in China today on the reception of Shakespeare can be clearly seen in the Shakespearean criticism and productions of the 1980s. It is easy to see that the main concern of the Shakespeare industry in China during this period has been a Chinese version of humanism: Shakespeare's works are viewed and interpreted from the perspective of human nature and human rights and combined with the social and political issues pertinent to contemporary China. In the 1950s and 1960s humanism was occasionally mentioned in Chinese interpretations of Shakespeare's works, but it was only regarded as an ideology in the early stage of capitalism and never linked with the social context of China.

Today humanism has not only become a prime topic of Shakespeare criticism in China but since 1978 it has been closely related to social and political issues by Chinese critics. In an article written in 1979, for example, Yuan Kun comprehensively discusses the historical and immediate significance of Shakespeare's humanism. He believes that Shakespeare represented in his works a humanism that was a prevailing and progressive ideology during the Renaissance, showing through his characters how humanism could be used as an ideological weapon against feudalism. Yuan also believes that this humanism was not the outmoded bourgeois idea that was condemned by the Gang of Four in the Cultural Revolution. Rather, it was of great significance to Chinese society after the Cultural Revolution because the people needed humanism to sweep away feudalism under the cover of socialism.[40] Students are also much taken with the topic. In a selection of Shakespeare criticism edited by the Shakespeare Society of Jilin Province, an article written by three postgraduate students of Jilin University discusses their understanding of Shakespeare's dramatic merits, highly praising Shakespeare's revelation of human nature and the roots of good and evil.[41] Commenting on the practical significance of Shakespeare's humanistic ideal to Chinese society, they wrote:

> Shakespeare tells us that the emancipation of individuality is of great importance to the progress of a modern society. Any restriction of the rational demands and rights of man will hamper the initiative and creativity of people. . . . Shakespeare also tells us that the progress of social development is never smooth, as we see in his tragedies. This should be especially understood by Chinese people, who have just experienced the disaster of the Cultural Revolution.[42]

That the Chinese on Shakespeare endeavor to relate particular social issues in Shakespeare's plays to those of contemporary China has become quite apparent. For example, numerous critics apply the power struggles in Shakespeare's plays to the political situation in China. They do so because the Chinese are disappointed with the existing political system and try to understand why Communist leaders, including Mao Tse-tung himself, who have been claimed to be great liberators of the people are politically degenerate. Many Chinese intellectuals believe that Shakespeare answers this question well: in his plays he clearly demonstrates that an autocratic political system must lead to corruption and oppression and that the passion for power is a fundamental source of disorder in society.[43] I should point out, however, that such discussions must be undertaken carefully and indirectly, for the amount of tolerance available for those who criticize the existing political policies and particularly the leadership of the party is limited.

Great concern about human rights in China can often be found in theatrical humanist approaches to Shakespeare. The insightful speech by a scholar, Ding Tao, delivered at a conference during the Inaugural Chinese Shakespeare Festival, addressed this issue. His topic was the staging of Shakespeare's plays from the standpoint of the modern age, with emphasis on the significance of Shakespeare's humanism for contemporary China. Ding maintained that Shakespeare's plays showed us how people were released from the ideological shackles of the Middle Ages and that the Chinese also faced an arduous task to emancipate themselves from outmoded spiritual fetters and to vindicate human rights and dignity. Thus he believed that to present Shakespeare's plays was, in a sense, to present modern-day China.[44] Other examples associating Shakespeare's works with the social context of China can be seen in amateur readings and discussions. For instance, many Chinese readers share an opinion that Shakespeare's sonnet 66 ("Tir'd with all these, for restful death I cry") vividly mirrors the Cultural Revolution. Iago and Edmund are also frequently associated with the political speculators, careerists, social climbers, informers, and villains during and after the Cultural Revolution.

Shakespeare productions in China since 1978 have tended to approach the dramatist in a humanist way. A generally recognized unwritten principle in Chinese theatrical circles since the 1980s is that a successful Shakespeare production must be one that represents the "original intention" of the dramatist, and that this "original intention" is, in fact, commonly explained as his humanist philosophy. To ensure audience and critical acclaim, therefore, Chinese directors make every effort to embody this idea, which is basically a mixture of Western values and Chinese philosophy, shaped by the country's contemporary social and political contexts. Critics also welcome a combination of this approach and other interpretations, as well as varied stage techniques, as I discussed in chapter 5 and above. As a modernized Shakespeare production, *Love's Labor's Lost* by the Jiangsu Spoken Drama Troupe in April 1986, displayed an obvious humanist approach in a warm and cheerful atmosphere, eliciting especially favorable reactions from young Chinese audiences. Xong Guo Dong, the director, sees the theme of the play as the liberation of human nature from unreasonable spiritual shackles, so he tried to present a "comedy of emancipation" with humanist thoughts and emotions. The treatment of the theme was centered on how the characters free themselves from asceticism. The absurdity of this asceticism, Xong believed, was not exaggerated by the dramatist because the asceticism imposed on the Chinese people during the Cultural Revolution was much more pronounced than that of this play.[45]

Other sinicized Shakespeare productions in the 1980s also conveyed a similar humanist idea. For example, the opera *Twelfth Night* by the Shanghai Shaoxing Opera Troupe in April 1986 was adapted to represent the Chinese understanding of humanism. According to the director, Hu Wei Min, Chinese audiences would be sympathetic to the humanism in Shakespeare's plays due to their experiences in the Cultural Revolution. Referring to his intention to mingle Shakespearean and Chinese styles in the production, Xong pointed out that the most important aspect of Shakespearean is his humanism, so the production must fully represent Shakespeare's affirmation of human value and dignity, praise of human nature, and celebration of individuality.[46]

In 1991 Jean Marsden wrote,

> When Ben Jonson said of Shakespeare that "he was not of an age but for all time," he could not have realised the double implications of his words. While Jonson's lines were written in praise of Shakespeare's timeless appeal, they can also be seen to describe an ongoing process of literary and cultural appropriation in which each new generation attempts to redefine Shakespeare's genius in contemporary terms, projecting its desires and anxieties onto his work.[47]

This view can be proved even by the short history of Shakespeare's in China. We have seen that the Chinese have three ways of understanding Shakespeare in different social and political contexts. The Confucian perspective helps the Chinese to see the similarity between Shakespeare's works and their cultural tradition and to find many open approaches to Shakespeare's thoughts and art. The Confucian philosophy urges followers to pay attention to the qualities emphasized by their cultural tradition such as public service, moral and political duties, the maintenance of order and harmony in society, and so forth. Traditional aesthetic tastes and literary bias enable the Chinese to bestow different interpretations on Shakespeare's plays. A Marxist approach helps the country to accept the dramatist in a harsh political climate and offers the people a philosophical and analytical method of evaluating his works. The Chinese are inclined to appreciate Shakespeare's plays in the light of English and European historical contexts as influenced by Marxist dialectic and historical materialism. Contributing to a deeper understanding and warmer reception of Shakespeare by the Chinese, the humanist approach spurs on the people to find in Shakespeare's plays the qualities lacking in their traditional culture. From this perspective Shakespeare's world is closely connected to one's own experiences, desires, and anxieties and the social and political contexts of China. The dramatist is therefore regarded as a contemporary and an inspirational leader, so his drama is seen as a mirror of changing society. Humanist ideas in Shakespeare's plays such as liberal and competitive individualism, the celebration of human nature and rights, freedom, and equality are taken as powerful ideological weapons by which the people can carry out social reform and enliven many aspects of China's cultural life. This approach has, in fact, paved the way for the participation of Shakespeare's drama in the making of institutions in contemporary China, which I discussed in chapter 5.

In the actual reading, criticism, and production of Shakespeare in China, however, these three major approaches are often mingled, although any one particular approach can be singled out. In one Shakespeare production, two or three different perspectives may be smoothly mixed together, especially when the play is performed in Chinese style, as I analyzed in chapter 5. It is easier to find different approaches in the same piece of writing. For example, when Zhang Yang dealt with Shakespeare's historical concept, he associated Shakespeare's idea with the political situation in China in terms of humanism. Yet the method of analysis he used was Marxist historical materialism. It is also very common for the three approaches to overlap in one's mind. If a Chinese intellectual saw a production of *Timon of Athens*, for example, his or her immediate reaction might be linked with the prevailing worship of money found in contemporary China. Marx's condemnation of the negative value of money would further reinforce this initial impression. But deep in the viewer's consciousness the conventional moral principle of *yi* and *li* would also be operating. *Hamlet* is another play that is likely to arouse such multiple responses among Chinese audiences. In sum, then, it can be said that these three approaches have been most responsible for Shakespeare's thorough assimilation into Chinese culture.

7

Conclusion

THE discussion of Shakespeare's impact on and assimilation into Chinese culture undertaken in chapters 5 and 6 will, I hope, contribute to a deeper understanding of the earlier topics in this book in that they have provided a broad social and cultural background for the examination of the interaction between Shakespeare and traditional Chinese drama. Against this background we can see more clearly the different positions and functions of the two types of drama present in the cultural landscape of China and more fully understand the reasons for the vigorous growth of Shakespeare and the decline of traditional Chinese drama. As I analyzed in the last two chapters, Shakespeare, as an "institution maker," has provided an ideological foundation for the individualistic values and social ideals that a changing Chinese society has desperately needed to build up its new political economy. By contrast, the conventional ideology and values perpetuated by traditional Chinese drama are not—at least in the short term—suitable for a modern developed country. The Cultural Revolution made China a grim society, causing estrangement and caution among its people. The universal love that the Chinese have for Shakespeare's works helps to reconcile the conflicts of a fractured society. So far neither a family love of traditional Chinese drama nor a class love of socialist literature has been able to accomplish this task.

Artistically Shakespeare caters to the new aesthetic taste, which sees traditional Chinese drama as cold and rigid. It is not difficult to understand why the Chinese prefer the realistic tragic endings of Shakespearean tragedies to the fake happy endings of traditional Chinese tragedies. Although the patterns of the "forest utopia" in Shakespeare's comedy and the "garden paradise" in traditional Chinese comedy bear some similarities, the Chinese feel that the "forest utopia" device is more familiar to them because it can be directly associated with the reality of today's China and its social practices, whereas the "paradise garden" is only an embodiment of the remote past.

The favor that the Chinese show toward other characteristics of Shakespeare such as characterization and his poetic and romantic styles, for example, also accounts for his vigor in the country and for the decline of traditional Chinese drama.

It is clear that the interaction between Shakespeare and traditional Chinese drama has been greatly affected by the country's political situation, or, more precisely, by the attitude of the political and cultural elite towards Western culture. This can be seen in the development of the May Fourth New Cultural Movement, the Cultural Revolution, and the reform movement since 1980. Even during the present reform movement, which has seen a sharp increase in Shakespeare's reputation in China, the interaction between Shakespeare and traditional Chinese drama continues to be affected by the political struggle between the reform and the conservative lines. The latter has strongly opposed the influence of the West and the people's increasing demands for democracy, calling it "antibourgeois liberalization." It was no accident that the influential Inaugural Chinese Shakespeare Festival was held in 1986 because in that year the reform politicians prevailed over their conservative foes and Chinese intellectuals enjoyed more freedom than ever before.

After the political events at Tiananmen Square in 1989, the Chinese government—to slow down the influence of the West—launched a campaign to promote traditional Chinese culture. Accordingly, the theatrical activity of traditional Chinese drama, funded by the government, has been revived with the cultural authority's staging of festivals, contests, and television programs. While it can be helpful to revitalize traditional Chinese drama, the obvious underlying political purpose may undermine the effect of all these efforts.

By contrast, the once large-scale activity concerning Shakespeare has been adversely affected by the political climate. The second Chinese Shakespeare Festival, which was to take place in April 1990, was postponed for two years and finally canceled, owing to the lack of critical support from the government.

More recently, however, the signs are encouraging. With an upsurge in economic reform, a new political climate has appeared since the summer of 1992. Inspired by this favorable situation, Chinese Shakespeare scholars and theatrical workers have carried out a series of large-scale activities.

In May 1993 an international conference on Shakespeare studies was held in Wuhan, organized by Wuhan Shakespeare Center and Wuhan University. It was the first time that the country's Shakespearean scholars had convened an international conference on Shakespeare and also the first opportunity for them to exchange academic ideas with their Western counterparts. More than sixty Western and Chinese Shakespeare scholars, including those from Taiwan and Hong Kong, attended the conference. Fifty research papers were submitted, and scenes from *A Midsummer Night's Dream* and *As You Like It* were presented by students of the English Department at Wuhan University.

The next year brought an even greater event—the Shanghai International Shakespeare Festival, organized by the Shakespeare Association of China, the Shanghai City Council, and the Shanghai Drama Institute. In September 1994, ten Shakespeare productions by German, British, and Chinese drama companies were staged in China's biggest city. They were:

Romeo and Juliet, by the Nuremberg Youth Theater Company (Germany)

Twelfth Night, jointly staged by the Edinburgh Royal Lyceum Theatre Company and the Salisbury Playhouse (U.K.)

Macbeth, by The Workshop Theater of the Drama Department, Leeds University (U.K.)

Othello, by the Shanghai People's Art Theater

The Revenge of the Prince (Hamlet), by the Shanghai Shaoxing Opera Troupe

Hamlet, jointly staged by the Taiwan Ping Feng Workshop and the Shanghai Modern People's Theatre

The Merchant of Venice, by the Drama Troupe of Fudan University

The Merchant of Venice, by the Shanghai Children's Art Theater

Henry IV (parts 1 and 2), by the Shanghai Drama Institute

Troilus and Cressida, by the Harbin Opera Theater

In addition, two radio plays—*A Midsummer Night's Dream* and *As You Like It* by the Shanghai People's Radio Station—and a campus production of *The Merry Wives of Windsor* by the Northeast Normal University were also presented during the festival. Of the Chinese productions, *Henry IV* and *Troilus and Cressida* were performed for the first time on the Chinese stage. The latter was also the first production presented as a Western-style opera in China.

Displaying a great variety of performing styles and interpretations, the festival was very successful. Chinese critics and audiences seemed more open-minded than ever before, which allowed theatrical professionals to adapt the plays more freely than they could for the 1986 Chinese Shakespeare Festival. For example, the director and adaptor of the Shaoxing opera's *The Revenge of the Prince* staged the play entirely in the Shaoxing opera style without worrying about the loss of a Shakespeare style. In the jointly performed *Hamlet,* the original plot was changed to reflect modern-day events, which would not have been accepted by an audience eight years earlier. New ideas were very obvious in some productions. In *The Merchant of Venice* by the Drama Troupe of Fudan University, for example, Shylock was presented as a positive character, with his business philosophy and complaints about the suffering of Jews handled sympathetically. This treatment apparently derived from the impact of the country's recent economic reforms.

The festival was supported by a campaign to further popularize Shakespeare among Shanghai citizens, especially young people. Many activities publicized the event such as articles in newspapers, television and radio programs, an exhibition, lectures, seminars, a competition, and even the sale of Shakespeare T-shirts. The city stood to benefit from the festival both politically and economically since it would help to establish the image of Shanghai as an international metropolis, one sought by the city after it was declared a special economic zone a few years ago. From a cultural standpoint the festival was part of a recent campaign throughout the country— in a sense a new cultural revolution—to emphasize the value of high-level art and literature over vulgar cultural products and to save the nation's cultural heritage from the corrosive influence of commercialism and money worship. Once again Shakespeare is a highly held banner in this new revolution.

What bias-free conclusions can we draw about the significance of the interaction between Shakespeare and traditional Chinese drama and culture? Perhaps Shakespeare's greatest contribution to China lies in the effect he has had on the vitalization of traditional Chinese drama. Through the immensity of his popularity in China, Shakespeare has forced the Chinese to examine the weaknesses of their own dramatic tradition and has helped them to recognize that the future path for traditional Chinese drama lies in self-improvement and development by adopting the best qualities of other dramatic traditions while retaining its own distinctiveness.

The interaction between Shakespeare and Chinese culture has also had a great impact on China. The dramatist has significantly influenced the institution of China's new ideology by providing powerful ideological concepts and new values and by helping to generate a new culture and body of literature in the country. Moreover, Shakespeare's rapid assimilation into Chinese culture serves as one more indication of his universal appeal and compatibility with foreign cultures.

It is clear that the significance of the interaction between Shakespeare and traditional Chinese drama is not limited to theatrical circles. The relationship between the two types of drama, in fact, reflects the interaction between two great cultural traditions. Like traditional drama, the entire Chinese cultural tradition has been in crisis since the beginning of the twentieth century. But as wise people have pointed out, Chinese culture would eventually regenerate itself through an exchange with Western culture. The interaction between Shakespeare and traditional Chinese culture has proved this to be true. The real crisis actually has come from the country's isolation from the outside world, rather than the influence of other cultural traditions. It is wrong to think of Western culture as conflicting with Chinese culture. In the long term the two cultural traditions can only complement each other, as we have seen in the process of Shakespeare's assimilation into Chinese culture. The prosperity of Japan shows that Western culture can be successfully mingled with a cultural tradition that has been thought to be very similar to Chinese culture. Recently Chinese scholars have predicted that the future of the world will depend on the renaissance of Chinese culture because they think Western culture has reached its peak and shown its own signs of crisis.[1] It is difficult to know now whether this prediction will come true, but one can say with some certainty that the cultural gap between the two great civilizations will be gradually bridged by their closer and more frequent exchanges and that their eventual combination will vastly contribute to the material and cultural prosperity of the world.

In her discussion of the intercultural tendencies of postmodern theater, a Western critic recently commented on whether a "world theater" and a "world culture" would appear in the future:

> It may well be that this type of interculturality reflects a general development in the culture of post-modern societies (and even in some societies in the Third World): one can observe a certain tendency of different cultures to merge into one world-culture. Whether such a world-culture will in fact arise and what it will look like is, for the time being, impossible to predict. Perhaps the search for a universal theatrical language in post-modern theater indicates that the theater has already passed into this new era.[2]

Certainly the interaction between Shakespeare and traditional Chinese drama can be included in the intercultural tendencies of postmodern theater. If a "world theater" does emerge, the blending of Shakespeare and traditional Chinese drama surely will have contributed to both its establishment and the founding of a "world culture."

Appendix: The Development of Traditional Chinese Drama

Pre-Qin Period (770–221 B.C.)	Also called Spring and Autumn Period. In embryonic stage, in the form of dancing and singing. Earliest actors were skilled court jesters.
Han Dynasty (206 B.C.– A.D. 220)	Called "Variety Plays" in early form; mixture of dance, song, acrobatics, martial art, and simple acting.
Tang Dynasty (618–907)	Short comedy satirizing corrupt officers, usually performed by two actors. Song and dance dramas praising kings' deeds, performed with masks, also popular.
Song Dynasty (960–1279)	Mature period. Dramatic form fully developed, with 5 role types. Mainly satirical comedy representing townspeople and lowlife types. More than 200 plays written but very few survive.
Yuan Dynasty (1279–1368)	Golden age of traditional drama. Main form called *zaju*, a combination of speech, singing, dancing, and acrobatics. Poetic description and stylized movements. Four acts plus prologue. Many different types of roles. Facial makeup used. In some plays only the leading male or female role could sing. Comedy, tragedy, and historical plays written. Broad depiction of society, including serious social problems. More than 100 playwrights and 600 plays (160 extant). Half of the greatest tragedies and comedies written in this period, such as Guan Han Qing's *An Injustice to Dou E*, Ji Jun Xiang's *The Orphan of the House of Zhao*, and Wang Shi Pu's *The Romance of the Western Chamber*.
Ming Dynasty (1368–1644)	Period of continued development. Main dramatic form called *chuanqi* (romance); more lengthy than *zaju* of Yuan dynasty. Diverse and flexible performing methods. Every type of role allowed to sing. Variety of music used, with "Kun tone" (Kunju opera) dominating in later

253

years of dynasty. Plots more complex. More than 100 playwrights, including the great dramatist Tang Xian Zu (*The Peony Pavilion*), and 1,000 plays, including tragedies and comedies.

Qing Dynasty (1644–1911)	*Chuanqi* (mainly in Kunju style) remained dominant until later years of dynasty, when many types of local drama flourished with differing musical styles and languages. Patriotism a major theme. Many great tragedies (such as Kong Shang Ren's *The Fan of Peach Blossom* and Hong Sheng's *The Hall of Longevity*) and famous comedies (as Li Yu's *The Error of a Kite*).
Modern China (1919–1994)	Gradual decline as modern tastes changed, but still remains one of the major dramatic entertainments, especially for the older generation and rural people. Performing techniques much improved but new plays rarely written. Some new plays in the Cultural Revolution very popular yet damaged by the political ambitions of Mao's wife. Main forms include Beijing, Kunju, Shaoxing, Huangmei, and Guangdong operas and 20 other types of local drama, with numerous outstanding actors such as Mei Lan Fang and Zhou Xin Fang. Recently popular once more, due to changes reflecting modern tastes.

Notes

INTRODUCTION

1. Hanna Scolnicov, introduction to *The Play Out of Context*, ed. Hanna Scolnicov and Peter Holland (Cambridge: Cambridge University Press, 1989), 1.

2. See, for example: He Qi Xin, "China's Shakespeare," *Shakespeare Quarterly* 37 (Summer 1986): 149–59; Philip Brockbank, "Shakespeare Renaissance in China," *Shakespeare Quarterly* 39 (Summer 1988): 195–204; and Zha Pei De and Tian Jia, "Shakespeare in Traditional Chinese Operas," *Shakespeare Quarterly* 39 (Summer 1988): 204–11.

3. Yi Yu, "The Exchange between Oriental Theatre and Western Theatre," in *A Selection of Comparative Drama*, ed. Xia Xie Shi and Lu Run Tang (Beijing: Chinese Drama Press, 1988), 118–48.

4. Jonathan Dollimore and Alan Sinfield, foreword to *Political Shakespeare: New Essays in Cultural Materialism*, ed. Jonathan Dollimore and Alan Sinfield (Manchester: Manchester University Press, 1985), viii.

5. See, for example: Chen Xing He, "*Hamlet* and *The Orphan of the House of Zhao*," *Journal of Nanjing Teacher's College* 2 (March 1983): 22–27; Chen Sou Zhu, "*The Peony Pavilion* and *Romeo and Juliet*," *Tang Xian Zu Studies: A Selection* (Beijing: Chinese Drama Press, 1984), 224–54; Ye Xiao Fan, "*The Sad Story of Lady Wang* and *Romeo and Juliet*," in *A Selection of Comparative Literature* (Tianjing: Nankai University Press, 1984), 107–25; Fang Ping, "Cleopatra and Lady Yang in *The Hall of Longevity*," *Literature and Art Studies* 2 (Summer 1985): 116–24; Hong Xin, "*Othello* and *The Story of a Jade Hairpin*," *Theatre World* 3 (May 1986): 86–87; and Xu Hao Yu, "*Macbeth* and *The Orphan of the House of Zhao*," *Chinese Literature Studies* 1 (Spring 1988): 56–61. All of the above articles are available only in Chinese.

CHAPTER 1. TRAGEDY AND COMEDY

1. Dieter Mehl, *Shakespeare's Tragedies: An Introduction* (Cambridge: Cambridge University Press, 1986), 8–9.

2. See *The Ten Greatest Classical Chinese Tragedies*, ed. Wang Ji Si (Shanghai: Shanghai Literature and Art Press, 1983), hereafter cited as *Classical Chinese Tragedies*.

3. Philip H. Highfill, Kalman A. Burnim, and Edward A. Langhans, eds., *A Biographical Dictionary of Actors, Actresses, Musicians, Dancers, Managers, and Other Stage Personnel in London, 1660–1800*, 14 vols. (Carbondale: Southern Illinois University Press, 1984), 4:31, 10:395.

4. Arthur Murphy, "The Orphan of China: A Tragedy," in *The British Drama: A Collection of the Most Esteemed Tragedies, Comedies, Operas, and Farces in the English Language* (1832; reprint, London: Jones and Co., 1974), 1394.

5. The original thought of Confucius was quite humane and benevolent. Yet increasingly strict moral principles were added by later philosophers due to the need of the feudal rulers to strengthen their absolute monarchy.

6. In A.D. 755 General An Lu Shan launched an armed rebellion against Emperor Tang Ming and occupied the capital city, Chang An. The rebellion, however, was quickly put down.

7. Geoffrey Brereton, *Principles of Tragedy* (London: Routledge and Kegan Paul, 1968), 17.

8. Some Chinese scholars argue that there are epics in early Chinese poetry such as "Sheng Ming" and "Gong Liu" in *The Book of Songs*. These poems are too short and simple to be classified as epics, however.

9. A. C. Bradley, *Shakespearean Tragedy* (London: Macmillan and Co., 1905), 28.

10. Lady Yang was praised by the Chinese as one of the four most beautiful women in Chinese history.

11. See John Drakakis's introduction to *Alternative Shakespeare,* ed. John Drakakis (London: Methuen, 1985), 6–9.

12. The quoted Chinese title is the name of the tune to which the verse for singing is set.

13. Dorothea Krook, *Elements of Tragedy* (New Haven: Yale University Press, 1969), 15.

14. Cheng Chao Xiang, "On Tragic Protagonists," *Journal of Beijing University* 5 (September 1987): 81.

15. In ancient China people believed that if some injustice occurs, nature can respond to human behavior and uphold justice.

16. M. S. Silk and J. P. Stern, eds., *Nietzsche on Tragedy* (Cambridge: Cambridge University Press, 1981), 72.

17. Bradley, *Shakespearean Tragedy,* 29.

18. The five elements have been successfully used in Chinese medicine to explain various physiological and pathological phenomena, although it seems farfetched to use them to interpret some other phenomena in the physical world, especially in human society.

19. W. R. Elton, "Shakespeare and the Thought of His Age," in *The Cambridge Companion to Shakespeare Studies,* ed. Stanley Wells (Cambridge: Cambridge University Press, 1986), 28.

20. Liu Zai Fu, "On Literary Studies," *Wen Hui Monthly* (Shanghai) 2 (February 1988): 2–7.

21. Wu Guo Qin, *The History of Traditional Chinese Drama* (Shanghai: Shanghai Literature and Art Press, 1980), 168.

22. There are some exceptions in this respect; for instance, Thomas Hobbes, the English political philosopher, advocated an absolute sovereign.

23. Catherine Belsey, "Disrupting Difference: Meaning and Gender in the Comedies," in *Alternative Shakespeare,* ed. John Drakakis (London: Methuen, 1985), 167–77.

24. See Hugh Grady, *The Modernist Shakespeare* (Oxford: Clarendon Press, 1991), 235–45.

25. Mehl, *Shakespeare's Tragedies,* 1.

26. Ibid.

27. See pre-Qin literature, e.g. *The Book of Songs* and *Li Sao* by the great Chinese poet Qu Yuan.

28. This quiet sadness is especially evident in traditional Chinese music, as for instance, the famous Cantonese music.

29. See *The History of Chinese Literature,* ed. Literature Institute of the Chinese Academy of Social Sciences, 3 vols. (Beijing: People's Literature Press, 1978), 1:186–202, 2:320–34, 617–32.

30. Cai Zhong Xiang, *The Highlights of Classical Chinese Dramatic Theory* (Beijing: Chinese People's University Press, 1988), 30.

31. Silk and Stern, eds., *Nietzsche on Tragedy,* 327.

32. James L. Smith, *Melodrama* (London: Methuen, 1973), 64–65.

33. Wang Ji Si, preface to *The Ten Greatest Classical Chinese Comedies,* 13–15.

34. A. R. Humphreys, introduction to *Much Ado About Nothing,* the Arden Shakespeare, ed. A. R. Humphreys (London: Methuen, 1981), 68.

35. Kenneth Muir, *Shakespeare's Comic Sequence* (Liverpool: Liverpool University Press, 1979), 51.

36. David M. Bergeron and Geraldo U. De Sousa, *Shakespeare: A Study and Research Guide* (Lawrence: University Press of Kansas, 1987), 140–41.

37. Northrop Frye, *A Natural Perspective* (New York: Columbia University Press, 1965), 46.

38. Ibid., 73–78.

39. Ibid., 119–22.

40. Tang Xian Zu (1550–1616), the author of *The Peony Pavilion* and one of the greatest Chinese dramatists, is often compared by Chinese critics to Shakespeare, partly because of their remarkable dramatic merits and partly due to the interesting fact that they were contemporaries and died in the same year. Tang's four major plays, including *The Peony Pavilion,* are called the "four dreams" because each of them has scenes involving a dream. *The Peony Pavilion,* together with *Macbeth,* was performed by a Chinese drama company at the 1987 Edinburgh Festival. See chapter 4 for an account of this event.

41. The argument occurred mainly in the Ming dynasty. Almost all the critics who insisted on moralization, such as the well-known playwright Wang Shi Zhen (1526–90), thought that *The Story of a Pipa* was much better than *The Secluded Boudoir* because the former was written to enhance decency and the latter to present passion. In this argument *The Romance of the Western Chamber* was also criticized by the orthodox critics as a poor play to represent lasciviousness. Yet more broad-minded critics and writers believed that *The Secluded Boudoir* and *The Romance of the Western Chamber* were better than *The Story of a Pipa.* For example, the famous thinker and writer Li Zhi (1527–1602), who initiated a literary movement to emphasize emotion in dramatic creations, thought that *The Secluded Boudoir* and *The Romance of the Western Chamber* were full of real feelings and emotions, hence they were more moving than *The Story of a Pipa* because the latter was affected and distorted by the feudal ethical code and had not as much real emotion as the first two. For details of the argument see Cai, *Highlights of Classical Chinese Dramatic Theory,* 25–35.

CHAPTER 2. GENERAL ARTISTIC CHARACTERISTICS AND THE RELATED CULTURAL CONTEXTS

1. Karl Jaspers, *Tragedy Is Not Enough,* trans. Harald A. T. Reiche, Harry T. Moore, and Karl W. Deutsch (Hamden, Conn.: Archon Books, 1969), 32–33.

2. Samuel Johnson, "Preface to Shakespeare," *Shakespeare Criticism: A Selection*, ed. D. Nichol Smith (Oxford: Oxford University Press, 1926), 98.

3. Philip Sidney, "An Apology for Poetry," in *Elizabethan Critical Essays*, ed. G. Gregory Smith, 2 vols. (Oxford: Clarendon Press, 1904), 1:199.

4. Li Yu (1611–80), a well-known dramatist and critic in the Qing dynasty, was noted for his comedy *The Errors of a Kite* and his book *On Drama*, which was the most influential writing on theatrical theory in seventeenth-century China. He was also a supervisor of a private drama company.

5. Li Yu, *On Drama* (1658; reprint, Changsha: Hunan People's Press, 1980), 42.

6. Ma Shuo Rong, "An Artistic Comparison Between Shakespeare and Traditional Chinese Drama," *Shakespeare Studies* (Shakespeare Association of China) 2 (October 1984): 238.

7. G. W. F. Hegel, *Aesthetik*, trans. Zhu Guang Qian, 3 vols. (Beijing: Commercial Press, 1980), 3:334.

8. Cai, *Highlights of Classical Chinese Dramatic Theory*, 43.

9. Roland Mushat Frye, *Shakespeare: The Art of the Dramatist* (London: Allen and Unwin, 1981), 228.

10. J. I. M. Stewart, "Shakespeare's Men and Their Morals," in *Shakespeare Criticism 1935–1960*, ed. Anne Ridler (Oxford: Oxford University Press, 1970), 290.

11. The translation of this passage is by Shih Chung Wen, *The Golden Age of Chinese Drama: Yuan Tsa-chu* (Princeton: Princeton University Press, 1976), 20–21.

12. Caroline F. E. Spurgeon, "Leading Motives in the Imagery of Shakespeare's Tragedies," in *Shakespeare Criticism 1910–1935*, ed. Anne Ridler (Oxford: Oxford University Press, 1962), 18.

13. Wolfgang H. Clemen, *The Development of Shakespeare's Imagery* (London: Methuen, 1953), 54–55.

14. Shih, *The Golden Age of Chinese Drama*, 159–60.

15. Edward A. Armstrong, *Shakespeare's Imagination* (Lincoln: University of Nebraska Press, 1979), 168.

16. The translation of these two passages is by Shih, *The Golden Age of Chinese Drama*, 135.

17. Wang Bo, "The Pavilion of Tengwang," in *Classical Chinese Literary Works*, ed. Zhu Dong Run (Shanghai: Shanghai Classic Press, 1980), 257.

18. Li Yu, "Yu Mei Ren," in *A Selection of Classical Chinese Poems*, ed. Lin Geng and Fen Yuan Jun, 4 vols. (Beijing: People's Literature Press, 1979), 2:562.

19. I am indebted here to a lecture given by Professor Han Jin Tai at Beijing Language Institute in June 1987.

20. Peter Jones, ed., introduction to *Imagist Poetry* (London: Penguin Books, 1972), 29.

21. Quoted by Arthur M. Eastman, *A Short History of Shakespearean Criticism* (New York: Norton, 1974), 40.

22. L. Mackinnon, *Shakespeare the Aesthete* (Basingstoke: Macmillan, 1988), ix.

CHAPTER 3. THE IMPACT OF SHAKESPEARE ON TRADITIONAL CHINESE DRAMA

1. Quoted in "Shakespeare's Plays in China," *The Drama* (Beijing) 4 (April 1954): 3.

2. Quoted in Cao Wei Feng, "Shakespeare in China," *Literature and Art Monthly* (Beijing) 4 (April 1954): 7.

3. Quoted in Zhang Si Yang, Xu Bin, and Zhang Xiao Yang, *A General Survey of Shakespeare* (Beijing: Chinese Drama Press, 1989), 516. Further page references to this work are given after the pertinent quotations.

4. Player Meng was a very famous and perhaps the earliest actor in Chinese history. He served as a clown in the court during the pre-Qin period (475–221 B.C.). Surviving stories recount how he mocked and criticized the bad behavior of the king through his speech and performance.

5. *The Diary of Guo Song Tao*, ed. Hunan People's Press, 3 vols. (Changsha: Hunan People's Press, 1982), 3:267–68.

6. Ibid., 3:641.

7. Ibid., 3:743.

8. Yan Fu, *The Evolution of Nature* (1894; reprint, Beijing: Science Press, 1971), 57.

9. Ibid.

10. Yan Fu, *An Elementary Introduction to Logic* (1908; reprint, Beijing: Commercial Press, 1981), 56.

11. Liang Qi Chao, "Yin Bin Room's Notes on Poetry," *Xin Min Monthly* (Shanghai) 5 (May 1902): 8.

12. *The Complete Works of Lu Xun*, 30 vols. (Beijing: People's Literature Press, 1980), 1:64.

13. Ibid., 1:35.

14. Ibid., 1:52.

15. Preface to *The Strange Tales from Overseas* (Shanghai: Da Wen Press, 1903), 1.

16. Lin Shu, preface to *The Mysterious Stories of the English Poet* (Shanghai: Commercial Press, 1904), 1.

17. Guo Mo Ruo, "My Childhood," *The Complete Works of Guo Mo Ruo*, 15 vols. (Chengdu: Sichuan People's Press, 1982), 1:118.

18. Qiu Ke An, "The Translating Technique in the Translation of Shakespeare's Plays," *People's Daily* (Beijing), overseas edition, 13 June 1991, 7.

19. Sun Da Yu, preface to the translation of *King Lear*, trans. Sun Da Yu (Shanghai: Commercial Press, 1948), 2–4.

20. See above, n. 18.

21. Cao Shu Jun and Sun Fu Liang, *Shakespeare on the Chinese Stage* (Harbin: Harbin Press, 1989), 77.

22. Ibid., 86–87.

23. Ibid., 91–92.

24. Cao, "Shakespeare in China," 12.

25. Guan Cha Jia, "The Column of Theatrical Criticm," *Da Gong Newspaper* (Shanghai), 9 June 1937, 3.

26. Zhang He, *Modern Drama in China* (Changchun: Jilin University Reference Department, 1979), 45.

27. Li Hong, *Modern Drama Studies* (Changchun: Jilin University Reference Department, 1980), 88.

28. Wang Yi Qun, "The Development of the Theatrical Shakespeare on the Chinese Stage," in *Shakespeare in China*, ed. Shakespeare Association of China (Shanghai: Shanghai Literature and Art Press, 1987), 96.

29. Ibid., 97–98.

30. Brockbank, "Shakespeare Renaissance in China," 195.

31. Cao and Liang, *Shakespeare on the Chinese Stage*, 59.

32. Meng Xian Qiang, ed., *Shakespeare Criticism in China* (Changchun: Jilin Education Press, 1991), 16–17.

33. Lu, *Complete Works*, 1:328.

34. Ibid., 1:329.

35. Hu Shi Zhi, "The Evolution of Literature and Drama Reform," *New Youth* (Beijing) 5 (May 1918): 24.

36. Tian Han, preface to the translation of *Hamlet*, trans. Tian Han (Shanghai: Commercial Press, 1922), 1.

37. Player Meng was a clown in the pre-Qin period. One day he wore the clothes of the late Prime Minister Sun Shu Ao and went to see the king. He acted so well that the king thought the dead prime minister had come back to life. Later people used the expression "the costume of Player Meng" to imply high skill in acting and theatrical activity.

38. Qian Xuan Tong, *Chinese New Literature* (Shanghai: Commercial Press, 1954), 79–80.

39. Wu Guo Qin, *The History of Traditional Chinese Drama* (Shanghai: Shanghai Literature and Art Press, 1980), 167.

40. Meng, *Shakespeare Criticism in China*, 44.

41. Zhang Fa, *Chinese Culture and Tragic Concepts* (Beijing: Chinese People's University Press, 1989), 120–21.

42. Ibid., 121.

43. Ding Jia Sheng, "Thinking Deeply of the Impact," in *Shakespeare in China*, ed. Shakespeare Association of China (Shanghai: Shanghai Literature and Art Press, 1987), 87–88.

44. Interview with the performers of Beijing Opera from five cities at a symposium held in Beijing, 4 May 1987.

45. See above, n. 2, 89–90.

46. Interview with students from Qinghua University at Beijing Haidan Theater, 18 March 1986.

47. Speech of Mr. Tong at the academic discussion held in the Central Drama Academy, Beijing, on 18 April 1986, from author's notes.

48. Meng, *Shakespeare Criticism in China*, 39.

49. Huang Yue Hua, ed., *Publication Reference Material* (Changchun: Jilin University Reference Department, 1990), 55.

CHAPTER 4. SHAKESPEARE ON THE CHINESE STAGE

1. Huang Zuo Lin, "The Prospects of Shakespeare's Plays on the Chinese Stage: A Speech Given at the Seminar of China's Inaugural Shakespeare Festival," in *Shakespeare in China*, ed. Shakespeare Association of China (Shanghai: Shanghai Literature and Art Press, 1987), 13.

2. Ibid., 14.

3. Zhang An Jian, "The Treasure Shakespeare Has Left Us: A Reflection on the Inaugural Chinese Shakespeare Festival," in *Shakespeare's Triple Play: Research, Performance, and Teaching*, ed. Zhang Si Yang, Men Xian Qiang, and Xu Bin (Changchun: Northeast Normal University Press, 1988), 218.

4. Lu Gu Shun, "Reflections after the Curtainfall," in *Shakespeare in China*, ed. Shakespeare Association of China (Shanghai: Shanghai Literature and Art Press, 1987), 35.

5. John Willett, ed., *Brecht on Theatre* (London: Methuen, 1964), 91–99.

6. The information given here is based on my own observations.

7. Interview with Shao Hong Cao at the Institute of Traditional Chinese Drama in Beijing on 25 January 1984.

8. Speech of Ma Yong An at the seminar held in Central Drama Academy in Beijing, 20 April 1986, during the Inaugural Chinese Shakespeare Festival.

9. Hu Wei Min, "Notes on Directing *Twelfth Night* in the Form of Shaoxing Opera," in *Shakespeare in China*, ed. Shakespeare Association of China (Shanghai: Shanghai Literature and Art Press, 1987), 128.

10. Hu Wei Min, "The Combination of Chinese Theatre and Western Theatre," *Wenhui Daily* (Shanghai), 20 April 1986, 2.

11. The Chinese version of this play was kindly provided by Zhou Shui He, the adaptor of the play.

12. Fernau Hall, *Daily Telegraph*, 28 August 1987, quoted in "Edinburgh International Festival Supplement 1987," *London Theatre Record*, 13–26 August 1987, 33.

13. Ibid.

14. Alfred Weiss, "The Edinburgh Festival, 1987," *Shakespeare Quarterly* 39 (Summer 1988): 85.

15. *Scotsman*, 29 August 1987, quoted in "Edinburgh International Festival Supplement 1987," *London Theatre Record*, 13–26 August 1987, 34.

16. Ibid.

17. Jin Zhi, "An Experiment with Misgivings—Thoughts Related to the Adaptation of *Much Ado About Nothing* into the Form of Huangmei Opera," in *Shakespeare in China*, ed. Shakespeare Association of China (Shanghai: Shanghai Literature and Art Press, 1987), 147.

18. Ibid., 153.

19. Speech of Zhang Qi Hong at the seminar held in the Central Drama Academy in Beijing, 15 April 1986, Inaugural Chinese Shakespeare Festival.

20. Brockbank, "Shakespeare Renaissance in China," 197.

21. Interview with Zhang Qi Hong at the seminar held in Central Drama Academy in Beijing, 15 April 1986, Inaugural Chinese Shakespeare Festival.

22. Impromptu speech of a teacher at Beijing Foreign Language Institute at the seminar held in Central Drama Academy in Beijing, 17 April 1986.

23. Speech of Zhang Li Wei at the seminar held in the Central Drama Academy in Beijing, 14 April 1986.

24. Speech of Jin Nai Qian at the seminar held in the Central Drama Academy in Beijing, 19 April 1986.

25. Xong Guo Dong, "Performing Shakespearean Plays in the Modern Manner," *Bulletin of the Inaugural Chinese Shakespeare Festival* (Shanghai: Shanghai Drama Institute, 1986), 2:2.

26. Li Jun Dong, "Art News," *People's Daily* (Beijing), 31 December 1994, 3.

CHAPTER 5. LOOKING AHEAD: SHAKESPEARE IN THE CULTURAL LANDSCAPE OF CHINA

1. Tian Han, "The Evolution of Shakespearean Theatre in the West," *Nanguo Monthly* (Beijing) 4 (April 1929): 26–35.

2. The biographical information in this paragraph derives from Cao Shu Jun, *The Biography of Cao Yu* (Beijing: China Youth Press, 1989), 35–39.

3. Li Zi Po, "Cao Yu's Talk about Drama," *Short Play Writing* (Beijing) 11 (November 1981): 53.

4. Cao Yu, "Talking with the Playwrights about Reading and Writing," *Play Writing* (Beijing) 10 (October 1982): 5.

5. Ibid., 6.

6. Ibid., 7.

7. Ibid., 9.

8. Guo Mo Ruo, "My Childhood," *Selected Works*, 6:114.

9. Guo Mo Ruo, "From *Hu Fu* to the Essence of Tragedy," *Guo Mo Ruo on Literary Creation* (Shanghai: Shanghai Literature and Art Press, 1983), 19.

10. Guo Mo Ruo, "How I Wrote *The Chinese Cherry Bush*," in *A Selection of Guo Mo Ruo's Plays* (Beijing: People's Literature Press, 1958), 36.

11. "Qu Yuan and *King Lear*," *The Selected Works of Guo Mo Ruo*, 3:317–18.

12. Ibid., 3:319–22.

13. Huang Shi Mo, *Guo Mo Ruo's "Qu Yuan"* (Chengdu: Sichuan People's Press, 1981), 128.

14. Yu Shang Yuan, "Why Should We Stage Shakespeare's Plays?" *Zhongyang Daily* (Nanjing), 18 June 1937, 4.

15. Cao and Sun, *Shakespeare on the Chinese Stage*, 174–75.

16. Huang Yue Hua, ed., *Theatre Research Reference Material* (Changchun: Jilin University Reference Department, 1986), 15–16.

17. Zhu Yan Ping, "How I Acted Wu Song," *Television and Film Weekly* 21 (May 1987): 4.

18. See Chen Ming, "What's Wrong with the Current Dramatic Creation," in *A Selection of Drama Studies*, ed. Huang Yue Qin (Changchun: Jilin University Reference Department, 1984), 44–49, and Jiao Zu, "Where Is Our Theatre Going?" *Drama Studies* 4 (July 1985): 5–11.

19. Interview with Mrs. Li Yue Qin, September 1985, Beijing.

20. Professor Meng Xian Qiang to author, 5 October 1988.

21. Edward Berry, "Teaching Shakespeare in China," *Shakespeare Quarterly* 39 (Summer 1988): 212–26.

22. "Programme of Foreign Literature Studies," *Postgraduate Studies in Chinese Universities from 1979 to 1984* (Beijing: State Education Commission, 1985), 108–15.

23. Interview with Professor Tao De Zhen in February 1987, Beijing Teacher's University.

24. Shan San Ya, "Special Report on the Art Festival of the 11th Asian Games," *Guangming Daily* (Beijing), 1 October 1990, 4.

25. "Art News," *Guangming Daily* (Beijing), 5 January 1992, 2.

26. "Statistics of the Living Conditions of the Chinese in the Past Decade," *People's Daily* (Beijing), 14 February 1991, 1.

27. Zhang Jun Chuan, "The First Attempt: Notes on the Symposium on the Radio Play *Macbeth*," in *Shakespeare in China*, ed. Shakespeare Association of China (Shanghai: Shanghai Literature and Art Press, 1987), 170.

28. *Jilin Radio and Television Weekly* (Changchun) 20 (May 1992): 2.

29. Zhang Yi, ed., *Modern Chinese Poets* (Changchun: Jilin University Reference Department, 1980), 102.

30. As reported by my former colleague Xu Bin, a lecturer at Jilin University.

31. Cao Wen Han, "A Note about the Creation of Shakespeare's Portrait," in *Shakespeare's Triple Play: Research, Performance, and Teaching*, ed. Zhang Si Yang,

Meng Xian Qiang, and Xu Bin (Changchun: Northeast Normal University Press, 1987), 257.

32. Xong Zhong Wu, "The Artistic Tendencies of the Contemporary Novel," *Literature Criticism* (Beijing) 3 (May 1986): 126–28.

33. Wen Jie, "My Creative Experience," in *The Discussion of Creative Writing by the Young Novelists*, ed. Wang Gang (Changchun: Jilin University Press, 1988), 22–24.

34. Xu Jing, "The Tendency of Contemporary Chinese Poetry," *Baihua Monthly* (Changchun) 4 (April 1985): 42.

35. Fan Hong, "The Evolution of Characterization from Moral Type to Individualization," *Jianghai Forum* (Tianjing) 5 (September 1981): 17.

36. Lan Ren Zhe, "The Main Methods of Contemporary Literary Criticism," *Literary Theory Studies* (Beijing) 3 (May 1982): 144–54.

37. Zhang Long Xi, "The Revival of the Gods," *Reading* (Beijing) 4 (July 1984): 36–41.

38. Cao and Sun, *Shakespeare on the Chinese Stage*, 80–81.

39. "The News Report," *People's Daily* (Beijing), 12 June 1986, 1.

40. Zheng Tu Sheng, "Gold, Yellow . . . ," *Education in China* (Beijing), 7 February 1993, 4.

41. Liu Run Wei, "Shakespeare, *Timon of Athens* and Marx," *Guangming Daily* (Beijing), 9 June 1993, 3.

42. Kang Ding, "The Russian International Shakespeare Conference," *Literature* (Beijing), 6 June 1991, 4.

43. Xie De Hui, "Money, the Desperate Beast," *People's Daily* (Beijing), 27 February 1989, 7.

44. Jing Zhong, "What Happened in the Dark," *Liaoyang Daily* (Shenyang), 3 July 1987, 2.

45. Han Xing, "A New Marriage Fad in Guangzhou," *The Youth* (Beijing) 5 (May 1990): 16.

CHAPTER 6. THE CHINESE VISION OF SHAKESPEARE

1. Zhang He, "What Should We Learn from Shakespeare?" *Literature and Art* (Beijing) 3 (Fall 1985): 18.

2. Cao and Sun, *Shakespeare on the Chinese Stage*, 49.

3. Bian Zhi Lin, "Preface to the Translation of *Hamlet*," in *Shakespeare Criticism in China*, ed. Meng Xian Qiang (Changchun: Jilin Education Press, 1991), 124–25.

4. Ibid., 127.

5. Bian Zhi Lin, "Shakespeare's Great Tragedy *Hamlet*," *Literary Studies* (Beijing) 2 (March 1956): 73–75.

6. Zhang, Xu, and Zhang, eds., *A General Survey of Shakespeare*, 1:361–63.

7. Ibid., 1:359.

8. Ibid., 1:360.

9. Cao and Sun, *Shakespeare on the Chinese Stage*, 102–5.

10. Ibid., 234.

11. Guo Mo Ruo, *Selected Works*, 3:319–22.

12. *King Lear*, in *The Complete Works of Shakespeare*, trans. Zhu Sheng Hao, 11 vols. (Beijing: People's Literature Press, 1978), 9:163–64.

13. Xu Bin, "On *King Lear*," in *Shakespeare in Our Times: A Criticism*, ed. Zhang Si Yang (Changchun: Jilin University Press, 1991), 122–23.

14. Interview with Professor Sun Jia Xiu at the Central Drama Academy, Beijing, June 1986.

15. Xu Qi Pin, "The Choice of Director," in *Shakespeare in China*, ed. Shakespeare Association of China (Shanghai: Shanghai Literature and Art Press, 1987), 112–17.

16. Interviews with teachers from twenty middle schools in northeast China at a conference held at Changchun Teacher's College, Changchun city, July 1986.

17. For example, "The Column of the Famous Quotations," *Jilin Youth* (Changchun) 9 (September 1985): 22.

18. "Lunyu: Datong," in *The Classical Chinese*, ed. Wang Li, 4 vols. (Beijing: Chinese Publishing House, 1978), 1:193.

19. Ibid.

20. From a discussion of Shakespearean histories at a conference held by the Shakespeare Society of Jilin Province in Changchun city, July 1986.

21. For example, "The Quotations of the Famous Figures in World Culture," *Cultural Life* (Beijing) 3 (May 1985): 30–31.

22. Zhang, Xu, and Zhang, eds., *A General Survey of Shakespeare*, 1:118.

23. Lecture by Cheng Ping at the conference held at the Central Drama Academy, 21 April 1986, Beijing.

24. Zhang, "The Treasure Shakespeare Has Left Us," 213.

25. *The History of Chinese Literature*, 2:322–23.

26. Zhu Dong Run, "Talks on Shakespeare's Poetic Quality," in *Shakespeare Criticism in China*, ed. Meng Xian Qiang (Changchun: Jilin Education Press, 1991), 54–55.

27. This reference was provided by Bao Guo An, a teacher at the Central Drama Academy, in his speech on the staging of *Macbeth*, 21 April 1986, Beijing.

28. Charles Lamb, "On the Tragedies of Shakespeare, Considered with Reference to Their Fitness for Stage Representation," in *Shakespeare Criticism*, ed. D. Nichol Smith (Oxford: Oxford University Press, 1926), 237–40.

29. Chen Jia, "The Political Ideas of Shakespeare in His Histories," *Journal of Nanjing University* 4 (July 1956): 150–70.

30. Zhu Wei Zhi, "On the *Merchant of Venice*," *Foreign Literature Studies* (Wuhan) 1 (Spring 1978): 19–28.

31. Li Fu Ning, "Shakespeare's *As You Like It*," *Journal of Beijing University* 4 (July 1956): 51–56.

32. Karl Marx, *Das Capital*, Chinese translation (Beijing: Central Translation Bureau, 1975), 152.

33. Dai Xing Dong, "The Description of Gold: Shakespeare's *Timon of Athens*," *Journal of Northeast Normal University* (Changchun) 1 (January 1981): 32–35.

34. Zhang Yang, "Shakespeare and the Concept of Nature During the Renaissance," *Journal of Jilin University* 1 (January 1986): 53–60.

35. Wan Ying Hua, "The Typical Characters and Typical Circumstances: Shakespearean Tragedies," *Journal of Hangzhou Teacher's College* 1 (February 1980): 51–55.

36. Central Translation Bureau, *The Literary and Artistic Theories of Marx and Engels* (Beijing, 1958), 145–47.

37. Zhang Si Yang, Xu Bin, and Zhang Xiao Yiang, *A Study of Shakespeare's Plays* (Changchun: Literature and Art Times Press, 1991), 1–12.

38. Zhang Xiao Yang, "The Staging of Shakespeare and the Artistic Taste of Our Times," *Foreign Literature Studies* (Wuhan) 1 (Spring 1989): 28–38.

39. Li Yi, "Interview with Liu Bin Yan," *The 1990s* (Hong Kong) 5 (May 1988): 25. Unfortunately this passage was particularly criticized by conservative leaders because they thought that Liu deliberately compared China to an inferior social period.

40. Yuan Kun, "On Shakespeare's Humanism," *Foreign Literature Studies* (Wuhan) 2 (Summer 1979): 124–28.

41. Feng Gang, Liu Yan Bing, and Li Li, "Our Understanding of Shakespeare's Plays," in *Shakespeare's Triple Plays: Research, Performance, and Teaching*, ed. Zhang Si Yang, Meng Xian Qiang, and Xu Bin (Changchun: Northeast Normal University Press, 1988), 276–78.

42. Ibid., 279–80.

43. Cf. Zhang Yang, "Shakespeare's Historical Concept," *Journal of Liaoning University* (Shenyang) 5 (September 1988): 9–15.

44. Speech by Ding Tao at a conference held in the Central Drama Academy, Beijing, 17 April 1986.

45. Xong Guo Dong, "The Conception of the Direction of *Love's Labor's Lost*," in *Shakespeare in China*, ed. Shakespeare Association of China (Shanghai: Shanghai Literature and Art Press, 1987), 142–43.

46. Hu Wei Min, "Notes on Directing *Twelfth Night*," 133.

47. Jean I. Marsden, introduction to *The Appropriation of Shakespeare: Post-Renaissance Reconstructions of the Works and the Myth*, ed. Jean I. Marsden (Hemel Hempstead: Harvester Wheatsheaf, 1991), 1.

CHAPTER 7. CONCLUSION

1. See, for example, Liang Shu Ming, "Chinese Culture and Western Culture," *Wenhui Newspaper* (Shanghai), 1 April 1985, 4.

2. Erika Fischer-Lichte, "Intercultural Aspects in Post-Modern Theatre: A Japanese Version of Chekhov's *Three Sisters*," in *The Play Out of Context*, ed. Hanna Scolnicov and Peter Holland (Cambridge: Cambridge University Press, 1989), 184.

Bibliography

Armstrong, Edward A. *Shakespeare's Imagination*. Lincoln: University of Nebraska Press, 1979.

Belsey, Catherine. "Disrupting Difference: Meaning and Gender in the Comedies." In *Alternative Shakespeare*, ed. John Drakakis. London: Methuen, 1985.

Berry, Edward. "Teaching Shakespeare in China." *Shakespeare Quarterly* 39 (Summer 1988): 212–16.

Bergeron, David M., and Geraldo U. De Sousa. *Shakespeare: A Study and Research Guide*. Lawrence: University Press of Kansas, 1987.

Bian Zhi Lin. "Preface to the Translation of *Hamlet*." In *Shakespeare Criticism in China*, edited by Meng Xian Qiang, 120–39. Changchun: Jilin Education Press, 1991.

———. "Shakespeare's Great Tragedy, *Hamlet*." *Literary Studies* (Beijing) 2 (March 1956): 70–137.

Bradley, A. C. *Shakespearean Tragedy*. London: Macmillan Co., 1905.

Brereton, Geoffrey. *Principles of Tragedy*. London: Routledge and Kegan Paul, 1968.

Brockbank, Philip. "Shakespeare Renaissance in China." *Shakespeare Quarterly* 39 (Summer 1988): 195–204.

Cai Zhong Xiang. *The Highlights of Classical Chinese Dramatic Theory*. Beijing: Chinese People's University Press, 1988.

Cao Shu Jun. *The Biography of Cao Yu*. Beijing: China Youth Press, 1989.

Cao Shu Jun and Sun Fu Liang. *Shakespeare on the Chinese Stage*. Harbin: Harbin Press, 1989.

Cao Wei Feng. "Shakespeare in China." *Literature and Art Monthly* (Beijing) 4 (April 1954): 29–34.

Cao Wen Han. "A Note About the Creation of Shakespeare's Portrait." In *Shakespeare's Triple Play*, edited by Zhang Si Yang, 257–64. Changchun: Northeast Normal University Press, 1987.

Cao Yu. "'Shakespeare Also Belongs to China': The Closing Speech at the Inaugural Chinese Shakespeare Festival." *Drama* (Beijing), 5 June 1986, 1.

———. "Talking with the Playwrights about Reading and Writing." *Play Writing* (Beijing) 10 (October 1982): 4–17.

Central Translation Bureau. *The Literary and Artistic Theories of Marx and Engels*. Beijing, 1958.

Chen Ge. "Humanism in *The Merchant of Venice*." *Journal of Songliao* 1 (February 1985): 82–84.

Chen Jia. "The Political Ideas of Shakespeare in His Histories." *Journal of Nanjing University* 4 (July 1956): 150–70.

Chen Ming. "What's Wrong with the Current Dramatic Creations?" In *A Selection of Drama Studies*, edited by Huang Yue Hua, 44–49. Changchun: Jilin University Reference Department, 1984.

Chen Sou Zhu. "*The Peony Pavilion* and *Romeo and Juliet*." In *Tang Xian Zu Studies: A Selection*, 224–54. Beijing: Chinese Drama Press, 1984.

Chen Xing He. "*Hamlet* and *The Orphan of the House of Zhao*." *Journal of Nanjing Teachers College* 2 (March 1983): 22–27.

Cheng Chao Xiang. "On Tragic Protagonists." *Journal of Beijing University* 5 (September 1987): 73–81.

Clemen, Wolfgang H. *The Development of Shakespeare's Imagery*. London: Methuen, 1953.

Confucius. "Lunyu: Datong." In *The Classical Chinese*, edited by Wang Li. 4 vols. Beijing: Chinese Publishing House, 1978.

Dai Xing Dong. "The Description of Gold: Shakespeare's *Timon of Athens*." *Journal of Northeast Normal University* (Changchun) 1 (January 1981): 32–35.

Ding Jia Sheng. "Thinking Deeply of the Impact." In *Shakespeare in China*, edited by the Shakespeare Association of China. Shanghai: Shanghai Literature and Art Press, 1987.

Dollimore, Jonathan, and Alan Sinfield, eds. *Political Shakespeare: New Essays in Cultural Materalism*. Manchester: Manchester University Press, 1985.

Drakakis, John, ed. *Alternative Shakespeare*. London: Methuen, 1985.

———. *Shakespearean Tragedy*. London: Longman, 1992.

Eastman, Arthur M. *A Short History of Shakespearean Criticism*. New York: Norton, 1974.

Elton, W. R. "Shakespeare and the Thought of His Age." In *The Cambridge Companion to Shakespeare Studies*, ed. Stanley Wells. Cambridge: Cambridge University Press, 1986.

Fan Hong. "The Evolution of Characterization from Moral Type to Individualization." *Jianghai Forum* (Tianjing) 5 (September 1981): 15–20.

Fang Ping. "Cao Yu and Shakespeare." *Shakespeare Studies* (Shakespeare Association of China) 2 (October 1984): 193–231.

———. "*Cleopatra* and Lady Yang in *The Hall of Longevity*." *Literature and Art Studies* (Beijing) 2 (Summer 1985): 116–24.

Feng Gang, Liu Yan Bing, and Li Li. "Our Understanding of Shakespeare's Plays." In *Shakespeare's Triple Play*, edited by Zhang Si Yang. Changchun: Northeast Normal University Press, 1988.

Fischer-Lichte, Erika. "Intercultural Aspects in Post-Modern Theatre: A Japanese Version of Chekhov's *Three Sisters*." In *The Play Out of Context*, edited by Hanna Scolnicov and Peter Holland. Cambridge: Cambridge University Press, 1989.

Fokkema, D. W., and E. Kunne Ibsch. *Theories of Literature in the Twentieth Century*. London: C. Hurst & Co., 1977.

Frye, Northrop. *A Natural Perspective*. New York: Columbia University Press, 1965.

Frye, Roland Mushat. *Shakespeare: The Art of the Dramatist*. London: Allen & Unwin, 1982.

Grady, Hugh. *The Modernist Shakespeare*. Oxford: Clarendon Press, 1991.

Guan Cha Jua. "The Column of Theatrical Criticism." *Da Gong Newspaper* (Shanghai), 9 June 1937, 3.

Guo Mo Ruo. *The Complete Works of Guo Mo Ruo.* Chengdu: Sichuan People's Press, 1982.

———. *Guo Mo Ruo on Literary Creation.* Shanghai: Shanghai Literature and Art Press, 1983.

———. "How I Wrote *The Chinese Cherry Bush.*" In *A Selection of Guo Mo Ruo's Plays.* Beijing: People's Literature Press, 1958.

———. *The Selected Works of Guo Mo Ruo.* Beijing: People's Literature Press, 1957.

Guo Song Tao. *The Diary of Guo Song Tao.* Changsha: Hunan People's Press, 1982.

Hall, Fernau. "The Kunju *Macbeth.*" *London Theatre Record,* 13–26 August 1987, 33.

He Qi Xin. "China's Shakespeare." *Shakespeare Quarterly* 37 (Summer 1986): 145–59.

Hegel, G. W. F. *Aesthetik.* Translated by Zhu Guang Qian. Beijing: Commercial Press, 1980.

Highfill, Philip H., Kalman A. Burnim, and Edward A. Langhans, eds. *A Biographical Dictionary of Actors, Actresses, Musicians, Dancers, Managers and Other Stage Personnel in London, 1660–1800.* 14 vols. Carbondale: Southern Illinois University Press, 1984.

The History of Chinese Literature. Edited by the Literature Institute of the Chinese Academy of Social Science. 3 vols. Beijing: People's Literature Press, 1978.

Hong Xin. "*Othello* and *The Story of a Jade Hairpin.*" *Theatre World* (Beijing) 3 (May 1986): 86–87.

Hsia, Adrian. "*The Orphan of the House Zhao* in French, English, German, and Hong Kong Literature." *Comparative Literature Studies* 25 (Winter 1988): 338–46.

Hu Shi Zhi. "The Evolution of Literature and Drama Reform." *New Youth* (Beijing) 5 (May 1918): 20–24.

Hu Wei Min. "The Combination of Chinese Theatre and Western Theatre." *Wenhui Daily* (Shanghai), 20 April 1986, 2.

———. "Notes on Directing *Twelfth Night* in the Form of Shaoxing Opera." In *Shakespeare in China,* edited by the Shakespeare Association of China, 123–38. Shanghai: Shanghai Literature and Art Press, 1987.

Huang Shi Mo. *Guo Mo Ruo's "Qu Yuan."* Chengdu: Sichuan People's Press, 1981.

Huang Yue Hua, ed. *Publication Reference Material.* Changchun: Jilin University Reference Department, 1990.

———, ed. *Theatre Research Reference Material.* Changchun: Jilin University Reference Department, 1986.

Huang Zuo Lin. "'The Prospects of Shakespeare's Plays on the Chinese Stage': A Speech Given at the Seminar of the Inaugural Chinese Shakespeare Festival." In *Shakespeare in China,* edited by the Shakespeare Association of China, 1–17. Shanghai: Shanghai Literature and Art Press, 1987.

Jaspers, Karl. *Tragedy Is Not Enough.* Translated by Harald A. T. Reiche, Harry T. Moore, and Karl W. Deutsch. Hamden, Conn: Archon Books, 1969.

Jiao Zu. "Where Is Our Theatre Going?" *Drama Studies* (Beijing) 4 (July 1985): 5–11.

Jin Liang Nian et al., eds. *The Concise History of Chinese Culture.* Shanghai: Shanghai Classics Press, 1987.

Jin Zhi. "An Experiment with Misgivings—Thoughts Related to the Adaptation of *Much Ado About Nothing* into the Form of Huangmei Opera." In *Shakespeare in China*, edited by the Shakespeare Association of China. Shanghai: Shanghai Literature and Art Press, 1987.

Johnson, Samuel. "Preface to Shakespeare." In *Shakespeare Criticism: A Selection*, edited by D. Nichol Smith, 89–142. Oxford: Oxford University Press, 1926.

Jones, Peter, ed. *Imagist Poetry*. London: Penguin Books, 1972.

Kang Ding. "The Russian International Shakespeare Conference." *Literature* (Beijing), 6 June 1991, 4.

Kong Geng Gong. "On the Sinicization of Shakespeare." *Foreign Literature Studies* (Wuhan) 4 (Winter 1986): 92–95.

Krook, Dorothea. *Elements of Tragedy*. New Haven: Yale University Press, 1969.

Lai Jian Ming. "The Victims of Love: Women in Shakespearean Tragedies." *Journal of Jiangxi University* 1 (January 1988): 23–28.

Lamb, Charles. "On the Tragedies of Shakespeare Considered with Reference to Their Fitness for Stage Representation." In *Shakespearean Criticism*, edited by D. Nichol Smith. London: Oxford University Press, 1926.

Lan Ren Zhe. "The Main Methods of Contemporary Literary Criticism." *Literary Theory Studies* (Beijing) 3 (May 1982): 144–54.

Leggatt, Alexander. *Shakespeare's Comedy of Love*. London: Methuen, 1973.

LeWinter, Oswald, ed. *Shakespeare in Europe*. London: Penguin Books, 1970.

Li Chang Chun. "*King Lear*—A Tragedy of Humanism." *Journal of Xiangtan University* 4 (July 1988): 135–41.

Li Fu Ning. "Shakespeare's *As You Like It*." *Journal of Beijing University* 4 (July 1956): 51–56.

Li Hong. *Modern Drama Studies*. Changchun: Jilin University Reference Department, 1980.

Li Jun Dong. "Art News." *People's Daily* (Beijing), 31 December 1994, 3.

Li Yi. "Interview with Liu Bin Yan." *The 1990s* (Hong Kong) 5 (May 1988): 22–26.

Li Yu. *On Drama*. 1658. Reprint. Changsha: Hunan People's Press, 1980.

Li Zi Po. "Cao Yu's Talk about Drama." *Short Play Writing* 11 (November 1981): 46–57.

Liang Qi Chao. "Yin Bin Room's Notes on Poetry." *Xin Min Monthly* 5 (May 1902): 8.

Liang Shu Ming. "Chinese Culture and Western Culture." *Wenhui Newspaper*, 1 April 1985, 4.

Lin Feng. "A Comparison of the Endings of *Hamlet* and *The Injustice to Dou E*." *Journal of Liaoning Teachers University* 3 (May 1985): 38–42.

Lin Geng and Feng Yuan Jun, eds. *A Selection of Classical Chinese Poems*. 4 vols. Beijing: People's Literature Press, 1979.

Lin Shu. *The Mysterious Stories of the English Poet*. Shanghai: Commercial Press, 1904.

Liu Bing Shan. "Shakespeare and Cao Xue Qin." *Journal of Henan University* 2 (March 1988): 46–50.

Liu Ren Wei. "Shakespeare, *Timon of Athens* and Marx." *Guangming Daily* (Beijing), 9 June 1993, 3.

Liu Zai Fu. *The Constitution of the Nature of Literary Characters*. Shanghai: Shanghai Literature and Art Press, 1986.

————. "On Literary Studies." *Wen Hui Monthly* (Shanghai) 2 (February 1988): 2–7.

Lu Gu Shun. "Reflections after the Curtainfall." In *Shakespeare in China*, edited by the Shakespeare Association of China. Shanghai: Shanghai Literature and Art Press, 1987.

Lu Xun. *The Complete Works of Lu Xun*. Beijing: People's Literature Press, 1980.

Luo Yi Tun. "Shakespeare in the Classroom at Sichuan University." *Foreign Literature Studies* (Wuhan) 3 (Fall 1985): 95–100.

Mackinnon, L. *Shakespeare the Aesthete*. Basingstoke: Macmillan Co., 1988.

Marsden, Jean I., ed. Introduction to *The Appropriation of Shakespeare: Post-Renaissance Reconstructions of the Works and the Myth*. Hemel Hempstead: Harvester Wheatsheaf, 1991.

Marx, Karl. *Das Capital*. Chinese ed. Beijing: Central Translation Bureau, 1975.

Ma Shuo Rong. "An Artistic Comparison Between Shakespeare and Traditional Chinese Drama." *Shakespeare Studies* (Shakespeare Association of China) 2 (October 1984): 232–42.

Mehl, Dieter. *Shakespeare's Tragedies: An Introduction*. Cambridge: Cambridge University Press, 1986.

Meng Xian Qiang, ed. *Shakespeare Criticism in China*. Changchun: Jilin Education Press, 1991.

Muir, Kenneth. *Shakespeare's Comic Sequence*. Liverpool: Liverpool University Press, 1979.

Murphy, Arthur. "The Orphan of China: A Tragedy." in *The British Drama: A Collection of the Most Esteemed Tragedies, Comedies, Operas and Farces in the English Language*, 2:1394–1414. London: Jones & Co., 1974.

Qian Xuan Tong. *Chinese New Literature*. Shanghai: Commercial Press, 1954.

Qiu Ke An. "The Translating Technique in the Translation of Shakespeare's Plays." *People's Daily* (Beijing), 13 June 1991, 7.

Ridler, Anne, ed. *Shakespeare Criticism 1910–1935*. Oxford: Oxford University Press, 1962.

————, ed. *Shakespeare Criticism 1935–1960*. Oxford: Oxford University Press, 1970.

Scolnicov, Hanna, and Peter Holland, eds. *The Play Out of Context*. Cambridge: Cambridge University Press, 1989.

Shan San Ya. "Special Report on the Art Festival of the 11th Asian Games." *Guangming Daily* (Beijing), 1 October 1990, 4.

Shih Chung Wen. *The Golden Age of Chinese Drama: Yuan Tsa-chu*. Princeton: Princeton University Press, 1976.

Sidney, Philip. "An Apology for Poetry." In *Elizabethan Critical Essays*, edited by G. Gregory Smith, 1:148–207. Oxford: Clarendon Press, 1904.

Silk, M. S., and J. P. Stern, eds. *Nietzsche on Tragedy*. Cambridge: Cambridge University Press, 1981.

Smith, James. L. *Melodrama*. London: Methuen, 1973.

Spurgeon, Caroline F. E. "Leading Motives in the Imagery of Shakespeare's Tragedies." In *Shakespeare Criticism 1910–1935*, edited by Anne Ridler. Oxford: Oxford University Press, 1962.

———. *Shakespeare's Imagery and What It Tells Us*. Cambridge: Cambridge University Press, 1935.

Stewart, J. I. M. "Shakespeare's Men and Their Morals." In *Shakespeare Criticism 1935–1960*, edited by Anne Ridler. Oxford: Oxford University Press, 1970.

The Strange Tales from Overseas. Shanghai: Da Wen Press, 1903.

Stone, George Winchester, and George M. Kahrl. *David Garrick: A Critical Biography*. Carbondale: Southern Illinois University Press, 1979.

Sun Da Yu. Preface to the translation of *King Lear*. Shanghai: Commercial Press, 1948.

Tian Han. "The Evolution of Shakespearean Theater in the West." *Nanguo Monthly* (Beijing) 4 (April 1929): 26–37.

———. Preface to the translation of *Hamlet*. Shanghai: Commercial Press, 1922.

Wan Ying Hua. "The Typical Characters and Typical Circumstances: Shakespearean Tragedies." *Journal of Hangzhou Teacher's College* 1 (February 1980): 51–55.

Wang Bo. "The Pavilion of Tengwang." In *Classical Chinese Literary Works*, edited by Zhu Dong Run. Shanghai: Shanghai Classic Press, 1980.

Wang Fan. "A Comparison of Falstaff and AQ." *Journal of Hebei University* 2 (March 1988): 63–69.

Wang Guo Wei. *A Collection of Wang Guo Wei's Writings on Traditional Drama*. Beijing: People's Literature Press, 1957.

———. *The History of Song and Yuan Drama*. Shanghai: Commercial Press, 1915.

Wang Ji Si, ed. *The Ten Greatest Classical Chinese Comedies*. Shanghai: Shanghai Literature and Art Press, 1983.

———, ed. *The Ten Greatest Classical Chinese Tragedies*. Shanghai: Shanghai Literature and Art Press, 1983.

Wang Qiu Rong. "Humanism and Shakespeare." *Literary Circles* (Shanghai) 5 (September 1981): 142–43.

Wang Yi Qun. "The Development of the Theatrical Shakespeare on the Chinese Stage." In *Shakespeare in China*, edited by the Shakespeare Association of China. Shanghai: Shanghai Literature and Art Press, 1987.

Wang Ying Hua. "The Typical Characters and Typical Circumstances: Shakespearean Tragedies." *Journal of Hangzhou Teachers College* 1 (January 1980): 51–55.

Wayne, Valerie, ed. *The Matter of Difference: Materialist Feminist Criticism of Shakespeare*. Hemel Hempstead: Harvester Wheatsheaf, 1991.

Weiss, Alfred. "The Edinburgh Festival, 1987." *Shakespeare Quarterly* 39 (Summer 1988): 79–89.

Wells, Stanley, ed. *Cambridge Companion to Shakespeare Studies*. Cambridge: Cambridge University Press, 1986.

———, ed. *Shakespeare: A Bibliographical Guide*. Oxford: Clarendon Press, 1990.

Wen Jie. "My Creative Experience." In *The Discussion of Creative Writing by the Young Novelists*, edited by Wang Gang. Changchun: Jilin University Press, 1988.

White, R. S. "The Year's Contributions to Shakespeare Studies: Critical Studies." *Shakespeare Survey* 40 (1987): 185–210; 41 (1988): 193–213; 44 (1991): 205–23.

Willett, John, ed. *Brecht on Theatre*. London: Methuen, 1964.

Wu De Bao and Tu Hai Ming. "Chinese People—Ardent Admirers of Shakespeare." *Jiefang Daily* (Shanghai), 4 December 1984, 1.

Wu Guo Qin. *The History of Traditional Chinese Drama.* Shanghai: Shanghai Literature and Art Press, 1980.

Wu Jie Min and Zhu Hong Da. "Zhu Sheng Hao and Shakespeare." *Foreign Literature Studies* (Wuhan) 2 (Summer 1986): 16–21.

Wu Quan Tao. "*Romeo and Juliet* and *The Romance of the Western Chamber.*" *Journal of Ningbo Teacher's College* 3 (May 1984): 51–59.

Xia Xie Shi and Lu Run Tang, eds. *A Selection of Comparative Drama.* Beijing: Chinese Drama Press, 1988.

Xie De Hui. "Money, the Desperate Beast." *People's Daily* (Beijing), 27 February 1989, 7.

Xiu Shuo Fang. "Tang Xian Zu and Shakespeare." *Social Science* (Beijing) 2 (Summer 1978): 208–16.

Xong Guo Dong. "The Conception of the Direction of *Love's Labor's Lost.*" In *Shakespeare in China*, edited by the Shakespeare Association of China. Shanghai: Shanghai Literature and Art Press, 1987.

———. "Performing Shakespearean Plays in the Modern Manner." *Bulletin of the Inaugural Chinese Shakespeare Festival.* Shanghai: Shanghai Drama Institute, 1986.

Xong Zhong Wu. "The Artistic Tendencies of the Contemporary Novel." *Literary Criticism* (Beijing) 3 (May 1986): 124–33.

Xu Bin. "On *King Lear.*" In *Shakespeare in Our Times: A Selection of Shakespeare Criticism*, edited by Zhang Si Yang. Changchun: Jilin University Press, 1991.

Xu Hao Yu. "*Macbeth* and *The Orphan of the House of Zhao.*" *Chinese Literature Studies* (Beijing) 1 (Spring 1988): 56–61.

Xu Jing. "The Tendency of Contemporary Chinese Poetry." *Baihua Monthly* (Changchun) 4 (April 1985): 30–38.

Xu Qi Ping. "The Choice of the Director." In *Shakespeare in China*, edited by the Shakespeare Association of China, 112–17. Shanghai: Shanghai Literature and Art Press, 1987.

Yan Fu. *An Elementary Introduction to Logic.* 1908. Reprint. Beijing: Commercial Press, 1981.

———. *Evolution and Ethics and Other Essays.* Beijing: Science Press, 1971.

———. *The Evolution of Nature.* 1894. Reprint. Beijing: Science Press, 1971.

Ye Xiao Fan. "*The Sad Story of Lady Wang* and *Romeo and Juliet.*" In *A Selection of Comparative Literature*, 107–25. Tianjing: Nankai University Press, 1984.

Yi Yu. "The Exchange Between Oriental Theater and Western Theater." In *A Selection of Comparative Drama*, edited by Xia Xie Shi and Lu Run Tang, 118–48. Beijing: Chinese Drama Press, 1988.

Yu Shang Yuan. "Why Should We Stage Shakespeare's Plays?" *Zhongyang Daily* (Nanjing), 18 June 1937, 4.

Yuan Kun. "On Shakespeare's Humanism." *Foreign Literature Studies* (Wuhan) 2 (Summer 1979): 124–28.

Zha Pei De and Tian Jia. "Shakespeare in Traditional Chinese Operas." *Shakespeare Quarterly* 39 (Summer 1988): 204–11.

Zhang An Guo. "On the Dramatic Creation of Shakespeare and Guan Han Qing." *Journal of Guiyang Teachers College* 3 (May 1985): 58–59.

Zhang An Jian. "The Treasure Shakespeare Has Left Us—A Reflection on the Inaugural Chinese Shakespeare Festival." In *Shakespeare's Triple Play*, edited by Zhang
Si Yang, 203–26. Changchun: Northeast Normal University Press, 1988.

Zhang Fa. *Chinese Culture and Tragic Concepts.* Beijing: Chinese People's University Press, 1989.

Zhang Geng and Guo Han Cheng. *The History of Traditional Chinese Drama.*
Beijing: Chinese Drama Press, 1980.

Zhang Geng et al., eds. *The Encyclopedia of Traditional Chinese Drama.* Beijing:
Chinese Encyclopedia Press, 1983.

Zhang He. *Modern Drama in China.* Changchun: Jilin University Reference Department, 1979.

———. "What Should We Learn from Shakespeare?" *Literature and Art* (Beijing)
3 (Fall 1985): 16–21.

Zhang Jun Chuan. "The First Attempt: Notes on the Symposium on the Radio
Play *Macbeth*." In *Shakespeare in China*, edited by the Shakespeare Association
of China, 155–70. Shanghai: Shanghai Literature and Art Press, 1987.

Zhang Long Xi. "The Revival of the Gods." *Reading* 4 (July 1984): 36–41.

Zhang Si Yang. "Marx and Shakespeare." *Journal of Jilin University* 2 (March
1983): 74–84.

Zhang Si Yang and Meng Xian Qiang, eds. *Shakespeare in Our Times: A Selection
of Shakespeare Criticism.* Changchun: Jilin University Press, 1991.

Zhang Si Yang, Meng Xian Qiang, and Xu Bin, eds. *Shakespeare's Triple Play:
Research, Performance, and Teaching.* Changchun: Northeast Normal University
Press, 1988.

Zhang Si Yang, Xu Bin, and Zhang Xiao Yang. *A General Survey of Shakespeare.*
Beijing: Chinese Drama Press, 1989.

———. *A Study of Shakespeare's Plays.* Changchun: Literature and Art Times
Press, 1991.

Zhang Xiao Yang. "The Staging of Shakespeare and the Artistic Taste of Our Times."
Foreign Literature Studies (Wuhan) 1 (Spring 1989): 28–38.

Zhang Yang. "Shakespeare and the Concept of Nature During the Renaissance."
Journal of Jilin University 1 (January 1986): 53–60.

———. "Shakespeare's Historical Concept." *Journal of Liaoning University* (Sheng-
yang) 5 (September 1988): 9–15.

Zhang Yi, ed. *Modern Chinese Poets.* Changchun: Jilin University Reference Department, 1980.

Zhu Dong Run. "Talks on Shakespeare's Poetic Quality." In *Shakespeare Criticism
in China*, edited by Meng Xian Qiang, 52–57. Changchun: Jilin Education
Press, 1991.

———, ed. *Classical Chinese Literary Works.* Shanghai: Shanghai Classic Press,
1980.

Zhu Sheng Hao, trans. *The Complete Works of Shakespeare.* 11 vols. Beijing: People's Literature Press, 1978.

Zhu Wei Zhi. "On *The Merchant of Venice*." *Foreign Literature Studies* (Wuhan) 1
(Spring 1978): 19–28.

Zhu Yan Ping. "How I Acted Wu Song." *Television and Film Weekly* (Changchun)
21 (May 1987): 4.

Index